EMILY PURSER & LINDA PAUL

Translation: Übersetzung

Anglistik · Amerikanistik

studium
kompakt

Cornelsen

studium kompakt Anglistik • Amerikanistik

Translation: Übersetzung

Die Hochschulreihe studium kompakt Anglistik • Amerikanistik wurde mit den Verfasserinnen und Verfassern von Dr. Christian von Raumer konzipiert und mit der Verlagsredaktion entwickelt.

Verfasserinnen: Emily Purser & Linda Paul
Verlagsredaktion: Dr. Blanca-Maria Rudhart
Layout: Gisela Hoffmann
Technische Umsetzung: Ingo Ostermaier
Umschlagsgestaltung: Grafik Design Vera Bauer, Berlin

Die Deutsche Bibliothek – CIP-Einheitsaufnahme:
studium kompakt Anglistik • Amerikanistik:
Translation: Übersetzung / Emily Purser / Linda Paul.
    1. Aufl. – Berlin: Cornelsen, 1999
    ISBN 3-464-00627-1

Cornelsen online http://www.cornelsen.de

1. Auflage ✔   Druck 4 3 2 1 Jahr 02 01 2000 99

Druck: Saladruck, Berlin

ISBN 3-464-00627-1

Bestellnummer 6271

gedruckt auf säurefreiem Papier, umweltschonend
hergestellt aus chlorfrei gebleichten Faserstoffen

Contents

Foreword
Acknowledgments

0   Orientation   9
0.1 Intended readership
0.2 Translation in "Anglistikstudium"
0.3 Terminology
0.4 Theoretical basis

I   Recount – biographical   15
I.1 German and English examples
  1.1 Comparison and contrast
  1.2 Text and function
  1.3 Summary of language features
I.2 Guided translation exercises
  2.1 Text completion
  2.2 Evaluation and improvement
  2.3 Vocabulary extension
I.3 Independent translation
  3.1 Quick texts
  3.2 45-minute texts
  3.3 Exam practice

II   News Item – in brief   35
II.1 German and English examples
  1.1 Comparison and contrast
  1.2 Text and function
  1.3 Summary of language features
II.2 Guided translation exercises
  2.1 Text completion
  2.2 Evaluation and improvement
  2.3 Vocabulary extension
II.3 Independent translation
  3.1 Quick texts
  3.2 45-minute texts
  3.3 Exam practice

III   Report – generalised   **57**
III.1   German and English examples
  1.1   Comparison and contrast
  1.2   Text and function
  1.3   Summary of language features
III.2   Guided translation exercises
  2.1   Text completion
  2.2   Evaluation and improvement
  2.3   Vocabulary extension
III.3   Independent translation
  3.1   Quick texts
  3.2   45-minute texts
  3.3   Exam practice

IV   Narrative – fictional   **85**
IV.1   German and English examples
  1.1   Comparison and contrast
  1.2   Text and function
  1.3   Summary of language features
IV.2   Guided translation exercises
  2.1   Text completion
  2.2   Evaluation and improvement
  2.3   Vocabulary extension
IV.3   Independent translation
  3.1   Quick texts
  3.2   45-minute texts
  3.3   Exam practice

V   Procedure – constructional   **113**
V.1   German and English examples
  1.1   Comparison and contrast
  1.2   Text and function
  1.3   Summary of language features

V.2   Guided translation exercises
2.1   Text completion
2.2   Evaluation and improvement
2.3   Vocabulary extension
V.3   Independent translation
3.1   Quick texts
3.2   45-minute texts
3.3   Exam practice

VI   **Advertising – product**   **137**
VI.1   German and English examples
1.1   Comparison and contrast
1.2   Text and function
1.3   Summary of language features
VI.2   Guided translation exercises
2.1   Text completion
2.2   Evaluation and improvement
2.3   Vocabulary extension
VI.3   Independent translation
3.1   Quick texts
3.2   45-minute texts
3.3   Exam practice

Appendix   **175**
Answer Key
Glossary
Further Reading

This volume in the series is written in English, as it is a workbook for practical training in the language rather than a theoretical discussion of it. It offers students and teachers of "English as a Foreign Language" a course in translation, which can be used in classes and/or for individual work. It is designed to meet the needs of students of English Studies in German universities, but can also be used by learners and teachers at other levels and institutions of English language learning.

Translation classes are a standard part of English Studies in German universities, so the book aims to meet the needs of students who have to prepare for final examinations in translation, and the needs of their teachers. More than just providing 'texts-and-keys' for translation practice, this workbook offers a systematic handling of several different types of text. Through this it aims to teach transferable knowledge of the texts' grammatical features and of translation evaluation criteria. The book does not of course aim to train anyone to work as a professional translator: no non-native speaker of English should imagine they can learn to translate into English to a professional standard. What students of this course can achieve is a greater awareness of some key differences between English and German text, as well as greater proficiency producing English text.

Natural languages are very complex phenomena, and any systematic description and teaching of one will involve technical terms. I have used some terms from 'traditional grammar' with which readers will be familiar, but I also introduce readers to terms and categories which may be new. The approach to text translation used here draws on descriptions of English known as FUNCTIONAL GRAMMAR. The terms from functional grammar are capitalised throughout the book for easy recognition, and a glossary is provided at the back for reference. Terminology has been kept to a minimum though, as this book is not an introduction to language analysis or 'functional' descriptions of English per se.

The book is organised into six teaching chapters. Each chapter presents a different GENRE but all are organised in the same way. Firstly the reader's attention is focused onto the GENRE'S typical grammatical features, grammatical patterns that distinguish it from other GENRES and from its German language counterpart. Secondly, translation practice is guided through various grammar and vocabulary tasks. Finally, further text examples are given for timed and completely independent text translation practice. Tasks are supported by an Answer Key at the end of the book.

Users of the book need not follow the order of chapters given, but should work with those GENRES of greatest interest and use for their particular needs. The six GENRES and their representative text examples given have been selected either for their general relevance to English Studies or their frequency in students' daily experience of language. The number of chapters is motivated only by the standardisation of book length necessary for the series. It is actually unlikely that all six chapters will be covered within one teaching semester, but this depends on the level of each class or student. Teachers are encouraged to create their own further or alternative course components on the basis of the design and ideas presented here.

The material has been trialled with students at Potsdam University, to whom our thanks are due. Users of the material in this book are welcome to give criticism and feedback to the authors at any time, sending correspondence to:

purser@rz.uni-potsdam.de

or to either E. Purser or L. Paul at:
Universitat Potsdam
Institut fur Anglistik und Amerikanistik
Postfach 601553
14415 Potsdam.

Acknowledgments

The major source of concepts and descriptive techniques used in this book is the *Functional Grammar* of M.A.K. Halliday. He, colleagues working in Sydney in the 1980s, and those researchers and teachers who developed GENRE PEDAGOGY in Sydney, established the context for the approach to language teaching applied here. As this is a book for mainstream students and teachers of English in Europe, rather than a book for linguists already working with Systemic-Functional Linguistic theory, I have adapted and selectively rather than comprehensively used insights and concepts from this work.

The development of this workbook has benefited greatly from constructive criticisms from several colleagues in linguistics, especially Dr Melina Alexa, Prof Dr Susanne Carroll and Prof Dr Eija Ventola. Our special thanks also to Dr Hiltrud Wedde for proof-reading thoroughly and being involved for much of the project. To those students whose translation texts we have been able to use in the course and this publication, many thanks. Without their work and comments we would not have been able to identify the key areas of learning need and to develop our ideas for the design of the course represented here.

Emily Purser

0   Orientation

0.1   Intended readership   10

0.2   Translation in "Anglistikstudium"   10

0.3   Terminology   10

0.4   Theoretical basis   13

0.1
Intended readership

The course structure and materials provided in this workbook will be particularly useful for university departments of English Studies in Germany, but also potentially interesting to groups and individuals in other types of language education programmes – wherever translation classes are a part of foreign language education. The book does not include discussion of Translation Theory, as there are already many texts on the market doing so. Practical translation courses such as the one described by this book do play a role in the wider picture of Translation Studies however, and may be useful within programmes focusing on theory and the training of translators.

0.2
Translation in "Anglistikstudium"

From the point of view of the student doing a degree in English Studies at a German university, a translation course is an important, because compulsory, element of the programme, and many final examinations. Amongst teachers and curriculum developers, translation is often controversial and its pedagogical value disputed. Many teachers conducting such courses however understand the work as an opportunity to enhance and extend students' language awareness and text-making skills, and as an invaluable opportunity for close comparative linguistic explorations. Traditional 'grammar translation' methods, focusing on structures at and below clause level and tending to work with structures outside of any real context, are rightly passed over, but translation per se is not to be discredited for language teaching. This book focuses translation practice beyond the 'sentence', provides a wide range of translation tasks, authentic materials and ideas for classrooms, it covers many types of text, and its clear and practical 'language about language' facilitates comparative text analysis.

0.3
Terminology

In a functional approach to the study of language, the starting point for analytic description is **TEXT**, rather than the sentences and isolated grammatical structures of traditional and formalist grammars. Functional grammars explain the lexical and grammatical choices of TEXT (ie any coherent and cohesive stretch of discourse) in relation to **CONTEXT**, the social order it expresses and brings into being. To translate TEXT well, the CONTEXT must be recognised and understood. It is a semiotic complex on two levels. At the level of general culture, it is a structuring and patterning of language activity into a recognisable **GENRE**, and at the level of specific situation type into a recognisable **REGISTER**. The lexical and grammatical choices a speaker or writer actually makes as they produce TEXT are never random, but are suited to the particular CONTEXT in which their TEXT arises and has to function.

A GENRE is an activity which language is being used to do, and is organised into sequenced stages. For example, 'telling a story' is a recognised activity, and proceeds by first setting the scene and introducing the participants, then indicating the problem, then presenting the complication, then resolving the crisis, then rounding off or reorienting the story. A REGISTER is an identifiable situation in which a GENRE is carried out. It is described in terms of who is doing the activity to / with whom (TENOR), whether they are using speech or writing (MODE) and what they are talking about (FIELD). A story might thus be in a REGISTER describable as 'parent telling bedtime animal story to child', or a story might be '18th century literary genius writing metaphorically about political events for elite circle of readers'. Activities (GENRES) are so frequently carried out in such tightly codified configurations of situation (REGISTERS) in a culture that their expression results in formulaic **TEXT TYPES** (eg a weather report, a letter of condolence, a market research phone interview, or the biographical recounts examined in this book).

A GENRE is not restricted to any one REGISTER. You can recount in spoken or written language, you can recount the events of a meeting, of a day or of the entire life of an individual, a nation or the planet. The potential to vary what you are recounting about, with whom and in what medium are vast, but in all cases, there is something similar going on and that is what is identified with the GENRE label "recount". The importance of this insight to translation is that each GENRE has its own typical grammatical features, regardless of REGISTER variables (such as type of tense, PARTICIPANTS, PROCESSES and COHESIVE DEVICES). The main language features of each GENRE, in German and in English, are discussed and summarised in the first section of each chapter.

The REGISTER of a text to be translated should also be examined, as students most frequently fail to translate all aspects of TEXT. The grammatical expression of MODE and TENOR, for example, in the following letter is illustrated by shifting lexical and grammatical choices. The original's REGISTER can be described as 'university professor formally informing staff, in writing, of an important upcoming event and commanding their presence':

Liebe Kolleginnen und Kollegen,
Unter bezug auf ein Rundschreiben von Prof. X bitte ich Sie im Namen
des Dekans, dringend um Ihre Anwesenheit zu der für den 11. Juli vom
Dekanat anberaumten Zusammenkunft der Institute in Vorbereitung
der Evaluationsbegehung durch den Wissenschaftsrat. Nähere Infor-
mationen aus dem Dekanat über den geplanten Ablauf des Tages
werde ich Ihnen umgehend mitteilen.
Mit freundlichen Grüßen,
Prof. Y

If the professor who wrote this message were talking rather than writing, and to a close friend rather than colleagues, she might have said something like:

Prof. X hat eine Mitteilung geschickt, dass wir alle hier sein müssen
am 11. Juli, und jetzt muss ich das weitergeben, das heißt, ich bitte
dich und alle anderen, an dem Tag hier zu sein, weil der Dekan will,
dass alle Institute zusammenkommen und diskutieren, wie wir vom
Wissenschaftsrat evaluiert werden, und wir wollen dafür ganz gut
vorbereitet sein. Und wenn ich selbst mehr darüber weiss, wie der
Dekan diesen Tag plant, sage ich dir Bescheid.

Translating all the meanings of the original letter appropriately requires finding grammatical forms to suitably represent its written MODE and formal TENOR, as well as the lexical items to represent its FIELD. The TENOR of the original (the formal, authoritarian relationship between the writer and the readers of this letter) is established by the use of titles and polite forms (*Sie, Ihnen, mfg*) and the indirect but still clear command (declarative rather than imperative MOOD). The MODE is written – meaning not simply that the message was received on a piece of paper, but that there are grammatical choices made which are typical of written language: one can speak formally or pretentiously like written language, and write in a 'spoken' style, such as in e-mails or in parts of novels. The typical 'written' aspects of the letter include the packing of information into just two clauses, with complex noun groups and nominalisations *(Zusammenkunft, Vorbereitung, Evaluationsbegehung, Ablauf)*. In the 'spoken' version of the message, the information is packaged into six times the number of clauses. Spoken language typically has many short and simple clauses with and quite complex relationships between them, while written language typically has fewer clauses and simple relationships, each clause packing a lot more information into complex nominal structures.

Other terms used throughout the book describe the clause grammar of texts mainly in terms of two areas of meaning – patterns of THEME and patterns of choice in TRANSITIVITY (PROCESS, PARTICIPANT and CIRCUMSTANCE). These are explained as they arise.

This book is based on the *Systematic Functional Grammar* of Michael Halliday, currently one of the most important models for language description and education. The use of the grammar to describe the texts presented in this volume however is very sparing rather than systematic. It is not the intention to overwhelm the reader with new concepts and terminology, but to select those concepts and metalanguage useful to teaching translation for language learning. Those readers who would like to learn more about Functional Grammar per se are directed to M.A.K. Halliday's *Introduction to Functional Grammar*. An excellent workbook designed as a companion to that book is Martin, Matthiessen and Painter's *Working with Functional Grammar*, and other very teacher-friendly introductory books are Gerot and Wignell's *Making Sense of Functional Grammar*, Gerot's *Making Sense of Text*, and Butt et al's *Using Functional Grammar: an explorer's guide*. Vastly more detailed studies of English grammar from the systemic-functional perspective are available in Jim Martin's *English Text: system and structure*, Suzanne Eggin's *Introduction to Systemic Functional Linguistics* and Christian Matthiessen's *Lexicogrammatical Cartography*. There are also now several functional grammars based on these works designed for teachers of English and English linguistics outside Australia: Graham Lock's *Functional English Grammar*, Thomas and Meriel Bloors' *Functional Analysis of English*, and Geoff Thompson's *Introducing Functional Grammar*.

0.4
Theoretical basis

I Recount – biographical

The term "recount", used widely in functional grammars, describes a language genre which records past events in chronological order – simply putting the facts on record, without explanation or commentary. Recounting might be the sole purpose of a given text, or might occur as part of a more complex genre. It can be done in various registers, ranging from the formal written record of an official chronicler, the record of personal events in a diary, to the accounts of social or personal events spoken between friends – each situation producing a different type of recounting text. This chapter focuses on the biographical blurb to be found on the back or inside cover of novels – a frequent and very regulated use of language.

I.1   German and English examples   16
  1.1 Comparison and contrast
  1.2 Text and function
  1.3 Summary of language features

I.2   Guided translation exercises   25
  2.1 Text completion
  2.2 Evaluation and improvement
  2.3 Vocabulary extension

I.3   Independent translation   30
  3.1 Quick texts
  3.2 45-minute texts
  3.3 Exam practice

The recount genre occurs in both German and English very frequently and in many text forms. In a recount, language is being used to make a record of past events in chronological order – just to put the facts on record, rather than to interpret them. Recounting often occurs within more complex genres, such as extended biographies, casual conversation or historical writing. It also occurs alone, such as in biographical blurbs and encylopaedia entries, simple chronicles and diary records. The short biographical recounts of writers below are a common form of simple recount and are chosen for this chapter's exercises because they are familiar, everyday texts with a direct relevance to English Studies. Longer biographies are often used in translation exams also, for which these shorter texts serve as preparation.

1 Margriet de Moor, Jahrgang 1941, studierte in Den Haag Gesang und Klavier. Sie machte Karriere als Sängerin, besonders mit Liedern des 20. Jahrhunderts. Kunstgeschichts- und Architekturstudium in Amsterdam. Mit ihren beiden Erzählungsbänden *Rückenansicht* (1988) und *Doppelporträt* (1989) machte sie zum ersten Mal als Schriftstellerin von sich reden. Es folgte der Roman *Erst grau dann weiß dann blau* (1991), für den sie 1992 eine der wichtigsten literarischen Auszeichnungen in den Niederlanden erhielt. 1993 erschien ihr zweiter Roman *Der Virtuose*.

(Margriet de Moor, *Bevorzugte Landschaft*, München, 1989.)

2 Robert Schneider, geb. 1961 in Bregenz, wurde für seinen Erstling mit dem Alemannischen Literaturpreis 1993, dem Robert-Musil-Stipendium und dem Preis Osterfestspiele Salzburg 1994 gewürdigt. Außerdem erhielt er den Abraham-Woursell-Award und für seine dramatischen Arbeiten den Drehbuchpreis des österreichischen Rundfunks und den Landespreis für Volkstheaterstücke in Baden-Württemberg (1990). Sein Monolog *Dreck* wurde als bestes Theaterstück 1993 bei den Potsdamer Theatertagen gekürt, die Hörspielfassung mit dem Civis '93 ausgezeichnet.

(Robert Schneider, *Schlafes Bruder*, Leipzig, 1994.)

3 Tilman Spengler, geboren 1947 in Oberhausen. Studierte in Heidelberg, Taipeh und München Sinologie, Politologie und Neuere Geschichte. 1980 und 1981 Gastdozent an der Chinesischen Akademie der Wissenschaften in Peking. Lebt in Ambach am Starnberger See.

(Tilman Spengler, *Chinesische Reisebilder*, Reinbeck bei Hamburg, 1996.)

1 Carol Shields was born and raised in Chicago and has lived in Canada since 1957. She studied at Hanover College and the University of Ottawa. Author of six novels, including *The Republic of Love*, which was shortlisted for the 1992 Guardian Fiction Prize, and *The Stone Diaries*, which was shortlisted for the 1993 Booker Prize. Carol Shields has also written three volumes of poetry and numerous short stories. She now lives in Winnipeg and spends each summer in France.   (Carol Shields, *Mary Swann*, London, 1993.)

2 Keith Oatley was born in London in 1939. He was educated at Cambridge and University College London, and has worked at the Universities of Sussex and Glasgow. He is a professor of psychology, and now lives and works in Toronto. He is married to a psychologist, Jennifer Jenkins, and has two sons and a daughter. *The case of Emily V.* won Best First Book of the 1994 Commonwealth Writers' Prize. It is his fifth book, but his first work of fiction.
                              (Keith Oatley, *The Case of Emily V.*, London, 1994.)

3 Jeanette Winterson is the author of five works of fiction, a comic book, two screenplays and most recently a collection of essays, *Art Objects*. She has received the Whitbread Award, the John Llewellyn Rhys Prize, and the E.M. Forster Award from the American Academy and Institute of Arts and Letters.
                              (Jeanette Winterson, *Gut Symmetries*, London, 1997.)

4 Eva Hoffman was born in Cracow, Poland, and emigrated to America at the age of thirteen. She was an editor of the New York Times Book Review and has written on a variety of cultural subjects. She is the recipient of the Guggenheim Fellowship, the Whiting Award and an award from the American Academy and Institute of Arts and Letters. She is currently living in London.
                              (Eva Hoffmann, *Lost in Translation*, London, 1991.)

1.1 Comparison and contrast

These texts are simple, and translating them from German into English may seem easy. They are designed to be read very quickly by a general reader, are short and contain few or no lexical or grammatical elements that will be new to an advanced student of English. Yet, students repeatedly make wrong lexical and grammatical choices when translating such biographical recounts, so the following exercises bring their specific language features to your attention. Seeing and understanding the patterns of these texts before attempting to translate these or similar ones will help you avoid the pitfalls that amateur translators make. A basic mistake inexperienced translators make is to use dictionaries alone, instead of examining

language patterns

other examples of the genre **in English**. The more experienced translator realises that there are specific lexical and grammatical choices typical of each genre and its register in its own language, and a translator must recognise and conform to these textual patterns. The following tasks help you identify language patterns typical of biographical recounts in German, and of biographical recounts in English.

Task 1 – identifying grammatical THEME

THEME – first element in a clause

Looking back at the various examples of biographical recount on the previous pages, perhaps the most obvious pattern to see across all of them is what comes first. The first element of a clause is known as its grammatical THEME. In both the German and English biographical recounts, all texts begin with the author. This is logical – first position signals what the text is about. But what comes first in the rest of the sentences through each text?

> Underline the beginnings of each sentence in each of the biographical recount texts and describe a pattern.

PROCESS
PARTICIPANT
CIRCUMSTANCE

Clauses consist of three types of element – a PROCESS, PARTICIPANTS and CIRCUMSTANCES. The PROCESS represents what is going on, the PARTICIPANTS represent who or what is involved in the event and the CIRCUMSTANCES represent where, when, how, with what the event takes place. In the English texts, THEME position is occupied only by a PARTICIPANT (the author or their work) or a CIRCUMSTANCE of time. In the German texts there is more variety. This is significant because it means that when you are translating from a German text into English, you will not necessarily be able to follow the same order of elements as the German text uses. It is much rarer in English to begin a sentence with a CIRCUMSTANTIAL element than it is in German. The dominant pattern in English is PARTICIPANT ^ PROCESS ^ CIRCUMSTANCE.

> Check how dominant this pattern is in English biographical recounts by collecting and examining further examples of your own.

Task 2 – identifying stylistic problems in German text

Translations into English by German speakers typically have certain stylistic errors. These are hard to recognise in a foreign language, so it might help you recognise them if you first see such problems in

German. Only one of the five versions of the biographical recount text below suits the genre. The others feature the sorts of inappropriate choices non-native users of German might make, and are given here to demonstrate the kinds of stylistic errors students often make when attempting to translate into English.

Decide which version would be acceptable to a publisher.

A Janina David wurde 1930 in Polen als einziges Kind einer jüdischen Familie aus der Mittelklasse geboren. Sie verlor ihre Eltern während des Krieges und ging nach ihrer Errettung aus dem Ghetto 1946 von ihrem Zuhause weg. Zwei Jahre wohnte sie in einem Waisenhaus in Paris und ging dann, kurz vor ihrem 18. Geburtstag, nach Australien. Sie kriegte die Australische Staatsangehörigkeit, war in Fabriken tätig und bekam eine Beihilfe für das Studium der Künste und Sozialwissenschaft an der Universität Melbourne. 1958 ging sie nach Frankreich zurück. Jetzt wohnt sie in London.

B Als einziges Kind einer bürgerlichen jüdischen Familie wurde 1930 in Polen Janina David geboren. Ihr Heimatland verließ sie 1946 nach ihrer Befreiung aus dem Ghetto und verlor ihre Eltern während des Krieges. Zwei Jahre verbrachte sie in Paris in einem Waisenhaus und dann emigrierte nach Australien kurz vor ihrem 18. Geburtstag. Die australische Staatsbürgerschaft erhielt sie, arbeitete in Fabriken und für das Studium der Geistes- und Sozialwissenschaften bekam sie ein Stipendium an der Universität Melbourne. Zurück nach Frankreich kehrte sie 1958. Sie lebt in London heute.

C Janina David wurde geboren in 1930 in Polen, das einzige Kind einer jüdischen bürgerlichen Familie. Sie verlor ihre Eltern während des Krieges und verließ Polen nach ihrer Befreiung aus dem Ghetto in 1946. Sie verbrachte zwei Jahre in einem Waisenhaus in Paris dann emigrierte nach Australien kurz vor ihrem 18. Geburtstag. Sie arbeitete in Fabriken, erhielt die australische Staatsbürgerschaft, und bekam ein Stipendium für das Studium der Geistes- und Sozialwissenschaften an der Melbourne Universität. Sie kehrte zurück nach Frankreich in 1958. Sie lebt jetzt in London.

D Janina David wurde 1930 in Polen geboren. Sie war das einzige Kind einer jüdischen Familie, die aus dem bürgerlichen Milieu kam. Sie hat ihre Eltern im zweiten Weltkrieg verloren und verließ 1946 ihr Land, nachdem sie aus dem Warschauer Ghetto rauskam. In Paris hat sie zwei Jahre lang in einem Waisenhaus gelebt und kurz bevor sie 18 wurde, ist sie nach Australien ausgewandert. Sie hat in verschiedenen Fabriken Arbeit gefunden und dann nach ein paar

Jahren hat sie die australische Staatsbürgerschaft bekommen. Danach kriegte sie ein Stipendium, um Geistes- und Sozialwissenschaften an der Uni Melbourne zu studieren. Dann ging sie 1958 nach Frankreich zurück und heute lebt sie in London.

E Janina David wurde 1930 in Polen als einziges Kind einer bürgerlichen jüdischen Familie geboren. Sie verlor ihre Eltern während des Krieges und verließ nach ihrer Befreiung aus dem Ghetto 1946 ihr Heimatland. Zwei Jahre verbrachte sie in einem Waisenhaus in Paris und emigrierte dann, kurz vor ihrem 18. Geburtstag, nach Australien. Sie erhielt die australische Staatsbürgerschaft, arbeitete in Fabriken und bekam ein Stipendium für das Studium der Geistes- und Sozialwissenschaften an der Universität Melbourne. 1958 kehrte sie nach Frankreich zurück. Heute lebt sie in London.

lexical choice

It is easy to decide which is the best text in German (check Answer Key if unsure). The other versions either make inappropriate lexical choices, use non-German word order or sound like spoken language.

Identify which lexical choices in version **A** are odd, and explain why.

When translating these texts into English, it is important to look for vocabulary in other examples of the same type of text **in English**, rather than just using a dictionary to translate words used in German texts. A fairly small set of verbs is regularly used in each language to represent education, artistic production and performance, so you need to be familiar with the usual choices.

List all the verbs used in the biographical recounts at the beginning of this chapter (and any other examples you have collected).

THEME

The way clauses throughout a text begin orientates the reader to what the text is about. First position is the grammatical THEME of the clause, and there must be a pattern, appropriate to the specific language, in the way all the THEMES through a text work together.

Identify what is odd, for a German text, about the way each sentence begins through versions **B** and **C**.

Biographical recounts printed on novels should be concise (publishing is expensive and the reader of these texts wants the information quickly). A good way to make text concise is 'nominalisation'. With nominalisation information can be packaged into a single noun group in one clause, so that the clause is 'lexically dense'. The examples below show how a message expressed over several clauses can be packaged into one clause. In the **b** versions, most of the information has been expressed through nouns rather than verbs:

LEXICAL DENSITY

1 a they suddenly left, which upset him and made him want to get back at them

1 b their sudden departure caused him distress and a desire for revenge

2 a he was upset because they left suddenly and then he wanted to get back at them

2 b his distress and desire for revenge was provoked by their sudden departure

> Find an example of nominalisation in version **E**, where an event is expressed as a noun, and then put the message into a more spoken style.

It is typical of concise, written text to use grammatically simple sentences, consisting of one or two clauses only. Spoken language on the other hand tends to string out information over more clauses.

number of clauses

> Name the grammatical feature which is used twice in version **D** and is also being used in the sentence which you are reading now and which is not a very suitable choice for a text that should be very concise and which makes the text sound rather more like a spoken text than a written one.

Both verbal forms, present perfect and simple past, are possible in English and German, but when translating into English you will not necessarily be able to use the same verbal forms as used in the German text. If the person is still living, English recounts tend to move into the present perfect towards the end of the text, in order to relate what has been recounted in the simple past to the present. The use and meaning of this form is not the same in German.

verbal form

> Explain why version **E** does not use the present perfect, and what effect its use has in version **D**.

Task 3 – identifying stylistic problems in English text

Stylistic problems are now presented in English text. Only one of the following English language versions of the Janina David text is a good translation of version **E** of the German text.

A In 1930 Janina David was born in Poland, the only child of a middle class Jewish family. She lost her parents during the war and left, after being rescued from the Ghetto in 1946, Poland. Two years she spent in an orphanage in Paris and emigrated then, shortly before her 18th birthday, to Australia. She was granted Australian citizenship, worked in factories and received a scholarship to study arts and social sciences at the University of Melbourne. 1958 she returned to France. Now she lives in London.

B Janina David was born in Poland in 1930 as an only child of a bourgeois Jewish family. She lost her parents in the war and left her homeland after her rescue out of the Ghetto in 1946. She was two years in an orphanage in Paris and then, shortly before her 18. birthday, left for Australia. She got the Australian citizenship, had jobs in factories and got a scholarship for the study of art and the social sciences at the Melbourne University. 1958 she went back to France. Today she is living in London.

C Janina David was born in Poland in 1930, the only child of a middle class Jewish family. She lost her parents during the war and, after being rescued from the Ghetto in 1946, left Poland. She spent two years in a Paris orphanage and then, shortly before her 18th birthday, emigrated to Australia. She was granted Australian citizenship, worked in factories and received a scholarship to study arts and social sciences at the University of Melbourne. In 1958 she returned to France and now lives in London.

D Janina David was born in Poland in 1930. She was the only child of a Jewish family which came from the bourgeois class. She lost her parents during the war and, after she had been rescued from the Ghetto in 1946, she left Poland. She spent two years in an orphanage in Paris and then she emigrated to Australia shortly before she turned 18. She found work in various factories and was granted Australian citizenship. She then received a scholarship in order to study arts and social sciences in Melbourne at the University. She returned to France in 1958 and lives in London currently.

Decide which version would be suitable for publication and explain what is wrong with the other versions, in terms of the following questions:

- What is odd about the beginnings of clauses, for a biographical recount, in English, in version **A**?
- What lexical and orthographic problems are there in version **B**?
- How would you describe and evaluate the clause grammar of version **D**?
- Of the basic types of PROCESS (Material, Mental, Relational) which types seem to occur most frequently in the biographical recount, based on these examples ?

1.2 Text and function

Not every text giving biographical information is 'recounting'. The texts below give biographical information about writers, but for a slightly different purpose than that of the biographical recounts seen so far in this chapter. The grammatical choices made to produce a text are carefully linked to the genre, and so when you are translating a text from your own language into a foreign language, you need to keep the specific genre's grammatical patterns in mind.

Task 4 – identifying situational context

The texts below feature some aspects of grammar which differ from the biographical recounts in this chapter.

1 Hilbert Meyer, Jahrgang 1941, ist seit 1975 Professor für Schulpädagogik an der Carl-von-Ossietzky-Universität Oldenburg. Er wurde durch zahlreiche Veröffentlichungen bekannt, vor allem durch sein *Trainingsprogramm zur Lernzielanalyse und den Leitfaden zur Unterrichtsvorbereitung.*

(Hilbert Meyer, *Unterrichtsmethoden*, Frankfurt/Main, 1987.)

2 Graham Lock teaches at the City University of Hong Kong. He has taught English and English Language Teaching in Singapore, Australia, and New Zealand. He has also published in the areas of phonology, Chinese sociolinguistics, and grammar teaching.

(Graham Lock, *Functional English Grammar*, Cambridge, 1996.)

3 Dell Hymes was born in Oregon. He has taught at Harvard, University of California Berkeley, University of Pennsylvania and University of Virginia, where he is Commonwealth Professor of Anthropology and of English. He has been President of the American Anthropological Association, the American Folklore Society, the Council on Anthropology and Education, and the Linguistic Society of America.

(Dell Hymes, *Ethnography Linguistics Narrative Inequality*, London, 1996.)

- In what kind of publication would the above texts likely appear?
- What is the purpose of giving the biographical information in this case, and how is the text function different from the biographies examined previously?
- How would *er wurde* in the Meyer text above be best translated for this context?
- How does the use of tenses in these texts differ from the use of tenses in the other biographies looked at before?

1.3 Summary of language features
The main grammatical features noticed in the biographical recount common to the German and the English versions are:

features in common

*Events are represented in chronological sequence.
*Texts begin with the person's name and most clause THEMES are unmarked.
*Simple verbal forms dominate.
*Most sentences consist of one clause only, and are linked by simple
conjunctions rather than complex grammatical relationships.
*Texts use conciseness devices – such as nominalisation, ellipsis of SUBJECT or
elements of the verbal group, and implicit conjunctive relations (temporal).
*Typical PROCESS types are Material and Relational.
*PARTICIPANTS are the person, their works and nominalised events.
*LEXIS is chosen from a restricted range, no colloquial items.
*LEXICAL DENSITY is not extremely high.
*Texts use almost no attitudinal LEXIS.

Though German and English biographies are very similar in function, there are certain key areas of difference in their grammatical realisation to remember when translating them: Word order, verbal form and the set of lexical choices typically used in each language.

grammatical differences between English and German

*All clauses in English biographies tend to begin with the person or their work. Other choices, such as CIRCUMSTANTIAL elements in first position in a clause, produce a 'marked' or unusual pattern. In German the first element of clauses throughout the text varies more, without producing a marked effect. If the ordering of elements in the German text is copied for a translation into

English, the translator runs the risk of producing a very odd, unsuccessful text in English.

*Present perfect tense is often used towards the middle or end of English texts about a living person, to relate a string of simple past events to the present situation. Use of present perfect in German is spoken style and not appropriate in such a recount.

*When a conjunctive ADJUNCT of time is present in English (rare), it is used together with a non-finite form of the verb (eg "after being rescued/ after joining").

*There is a set of lexical choices that recur in each language, therefore the range typically used in English texts should be learned, rather than translating German words from a dictionary. Word choices in English for this genre favour the more formal register of Latin-based words (eg "return" rather than "go back" and "receive" rather than "get").

Having identified the major language patterns of a type of recount, you have some preparation for translating such texts. The following exercises draw your attention to lexical and grammatical choices potentially available at several points in text production, some of which are simply wrong, others possible in some contexts but not for this genre. An understanding of which choices are and which are not possible in this genre will prepare you for independent translation work.

**I.2
Guided
translation
exercises**

2.1 Text completion
The following biographical recount was found in a German language novel.

Irina Korschunow, geboren und aufgewachsen in Stendal als Tochter einer deutschen Mutter und eines russischen Vaters, gehört zu den bekanntesten Kinder- und Jugendbuchautoren. Ihre Bücher wurden mit vielen Preisen ausgezeichnet und in zehn Sprachen übersetzt. Sie schrieb Drehbücher zu erfolgreichen Fernsehfilmen wie *Der Führerschein*, *Der Urlaub* und *Wie es geschah*. Sie ist Mitglied des PEN und lebt heute in der Nähe von München.

(Irina Korschunow, *Glück hat seinen Preis*, Berlin, 1983.)

Task 5 – completing gap translation text

Complete the translation by choosing from the words offered below. Refer back to the biographies at the beginning of the chapter as a guide.

Irina Korschunow was born and (1) ___ in Stendal, (2) ___ a German mother and a Russian father. She (3) ___ the most (4) ___ (5) ___. Her books (6) ___ many prizes and (7) ___ into ten languages. She (8)___ screenplays for such successful TV series as ... She is a member of PEN and (9) ___ near Munich.

(1) grew up, brought up, raised, reared, spent her childhood
(2) as the daughter of, as a daughter of, the daughter of, daughter of, to (omit reference to parents)
(3) belongs to, is among, is one of, counts among
(4) well-acquainted, well-known, familiar, popular, widely-read, known, renowned, famous, better-known
(5) writers of books for children and young people, child and youth book authors, writers for children and young people, children's writers, authors of children's and youth books, authors of children's and adolescent literature
(6) were awarded, won, received, got, have been awarded, have won, have received
(7) were translated, have been translated, are translated
(8) wrote, has written, was writing, had written
(9) currently lives, is now living, now lives, lives today, presently lives

2.2 Evaluation and improvement

The following biographical recount was found in a German translation of an Amy Tan novel.

Amy Tan wurde 1952 als Tochter chinesischer Auswanderer in Oakland, Kalifornien, geboren. Ihr Vater und ihr Bruder starben, als sie fünfzehn Jahre alt war. Ihre Mutter, Tochter einer wohlhabenden Familie in Schanghai, mußte drei Töchter aus erster Ehe in China zurücklassen; sie kehrte erst 1978 zum erstenmal in ihre Heimat zurück. Amy Tan lebt heute mit ihrem Mann in San Francisco. Ihr zweiter Roman, *Die Frau des Feuergottes*, war auch in Deutschland monatelang auf der Bestsellerliste.

(Amy Tan, *Töchter des Himmels*, München, 1990.)

Task 6 – evaluating student translations

Mark every mistake and stylistic problem you can find in the following student translations of the text, choose which functions best and explain your decisions.

A Amy Tan was born as a daughter of Chinese emigrants in Oakland, California, in 1952. At the age of fifteen her father and brother died. Her mother, a daughter of a wealthy family living in Shanghai, had to leave behind three daughters of her first marriage in China. It was not until 1978 that she returned for the first time to her homeland. Today Amy Tan is living with her husband in San Francisco. Her second novel has been among bestsellers for months even in Germany.

B Amy Tan, daughter of Chinese emigrants, was born in 1952 in Oakland, California. Her brother and her father died when she was 15 years old. Her mother, daughter of a well-to-do family in Shanghai, had to leave behind in China three daughters of first marriage. It was not until 1978 that she returned to her homecountry for the first time. Today Amy Tan and her husband live in San Francisco. Her second novel has been on the best selling list for several months even in Germany.

C Amy Tan was born in Oakland, California, in 1952 to Chinese emigrants. Her father and brother died when she was 15. Her mother, the daughter of a wealthy Shanghai family, had to leave three of her daughters from her first marriage behind in China and did not return to her native China until 1978. Amy Tan lives today with her husband in San Francisco. Her second novel was a bestseller for months, also in Germany.

Task 7 – improving the translation

Write your own translation of the text (in pairs or small groups if you are in a class) and compare with other students.

2.3 Vocabulary extension

Use a good bilingual dictionary and a thesaurus to answer the following questions.

Task 8 – Janina David text

- How many alternatives are there for "get"? It is a common and useful word in English, but does not suit this genre as it is mainly used in spoken English. Which alternatives would be suitable in a biographical recount?

- What does your dictionary suggest for translating *Milieu*, and what is the more frequent way of expressing the idea in English, when talking about the social "milieu" one was raised in?
- *Heimat*, *Heimatland*, *Heimkehr* are quite common expressions in German, but how do you translate them into English?
- What is the relationship or difference between "art" and "arts", between "arts" and "humanities", between "study" and "studies", between "social studies" and "social sciences"?
- How many words are suggested for *bürgerlich* in a good bilingual dictionary, and why is "bourgeois" not a good English translation in this context?

Task 9 – Amy Tan text

- How do the words below, probably listed in your dictionary as synonyms for "wealthy", differ in collocation and connotation?

affluent, loaded, rich, well-to-do, well-off, flush, prosperous, well-heeled, rolling in it, made of money, moneyed, opulent, comfortably-off, filthy rich, in the money, thriving

- Why is "even" (sometimes a good translation of *auch*) not appropriate in the Amy Tan translation?
- What is a good translation for *auch* in each sentence of the following fictional dialogue?

A Wenn ich es mir **auch** oft vorgenommen habe, ich lerne einfach nicht Auto fahren.
B Ich kann **auch** nicht Auto fahren.
C Mein Freund **auch** nicht.
A Ich könnte es **auch** nicht lernen... und wenn ich hundert Fahrstunden nehmen würde.
B Ja, das Geld ist **auch** nicht das Problem.
A Na ja, für mich wäre es aber **auch** ein Problem.

- *Auf der Bestsellerliste* would probably be translated as "was a bestseller", although "in the best selling lists" does exist in English. How would you translate the following English sentences into German?

"He is a bestselling author" and "his books have been selling well recently".

- "native China" is quite a good translation of *Heimat* in this text, but what would be good German translations of "a native Londoner", and "to go native"?

Task 10 – Emma Thompson text (text follows in part 3)

- How can *sie studiert Geschichte* and *sie studiert Medizin* be translated in at least four different ways?
- How would you translate the following into English? *Nach Absolvierung ihres Studiums will sie ins Ausland fahren*, and *neben dem Studium arbeitet sie als Kellnerin*.
- Would any of the following be acceptable translations for *erste Schauspielversuche* in this context, and if not, why?

  - she made a first effort to act
  - she made her first attempts at acting
  - she had a first go at acting
  - she tried to act for the first time
  - she experimented with acting
  - she did her first acting trials
  - she tested her acting skills for the first time

- Why would it be advisable to avoid trying to translate *Versuch* with the help of the dictionary in this context?
- How can the following be translated into English?

  Versuchsabteilung, Versuchsbeschreibung, Versuchskanninchen, Versuchsperson, Versuchsprojekt, Versuchsreihe, Versuchsstadium, Versuchsstrecke, versuchsweise

- *Hauptrolle* in this context would be "lead" or "leading role", not "main part", but can you find several ways of translating the following? *Er muß ständig die Hauptrolle spielen.*
- Which of the following abbreviations are used in English, and can you use any of them to translate the German *u.a.*?

  etc, aso, eg, ao, incl, ie, fe

- What is the difference between "sensibility, sensuality, sensitivity, sensitiveness and sensuousness", and between "sensible, sensitive, sensual, sensuous, and sensory"?
  (Contextualise each to show the difference of meaning.)

3.1 Quick texts

Use the following for further practice translating biographical recounts. Time yourself to complete each within ten to twenty minutes. Pay particular attention to the English versions of city and place names, names of university subjects, and appropriate titles of festivals in English. Check your English text with other students.

1 Robert Schneider, geb. 1961 in Bregenz, wurde für seinen Erstling mit dem Alemannischen Literaturpreis 1993, dem Robert-Musil-Stipendium und dem Preis Osterfestspiele Salzburg 1994 gewürdigt. Außerdem erhielt er den Abraham-Woursell-Award und für seine dramatischen Arbeiten den Drehbuchpreis des österreichischen Rundfunks und den Landespreis für Volkstheaterstücke in Baden-Würtemberg (1990). Sein Monolog *Dreck* wurde als bestes Theaterstück 1993 bei den Potsdamer Theatertagen gekürt, die Hörspielfassung mit dem Civis '93 ausgezeichnet.

2 Tilman Spengler, geboren 1947 in Oberhausen. Studierte in Heidelberg, Taipeh und München Sinologie, Politologie und Neuere Geschichte. 1980 und 1981 Gastdozent an der Chinesischen Akademie der Wissenschaften in Peking. Lebt in Ambach am Starnberger See.

The following information appeared next to an interview published in *Focus*. Use it to write a short prose biographical recount text in English.

3 EMMA THOMPSON
JAHRGANG 1959, Vater Theaterregisseur, Mutter Schauspielerin
AUSBILDUNG Studium in Cambridge, dort auch erste Schauspielversuche
ERSTE ERFOLGE 1985 Hauptrolle im Musicalhit *Me and My Girl*, 1986 TV-Miniserien, u.a. mit Kenneth Branagh, den sie 1989 heiratet
FILMDEBÜT mit *The Tall Guy* (1989). Danach in Branaghs *Henry V*, *Dead Again* and *Much Ado About Nothing*
OSCAR für *Howard's End* (1992), danach *Remains of the Day*, *In the Name of the Father*, *Carrington*

1995 Script für *Sinn und Sinnlichkeit* (Golden Globe) und Trennung von Branagh (*Focus* 10/ 1996)

3.2 45-minute texts

Time yourself to complete each of the following, slightly longer, texts within an hour.

1 Lion Feuchtwanger wurde 1884 in München geboren. Nach vielseitigen Studien gab er die Kulturzeitschrift *Der Spiegel* heraus, schrieb Theaterkritiken und arbeitete an der *Schaubühne* mit. Bei Ausbruch des Ersten Weltkrieges wurde Feuchtwanger in Tunis interniert, konnte jedoch fliehen. In München vom Wehrdienst suspendiert, nahm er die Übersetzung und Bearbeitung indischer, griechischer und spanischer Dramen wieder auf, zudem entstanden eigene Stücke und Antikriegsdichtung. 1918/19 begann die freundschaftliche Zusammenarbeit mit Brecht. Die bayrische Räterepublik erlebte er „in großer Nähe führender Männer". Die historischen Romane *Die häßliche Herzogin Margarete Maultausch* und *Jud Süß* brachten Feuchtwanger Weltruhm. 1925 siedelte er nach Berlin über. Als die Nazis die Macht übernahmen, war er auf Vortragsreise in den USA. Seine Bücher wurden verboten, Haus und Vermögen konfisziert. Sanary-sur-Mer, Feuchtwangers neuer Lebensort, war zeitweilig ein Zentrum deutscher Emigranten. Hier vollendete er u.a. die *Wartesaal*- und die *Josephus*-Trilogie. Ende 1936 fuhr er in die UdSSR (Moskau 1917, *Ein Reisebericht für meine Freunde*). 1940 internierten ihn die Franzosen. Ab 1941 lebte er in Kalifornien, wo große historische Romane, Erzählungen, Stücke und Essays entstanden. Feuchtwanger starb 1958 in Pacific Palisades.
(Lion Feuchtwanger, *Die Brüder* Lautersack, Berlin, 1977.)

2 Die amerikanische Schriftstellerin Djuna Barnes, die 1892 in Cornwall-on-Hudson geboren wurde, war eine Pendlerin zwischen der Alten und Neuen Welt. In Greenwich Village hatte sie sich bereits mit Reportagen und Interviews, Gedichten und Einaktern einen Namen gemacht, ehe sie 1920 nach Paris ging. Sylvia Beach, Gründerin der Buchhandlung „Shakespeare and Company" und Verlegerin des *Ulysses* von James Joyce, schreibt in ihren Erinnerungen: „Sie war ganz entschieden eine der talentiertesten und meiner Meinung nach eine der faszinierendsten Gestalten der literarischen Welt im Paris der Zwanzigerjahre". Zu dieser literarischen Welt gehörten u.a. Gertrude Stein, Ezra Pound, T.S. Eliot und James Joyce wie auch der Kreis um die amerikanische Millionärin Natalie Barney, Vorbild für den von Djuna Barnes anonym veröffentlichten *Ladies' Almanach*. Im gleichen Jahr erschien der Roman *Ryder* und 1935 ihr

Hauptwerk, der Roman *Nachtgewächs*. 1940 kehrte Djuna Barnes nach New York zurück, wo sie 1982 starb.
(Kyra Stromberg, *Djuna Barnes Leben und Werk einer Extravaganten*, Frankfurt a. M., 1992.)

3 Martin Luther King wurde in Atlanta, Georgia, geboren. Er studierte Theologie und wurde 1954 Baptistenpfarrer. In den fünfziger Jahren trat er als Kämpfer in der amerikanischen Bürgerrechtsbewegung hervor. Er gründete verschiedene Vereinigungen zur Förderung der Rassenintegration. Wie Gandhi plädierte er für gewaltlosen Widerstand und führte zahlreiche Demonstrationen durch. Im Laufe seines Lebens wurde er wiederholt inhaftiert, konnte jedoch 1956 als ersten Erfolg die Aufhebung der Rassenschranke in öffentlichen Verkehrsmitteln in Montgomery, Alabama, verzeichnen. Seit den Rassenunruhen 1964 sah er sich zunehmend von der „Black Power"-Bewegung, einer militanten Schwarzenbewegung, bedrängt. Er erhielt 1964 den Friedensnobelpreis. 1968 wurde er nach vorhergegangenen erfolglosen Anschlägen in Memphis, Tennessee, ermordet.
(Ellen Henrichs-Kleinen, *Englisch: Textinterpretationen*, Niedernhausen, 1992.)

3.3 Exam practice

Translate each of the following texts within one and a half hours. They are about the length and complexity of exam texts used in German universities. Use dictionaries if your *Prüfungsordnung* allows it.

1 Antonio Vivaldi wurde 1678 als ältestes von neun Kindern des Friseurs und sehr guten Laiengeigers Giambattista Vivaldi, der Mitglied des Orchesters von San Marco war, in Venedig geboren. Neben dem Violinenunterricht bei seinem Vater erhielt er eine geistliche Ausbildung und wurde am 18. September 1693 zum Priester geweiht. 1703 wurde Antonio Vivaldi an das „Ospediale della Pieta" als Geigenlehrer verpflichtet. An diesem öffentlich unterstützten Waisenhaus wurden junge Mädchen musikalisch ausgebildet. Die Konzerte des Orchesters waren Glanzpunkte im Musikleben der Stadt, und keiner der vielen Venedig-Besucher versäumte, sie zu hören. Hier konnte Vivaldi unter optimalen Bedingungen seinen Stil entwickeln, der in den *Vier Jahreszeiten* einen Höhepunkt fand. Später wandte sich Vivaldi auch der Oper zu und brillierte auf Konzertreisen durch Europa als Solist. 1741 starb er in Wien. Unter seinen zahlreichen Kompositionen sind die *Vier Jahreszeiten*-Konzerte die bekanntesten und beliebtesten. Die Konzerte sind 1725 als Nr. 1–4 seines Opus VIII *Il cimento dell armonia e dell inventione (Der Wettstreit von Harmonie und*

Erfindung) erschienen. Diese Werke von Vivaldi entsprachen auf besondere Weise den ästhetischen Vorstellungen der ersten Hälfte des 18. Jahrhunderts. In ihnen verbindet sich eine ausgewogene Form („armonia") mit besonders bildhaften und klangvollen Einfällen („inventione"). Der Partitur sind erklärende Sonette beigefügt, die wahrscheinlich von Vivaldi selbst verfaßt wurden. *(Weihnachtskonzertprogramm der Märkischen Energieversorgung AG, Netzeband, 1996.)*

2 Max Frisch ist der Sohn eines Züricher Architekten. Er begann bereits auf dem Gymnasium, Theaterstücke zu schreiben. Nach dem Abitur studierte er zwei Jahre Germanistik. Aus finanziellen Gründen mußte er das Studium abbrechen und sich als Journalist den Lebensunterhalt erwerben. In dieser Zeit unternahm er ausgedehnte Reisen. Nach einem zweiten Studium an der Schweizer Technischen Hochschule eröffnete er in Zürich ein Architektenbüro. Bei Kriegsausbruch wurde Frisch zum Militärdienst eingezogen. Am gleichen Tage begann er, obwohl er seit seinem ersten Roman *Jürg Reinhart* (1934) das Schreiben aufgegeben hatte, mit den Aufzeichnungen zum Tagebuch *Blätter aus dem Brosack* (1940). Es folgte ein zweiter Roman, *Die Schwierigen oder J'adore ce qui me brûle* (1943), der Entwicklungsroman eines Künstlers. Nach der Erzählung *Bin oder Die Reise nach Peking* (1945) errang Frisch mit dem Roman *Stiller* (1954) seinen ersten internationalen Erfolg. Er erzählt darin die Geschichte eines Bildhauers, der aus der Enge seiner bürgerlichen Existenz flieht und seinem eigenen Versagen als Künstler und Liebhaber entrinnen will, nach vielen Jahren als ein ganz anderer zurückkehrt und trotz verzweifelter Gegenwehr wieder in sein früheres Leben eingeschlossen wird. Das Thema des gespaltenen, ausbrechenden und schließlich doch scheiternden Menschen ist auch in Frischs Dramatik enthalten. Aufsehen erregten ferner der Bericht *Homo Faber* (1957) und das *Tagebuch 1946-49* (1950), ein aufschlußreiches Zeitdokument zur europäischen Nachkriegsentwicklung (...). Frisch ist neben Dürrenmatt der bedeutendste Schweizer Dramatiker der Gegenwart und einer der profiliertesten bürgerlichen Dichter der zeitgenössischen deutschsprachigen Literatur. Seine Stücke sind von der modernen amerikanischen Dramatik (Wilder), vom Wiener Volkstheater und von Bertolt Brecht beeinflußt. Er erhielt unter anderen den C.F.-Meyer-Preis der Stadt Zürich (1938), die Rockefeller Grant for Drama (1951), den W. Raabe-Preis (1955) und den Georg-Büchner-Preis der Deutschen Akademie für Sprache und Dichtung, zu deren Mitgliedern er zählt. Von seinen Hörspielen sind zu nennen: *Rip van Winkle* (1953) und *Herr Quixote* (1955).
(Schauspielführer Band III, Hrsg. K.-H. Berger et al., Berlin, 1964.)

The following text, though historical rather than biographical, is also recount.

Translate within two hours. Before beginning to translate, consider carefully the issues of word order, tense and lexis focused on through this chapter.

Zu Beginn des 19. Jahrhunderts gab es Anglistik nur als einen Teilbereich der Germanistik, die sich mit allen germanischen Sprachen beschäftigte, so wie sich heute noch die Romanistik mit allen romanischen Sprachen befasst. Davor gab es noch nicht einmal die Germanistik, sondern nur die klassische Philologie, die schon in der Antike von den Gelehrten in Alexandria wissenschaftlich betrieben wurde. Ihre Methoden übernahmen im Mittelalter die Theologen, um die in lateinischer, griechischer oder hebräischer Sprache überlieferten Dokumente des Christentums in ihrer Textgestalt zu sichern und ihre Inhalte exegetisch aufzuschließen. In der Renaissance kam dann eine ausgedehnte Beschäftigung mit der antiken Dichtung und Philosophie hinzu. Erst im 18. Jahrhundert machte man sich unter dem Einfluss der heraufziehenden Romantik daran, auch die frühe volkssprachliche Überlieferung mit den gleichen philologischen Methoden zu erforschen. So bildete sich neben der klassischen eine romanische und eine germanische Philologie heraus. Dabei wurden die Zeugnisse der althochdeutschen und altenglischen Dichtung anfangs weniger als Dichtung denn als sprachhistorische Dokumente studiert. Als dann aber Werke wie der altenglische *Beowulf* oder das mittelhochdeutsche *Nibelungenlied* in philologisch erarbeiteten Ausgaben allgemein zugänglich wurden, rückten auch die literarischen Aspekte ins Blickfeld. Da im 19. Jahrhundert das wachsende Nationalbewusstsein die politische Entwicklung Europas prägte, war es nur natürlich, dass die neueren Philologie, anders als die klassische Philologie, die Nation als das Subjekt der einzelnen Sprachen und Literaturen ansahen. Das führte 1872 zur Errichtung des ersten anglistischen Lehrstuhls in Straßburg und damit zur Ausgliederung der Anglistik aus der Germanistik, worauf sie sich rasch im Fächerkanon der deutschen Universitäten etablierte und wegen der großen Nachfrage nach Englischlehrern bald zu einem Massenfach wurde, das gegenwärtig von ca. 60 000 Studierenden an 59 deutschen Hochschulen studiert wird.

(Hans-Dieter Gelfert, *Einführung in das Studium, studium kompakt Anglistik · Amerikanistik*, Berlin, 1998.)

II News Item – in brief

A "news item" is a short, neutral account of a current event in the news media. This chapter focuses on the very brief items to be found in narrow columns in most daily newspapers.

II.1 German and English examples   36
1.1 Comparison and contrast
1.2 Text and function
1.3 Summary of language features

II.2 Guided translation exercises   48
2.1 Text completion
2.2 Evaluation and improvement
2.3 Vocabulary extension

II.3 Independent translation   51
3.1 Quick texts
3.2 45-minute texts
3.3 Exam practice

The news item is a common factual genre in both English and German. The news-in-brief items below are typical and simple texts, such as can be found in daily newspapers around the world. Like the short recount texts in Chapter I, these texts feature lexical and syntactic choices designed for a very quick read. They give a precise and concise account of events, with no obvious interpretation or comment on them. In these texts, just one event, deemed by the editors to be topical, generally interesting or amusing, is told. They are the focus of this chapter on the basis of their familiarity to readers and the fact that the German and English examples illustrate important grammatical differences. Newspaper texts featuring such patterns are frequently used in translation exams.

1 Roma verprügelt

In Sofia haben Skinheads mehrere Roma überfallen und dabei einen 15 Jahre alten Jungen getötet. Wie die bulgarische Polizei am Montag mitteilte, waren die Skinheads am Wochenende in ein leerstehendes Haus im Stadtzentrum eingedrungen und hatten dort sieben Roma verprügelt. Eines der Opfer habe sich gewehrt und sei aus dem Fenster geworfen worden.   (*F.A.Z.* 19.5.98)

2 Kriminalitätsbelastung in Frankfurt am Main am höchsten

Frankfurt, 3. Juni. Frankfurt am Main bleibt die Stadt mit der höchsten Kriminalitätsbelastung in Deutschland. Im vergangenen Jahr wurden dort mehr als 125 000 Straftaten gezählt, das sind 19 394 Delikte auf 100 000 Einwohner. Auf Platz zwei der gefährlichen Städte kam die Hansestadt Rostock mit 18 392 Straftaten auf 100 000 Einwohner, Hamburg (17 420) und Berlin (17 134) folgen auf den Plätzen drei und vier. Überdurchschnittlich viele Delikte wurden in den Städten in Ostdeutschland begangen: Magdeburg, Potsdam, Halle und Schwerin liegen deutlich vor weitaus grösseren Stadten im Westen.   (*F.A.Z.* 4.6.98)

3 Verwirrten aufgegriffen

Ferch – einen offenbar geistig verwirrten Mann hat die Polizei nach einer mehrtägigen Suche wohlbehalten aufgegriffen. Das Auto des 85jährigen aus Mönchengladbach war bereits in der Nacht zu Montag bei Ferch (Potsdam-Mittelmark) leer aufgefunden worden. Mit einem Polizeihubschrauber wurde den ganzen Montag das Gebiet abgesucht. Gestern morgen fanden die Beamten den Mann, bekleidet mit Oberhemd und Unterhose. Der entkräftete Rentner kam ins Krankenhaus.   (*Berliner Morgenpost* 20.5.98)

4 Brand im Mehrfamilienhaus

Potsdam – Nur knapp einer Katastrophe entgingen in der Nacht zu Donnerstag sechs Familien in einem Haus an der Bergholzer Strasse. Alle mussten das Haus zeitweilig räumen. Zwei der zwölf Hausbewohner kamen mit Rauchvergiftungen ins Krankenhaus, drei weitere, darunter ein Kind, mussten ambulant behandelt werden. Nach ersten Erkenntnissen war das Feuer in einer Erdgeschosswohnung neben einer Couch ausgebrochen. Die Polizei schliesst fahrlässige Brandstiftung nicht aus. *(Berliner Morgenpost 27.3.98)*

5 2 Mio. Moslems auf dem Berg Arafat
In brütender Hitze von 38 Grad beten rund zwei Millionen Moslems aus 100 Ländern auf dem Berg Arafat (Saudi-Arabien) – Höhepunkt der jährlichen Pilgerreise Hadsch. An diesem Berg soll der Prophet Mohammed vor etwa 1400 Jahren die letzte Sure des Korans verkündet haben. *(Bild 7.4.98)*

6 Seltene Tiger: Nachwuchs per Kaiserschnitt
Peking – Nur per Kaiserschnitt ist es gelungen, den äusserst seltenen Südchina-Tigern zu Nachwuchs zu verhelfen. Wie die chinesische Nachrichtenagentur Xinhua gestern berichtete, musste das 14jährige Tigerweibchen Xianghuan in einem Reservat im Südwesten Chinas den Eingriff über sich ergehen lassen, damit drei Junge zur Welt gebracht werden konnten, von denen eins starb. *(Berliner Morgenpost 8.6.98)*

7 Frauen als Priester
Baden-Baden – Für tiefgreifende Änderungen in der katholischen Kirche wie ein Ende des Zölibats, Frauen als Priester und die Wahl der Bischöfe durch die Ortskirche hat sich der Präsident des Zentralkomitees der deutschen Katholiken (ZdK), Hans-Joachim Meyer, ausgesprochen. Allerdings müsse sich die katholische Kirche „erst an diese Gedanken gewöhnen". Solche Veränderungen wurden sonst zu einer Zerreissprobe der Kirche fuhren. Im ZdK sind die katholischen Laienorganisationen in Deutschland zusammengeschlossen. Es veranstaltet unter anderem die Katholikentage. *(Berliner Morgenpost 23.2.98)*

1 Neo-Nazi violence soars by a quarter
Extreme right crime soared by one-third in Germany last year to the highest level seen since unification in 1990, and violence by the same group also rocketed by 27 per cent.
The domestic intelligence service and the constitutional watchdog said yesterday that criminal offences by far right activists had risen to 11,719 from 8,730 in 1996, or by 34 per cent.
Acts of violence by neo-Nazis, including attempted manslaughter and assault on foreigners, rose to 790 from 624, while the number of rightwing youths

prone to violence was estimated at 7,600, up from 6,400. Almost half of the violence took place in the east. (*The Guardian*, 7 May, 1998)

2 Three held over shooting

Detectives investigating the murder of a "supergrass" yesterday arrested three men.

The men were detained at separate addresses in Richmond and Hampton, in South-West London, and Sunbury, Surrey.

The men, aged 34, 40 and 49, are being held at police stations in Hampshire, where they were being interviewed about the death last February of James Lawson, who was shot at his home in Bow Field, Hook.

Mr. Lawson, aged 40, who was also known as Peter McNeil, was shot as he answered the door.

He became a "supergrass" nine years ago when he tipped off police about a Maffia plot to flood Britain with cocaine worth £ 20 million a week on the streets. (*The Guardian*, 8 May, 1998)

3 Rebel rally at Mecca pilgrimage

Two million muslims prayed on Mt Arafat yesterday at the climax of the haj pilgrimage. They were told by Sheikh Abdul Aziz bin Abdullah al Sheikh, the deputy mufti of Saudi Arabia, to spread the messsage of Islam peacefully.

But Iranian media said thousands of pilgrims had held a rally chanting "Death to America and Israel", despite a Saudi ban on political demonstrations at the haj. (*Daily Telegraph*, 7 April, 1998)

4 US tornado kills eight

A surprise tornado tore through a rural area of north-eastern US state of Georgia yesterday, ripping apart homes and damaging farm buildings and a primary school. At least eight people were killed and 80 injured. Six people, including two children, were killed in mobile homes near a high school, including a girl aged 13 whose home was dumped into a pond.

(*The Guardian*, 21 March, 1998)

5 £ 144,500 for Potter letter

A Beatrix Potter letter which had been consigned to the rubbish tip fetched £ 144,500 at auction at Sotheby's yesterday – a world record for memorabilia relating to the children's book writer.

The letter, containing the first pictures of Potter's creation Mr Jeremy Fisher, was rescued by a little girl in Connecticut, as her family moved home in 1978. It was bought by a New York book dealer, Raymond Wapner, on behalf of a private American collector.

The seven-page correspondence, penned by Potter from her home at Dunkeld, Tayside, had been expected to fetch up to £ 60,000. Potter drew the famous fictional frog in a picture-letter to Eric Moore, second son of her old governess, Annie Moore, in September 1893.   (*Daily Telegraph,* 8 May, 1998)

6 Media tycoon Rupert Murdoch launched withering attack on BBC bosses yesterday.

He lashed out at BBC Director-General John Birt and the "elitists" who tell viewers what they should watch on television.

Mr Murdoch said British TV chiefs treated the public like idiots who couldn't tell good TV programmes from bad.

"There seems to be a feeling that the public cannot be trusted," he said in a rare public appearance. "But the public can work out pretty quickly if it is being conned."

Mr Murdoch said viewers didn't care which channel their TV programme came from as long as it was good.   (*Daily Mirror,* 7 April, 1998)

7 Press complaints record
A record number of complaints were resolved by the Press Complaints Commission last year. The PCC's annual report reveals that 2,944 complaints were made in 1997 – seven out of 10 relating to accuracy in reporting – and nine out of 10 involving a breach of its code of practice were settled. The PCC said it underlined that self-regulation was the best way to handle complaints about press reporting.   (*The Guardian,* 7 May, 1998)

1.1 Comparison and contrast

News items are obtained from various news agencies around the world (*dpa, Reuter, AP, UP, AFP*) and share similar features, wherever and in whatever language they are published. Some refer to and quote studies of complex situations or of important public statements, others represent events as stories, or elaborate a reported event with brief explanation. Those texts which refer to a series of events rarely tell the plot like a recount, that is, in chronological order. Generally speaking, the main event will first be summarised into one topic sentence, which the rest of the text elaborates, expands or explains. So the facts or event deemed most important begin the text, then the text might elaborate with the **result**, work backwards to the **causes** and end with the **least important details**. In a longer news text the headline, and possibly sub-heading, together with the first paragraph should provide answers to the questions **who?** (the participants involved), **what?** (the event that took place), **when?** (the time of the

journalists' questions

event) and **where?** (the place of the event). Further details are then given about the circumstances in which the event took place – **how?** – and the motive – **why?**.

Yet, although general text functions may be the same in German and English news items, the texts typically feature important differences in grammatical structures and lexis. The following exercises bring the language features of the genre in English and in German to your attention, to help you avoid the typical mistakes students make translating such texts.

Task 1 – identifying grammatical differences

Looking carefully through the examples given of short news items taken from various German and English language newspapers, you will notice some obvious differences in each language's texts in several areas of grammar. There are differences in what comes first in the clause (THEME) and in the use of tenses. The grammar used for indirectly reporting speech differs: German texts can make use of a MOOD choice that does not exist in English (*Konjunktiv*) or use MODALITY (usually modal verbs), an English text generally reports speech with other grammatical strategies. The texts make different lexical choices: a different role is played in German and English news texts by the use of word play, attitudinal, exaggerated or amusing lexis, and sometimes by nominalisation. The texts may have quite different lexical densities in each language: this is tested by counting the number of 'content' words per clause and calculating a ratio in relation to the words in the whole text – the higher the ratio of content words to total words, the denser the text. Even the texts' layout differs.

> Note down as many differences as you can, looking at all the features above.

THEME

SUBJECT

The texts in German begin quite differently from those in English. The THEMES of the **first** clauses in German news texts may be CIRCUMSTANTIAL elements or affected PARTICIPANTS, or the clause's grammatical SUBJECT. THEME position in the English language texts is almost always filled by a noun that is the grammatical SUBJECT of the clause. When translating such texts into English, this observation must be put into practice. It would simply be wrong to begin an English language text of this kind with the same type of element (prepositional phrase or object) that is so often used to begin a

German language news item. Word order can be more flexible in German because its system of 'case' markings indicates the grammatical role of each clause element. It is possible to begin a German clause with various elements without producing a 'marked' effect. In English, first position typically conflates with grammatical SUBJECT, and variations to this are 'marked'.

Since short news items are concerned with topical events, CIRCUMSTANCES of time are likely to refer to the recent past, usually the day before. CIRCUMSTANCES are never at the beginning of English news items, unless the date has a particular significance, for example an anniversary.

> Look at the THEME choices throughout the texts, not just the first clause. Underline the beginnings of each sentence in both the English and German reports, and comment on what you notice.

The use of 'tenses' is not quite the same in each language, and this also needs to be born in mind when translating.   *verbal forms*

> List the verbs (in their given forms) used in each text, and explain the differences you observe in the use of tenses in the German and the English language texts.

When reporting speech, each language uses different grammar.   *reporting speech*

> List the occasions in the German texts where either *Konjunktiv* or modality is used to report speech indirectly, and consider how these could be translated.

> Calculate, compare and comment on the LEXICAL DENSITY of the texts in each language.   *LEXICAL DENSITY*

> List, compare and comment on those words you find in each language's texts that are not 'neutral' in what functional linguists call AFFECT.   *AFFECT*

> Find other examples of short news items in English and German and examine whether the patterns you have noticed dominate these also.

Task 2 – identifying stylistic problems in German text

Below are student translations into German of the English news items "Three held over shooting" and "£ 144,500 for Potter letter". Although grammatically possible, to the native speaker the texts have features that sound strange, and on close examination, they don't conform to the norms of German language news items in several respects.

Underline the words and grammatical features in translations 1 and 2 you think do not 'sound right'. On the basis of what you have noticed so far about such texts, critically comment on these fairly literal translations in terms of their acceptability as German news items.

1 Detektive, die im Mordfall an einem „Superspitzel" ermittelten, verhafteten gestern drei Männer.
Die Männer wurden an getrennten Adressen in Richmond und Hampton, in Süd-West-London und Sunbury, Surrey, festgenommen.
Die Männer, im Alter von 34, 40 und 49 Jahren, werden in Polizeirevieren in Hampshire festgehalten, wo sie über den Tod von James Lawson befragt werden, der im vorigen Februar in seinem Haus in Bow Field, Hook, erschossen wurde.
Der 40jährige Lawson, der auch unter dem Namen Peter McNeil bekannt war, wurde beim Öffnen der Haustür erschossen.
Er wurde vor neun Jahren ein „Superspitzel", als er die Polizei über ein Mafia-Komplott informierte, Kokain im Wert von 20 Millionen Pfund pro Woche im Straßenhandel nach Großbritannien einzuschleusen.

2 Ein Brief Beatrix Potters, der für den Müll bestimmt war, brachte gestern £144,500 bei einer Versteigerung bei Sotheby – eine Rekordsumme für Erinnerungsstücke der Kinderbuchautorin.
Der Brief, der erste Bilder von Potter's Geschöpf „Herr Jeremias Fischer" enthält, wurde von einem kleinen Mädchen in Connecticut gerettet, als ihre Familie 1978 umzog. Er wurde von Raymond Wappner, einem New Yorker Buchhändler, für einen amerikanischen Privatsammler gekauft.
Die siebenseitige Korrespondenz, von Potter in ihrem Zuhause in Dunkeld, Tayside geschrieben, sollte, so hatte man erwartet, £ 60,000 einbringen. Potter zeichnete die berühmte Froschfigur im September 1898 in einem illustrierten Brief an Eric Moore, den zweiten Sohn ihrer früheren Gouvernante, Annie Moore.

One reason the translations sound odd to the native speaker of German is that they have copied the THEMATIC pattern of the English source texts instead of conforming to the usual word order patterns of German text.

THEME

Another feature contributing to their inadequacy as German text is their 'spoken style', also copied from the English source texts. German news items often prefer *Nominalstil*, in which information is packed into noun groups, rather than being carried over several clauses. A better German translation of text **1** might therefore make use of nouns such as *Ermittlungen, Festnahme, Tatverdächtige, Polizeigewahrsam, Hinweise*, etc.

nominalisation

The two translations also begin in the simple past tense, probably influenced by the English. German news items, however, make greater use of the present perfect tense. The present perfect is sometimes used in English news items to stress how up-to-date the news is, but never in connection with a temporal ADJUNCT such as "yesterday".

verbal form

There are also several lexical items used in these translations that are not idiomatic German, or are very poor translations for reasons of style or accuracy. The items *Detektive, Superspitzel, getrennten Adressen, Komplott, einschleusen, einbringen, Sotherby* and *Geschöpf* need to be reconsidered.

The translations have also kept the paragraph layout of the English source texts. Even short news items in English, like longer newspaper articles, tend to paragraph, even if each paragraph only has one or two sentences. This layout is not, however, typical of German short news items, in which the whole story usually appears in one paragraph, or two at the most.

layout

Rewrite the two texts so that they read like published news items in German.

Task 3 – identifying stylistic problems in English text
Below are two student translations of German news items (**3**, p. 36/& **7**, p. 37) into English.

Explain what is wrong with them.

1 After a search lasting several days, the police have found an obviously mentally confused man alive and well. The car of the 85-year-old man from Mönchen-Gladbach had been found empty already in the night to Monday near Ferch (Potsdam-Mittelmark). With a police helicopter, the area was searched all day Monday. Yesterday morning police officers found the man dressed in a shirt and underpants. The exhausted old-aged pensioner was taken to hospital.

2 For far-reaching changes in the Catholic Church such as the end of celibacy, women priests and the election of bishops by the Churches of the Diocese the President of the Central Committee of German Catholics, Hans-Joachim Meyer has spoken out. However, the Catholic Church must "first get used to these ideas." Such changes would otherwise be a breaking test. In the Central Committee of German Catholics, the Catholic lay organisations of Germany are united. It organises among other things the 'Catholic Days'.

THEME

The choice of elements other than the grammatical subect as THEME make the English text sound very odd. In short news items the grammatical SUBJECT of clauses should generally be in THEME position.

NOUN GROUPS

The use of noun group structures taken from the German source texts (eg *eine mehrtägige Suche, einen offenbar geistig verwirrten Mann, der ganze Montag, Änderung*) is less appropriate in the English language news item. Meanings packed into a single noun group in the German text might be better expressed over further clause structures, including relative clauses, in English text versions of the short news item. There are also NOUN GROUPS in these translations that are either not idiomatic English or not suitable to the context, such as "in the night to Monday", "spoken out" and "breaking test".

verbs

The use of the present perfect tense in English is not appropriate in every instance where it is used in German. The use of "must" to translate the German *müsse* reporting speech indirectly is quite wrong.

layout

The text layout of these translations is also unusual. It would be better to paragraph the English version, noting that a new paragraph often indicates a change in THEME.

> Taking all of this into account, rewrite the translations into English to make them suitable for publication in an English language newspaper.

1.2 Text and function

In order to translate a text well, it is vital to know what kind of text you are dealing with. Not every short text in a newspaper is a straight news item, referring to events without comment.

Task 4 – identifying situational context

The following text features grammatical and lexical choices which differ from the news items in this chapter.

1 Foreign Secretary Robin Cook is said to have danced a jig of rage on discovering he and his minions had been elbowed out of the pre-Brussels talks on monetary union. Principal reason: the determination of Chancellor Gordon Brown to keep the snout of his peppery Caledonian rival out of economics. Prior to the election, Mr Brown sought to annex the FO's European operation. He didn't get his way. But isn't it curious the Europe Minister subsequently planted on Mr Robin Cook was none other than Doug Henderson, a trusted member of Mr Brown's inner court? (*The Daily Mail*, 16 June, 1998)

• How does the text above differ from a short news item?

Text **2** below also differs from the news item.

Identify a likely context for it and explain your view.

2 On the day of the tragedy, the boys of Windfield school had been confined to their rooms. It was a hot Saturday in May, and they would normally have spent the afternoon in the South field, some playing cricket and others watching from the shapely fringes of Bishop's Wood. But a crime had been committed. Six gold sovereigns had been stolen from the desk of Mr Offerton, the Latin master, and the whole school was under suspicion. All the boys were to be kept in until the thief was caught.

Rewrite both of texts **1** and **2** above as short news items for a newspaper.

Task 5 – headlines

Most news items are preceded by a headline. Headlines are one of the most distinctive features of any newspaper, and their grammar is distinctive enough to have been given a special name – "headlinese". English langue headlines, especially in longer news texts, are often difficult for non-native speakers to understand. They make extensive use of abbreviations, puns, alliteration, assonance, rhyme, archaisms

"headlinese"

and neologisms, deliberate ambiguity and cultural allusions. Special lexis, often emotive and suggestive, is used, and specific verb tenses are used: present tense, for example, is often used to refer to the past, simple past tense used for the past, and the future expressed by to+infinitive. Auxiliaries are generally omitted.

Very typical of the longer English language news text is the all-noun headline, such as: "STRIKE BAN SHOCK PROBE", and "Family Suicide Tragedy". These can be 'decoded' by working backwards; "there has been an investigation after the shock of the ban on strikes", and "there has been a tragic incident involving the suicide of a whole family". Some creativity is needed to translate headlines into English, so that they sound appropriately similar to the usual grammar of English language headlines. German headlines tend to be less cryptic, often using full verbal structures, and using less of the poetic features typical of English language headlines (such as puns and alliteration).

Discuss the grammar of the English headlines (taken from newspapers such as *The Daily Mirror*, *The Daily Mail*, *The Daily Telegraph*, *The Guardian*, *The Independent Weekend* and *The Times Higher Educational Supplement*) below, and then translate the German headlines (taken from newspapers like *Bild*, *BZ*, *Berliner Morgenpost*, *Der Tagesspiegel* and *Die Welt*) to suit publication in an English language newspaper.

1 Unversities count cost of innumeracy
2 POWs to sue Japan
3 Dirty dentist fondled gassed girl
4 Stowaway bride hope
5 Vehicle sales in top gear
6 Exam probe secrecy
7 Simon show suffers sound of silence
8 Lords a-fuming over bid to ban smoking
9 On a cruise along the Ouse
10 Driving ban for nine-in-car son of millionaire MP

11 Liebeskummer – Schüler erschoss sich im Wald
12 Ehemann mit Tasse mißhandelt
13 Tornados wüteten in Minnesota
14 Alarmierende Zunahme der Kriminalität bei Kindern
15 LKW-Kontrolle: über die Hälfte hatte Mängel

16 Forelle tötete Angler
17 Familie im Unglück – Flaschenpost brachte die Rettung
18 28 Millionen arbeiten schwarz
19 Verwirrter im Pyjama wollte Tankstelle in Brand setzen
20 USA und Iran nähern sich vorsichtig an

1.3 Summary of language features

The main grammatical features noticed in the short news item, common to the German and the English versions, are:

* Events are not represented in chronological sequence.
* Simple verbal forms dominate.
* Typical PROCESS types are Material and Verbal.
* Most sentences consist of one clause only, and are linked by no or simple conjunctions.

features in common

Though German and English news items are very similar in function, there are areas of difference in their grammatical realisation to remember when translating them: THEME choice, verbal form, NOUN GROUP structure, lexis and layout.

* The THEME of the first clause in English language short news items is always the grammatical SUBJECT of the clause. In German they can and often do begin with a CIRCUMSTANTIAL element or another PARTICIPANT.
* German news texts nominalise more than their English counterparts.
* Attitudinal lexis is a feature of the English language texts.
* Present perfect tense used in German news items is in most cases best translated into English with the simple past.
* *Konjunktiv* and modal verbs are used in German to indirectly report speech, not in English.
* The layout often differs, German texts favouring one paragraph.
* The grammar of headlines differs, English language press favouring cryptic, 'poetic' headlines, often comprising nouns only.

grammatical differences between English and German

Having identified the major language patterns of a type of news text, you have some preparation for translating such texts. The following exercises draw your attention to lexical and grammatical choices potentially available at several points in text production, some of which are simply wrong, others possible in some contexts but not for this genre. An understanding of which choices are and which are not possible in this genre will prepare you for independent translation work.

2.1 Text completion

The following news item appeared at the beginning of the chapter as an example.

In Sofia haben Skinheads mehrere Roma überfallen und dabei einen 15 Jahre alten Jungen getötet. Wie die bulgarische Polizei am Montag mitteilte, waren die Skinheads am Wochenende in ein leerstehendes Haus im Stadtzentrum eingedrungen und hatten dort sieben Roma verprügelt. Eines der Opfer habe sich gewehrt und sei aus dem Fenster geworfen worden.

Task 6 – completing gap translation text

Complete the translation by choosing from the words offered below.

Skinheads in Sofia (1) ＿＿ (2) ＿＿ Romanies and (3) ＿＿ killed a 15-year-old (4) ＿＿.
(5) ＿＿ the skinheads (6) ＿＿ an empty house in the centre of town at the weekend and (7)＿＿ seven Romanies. One of the (8) ＿＿ (9) ＿＿ and (10) ＿＿ thrown out of the window.

(1) have attacked, had attacked, attacked, were attacking, have been attacking
(2) several, a few, a number of, a group of
(3) thus, in so doing, thereby, (–)
(4) youth, lad, adolescent, boy
(5) as the Bulgarian police informed, according to Bulgarian police reports, in a communique of the Bulgarian police
(6) penetrated into, have penetrated into, had penetrated into, forced their way into (have/had), broke into (have/had broken into)
(7) have/had beaten, have/had hit, have/had thrashed, have/had assaulted
(8) sacrifices, victims, offertories
(9) put up a fight, has/would have put up a fight, (has/would have) defended himself, (has/would have) resisted
(10) is/would be/was thrown

48

2.2 Evaluation and improvement

The following news item also appeared as an example at the start of the chapter.

Frauen als Priester

Baden-Baden – Für tiefgreifende Änderungen in der katholischen Kirche wie ein Ende des Zölibats, Frauen als Priester und die Wahl der Bischöfe durch die Ortskirche hat sich der Präsident des Zentralkomitees der deutschen Katholiken (ZdK), Hans-Joachim Meyer, ausgesprochen. Allerdings müsse sich die katholische Kirche „erst an diese Gedanken gewöhnen". Solche Veränderungen würden sonst zu einer Zerreissprobe der Kirche führen. Im ZdK sind die katholischen Laienorganisationen in Deutschland zusammengeschlossen. Es veranstaltet unter anderem die Katholikentage.

Task 7 – evaluating student translations

Mark every mistake and stylistic problem you can find in the following student translations of the text above. Choose which functions best and explain your choice.

A Fundamental changes of the Catholic Church such as the end of celibacy, women as priests and the election of the bishops by the churches of the diocese, have been favoured by Hans Joachim Meyer, President of the Central Committee of German Catholics (ZdK). But, first of all, the Catholic Church has "to get used to these thoughts". Otherwise such changes would put a strain on the church. The Catholic lay organizations of Germany are joined in the ZdK. It organises, for example, the 'Catholic Days'.

B Hans Joachim Meyer, President of the Central Committee of German Catholics (ZdK) demanded fundamental reforms in the Catholic Church. He advocated the end of celibacy, the introduction of women as priests, and the election of bishops by the churches of the diocese. However, the Catholic Church has to get used to this idea first. Such reforms would otherwise put a hard strain on the churches, Meyer argued. The ZdK is the union of the Catholic lay organisations in Germany. It also arranges the 'Catholic Days'.

C Hans Joachim Meyer, President of the Central Committee of the German Catholics (ZdK) has pleaded for radical changes in the Catholic Church such as the end of celibacy, women for priests and the election of the bishops by the local churches. By all means, the Catholic Church has to get used to this thought gradually. Otherwise, these changes will lead to dramatic tensions within the church. In the ZdK the Catholic lay organisations of Germany are unified. It organises, for examples, the 'Days of Catholics'.

Task 8 – improving the translation

Write your own translation of the *Frauen als Priester* text and compare with other students.

2.3 Vocabulary extension

Task 9 – modal verbs

Translating *sollen* needs particular care. Occasionally "should" works, but it is far from the only option and is usually not the most appropriate way to translate indirect speech. Translating *wollen* is similary tricky; sometimes "want" or "would" work, but these are certainly not the only or most appropriate translations in every situation.

Decide on the best way to translate *sollen* and *wollen* in the following:

1 An diesem Berg soll der Prophet Mohammed vor 1400 Jahren die letzte Sure des Korans verkundet haben.
2 Jungen und Mädchen sollen in einzelnen Fächern wieder getrennt unterrichtet werden können.
3 Die Volksabstimmung soll endlich den Frieden bringen.
4 Dieser Roman sollte sein Durchbruch sein. (Vergangenheit)
5 Es sollte ein Gesetz geben, dass das Rauchen in Restaurants verbietet.
6 Das siebte Gebot lautet „Du sollst nicht stehlen".
7 Soll das dein Ernst sein?
8 Ihr Baby sollte im Mai kommen.
9 Die Pflanze ist hinüber, ich hätte ihr mehr Wasser geben sollen.
10 Mit ihrem ersten und einzigen Roman sollte Emily Bronte ihren Platz in der Geschichte der englischen Literatur sichern.
11 Edinburgh soll eine der schönsten Städte der Welt sein.
12 Sein Vortrag soll als Beitrag zur Völkerverständigung dienen.
13 Wir sollten eigentlich um 8 Uhr abfliegen, aber wegen des Nebels mussten wir bis zum Nachmittag am Flughafen rumsitzen.

1 Ein neues Buch will Shakespeares wahre Identität entdeckt haben.
2 Ich wollte gerade gehen, als das Telefon klingelte.

3 Sie will es nicht so gemeint haben.
4 Er will ein Ufo gesehen haben.
5 Wir wollen uns wieder vertragen.
6 Sie glaubt, sie kann immer nur machen, was sie will.
7 Das will nicht viel heißen.
8 Wie es das Schicksal so wollte, traf sie ihren Ex-Mann bei der Party.
9 Sie ist in der S-Bahn überfallen worden, aber niemand wollte ihr helfen.
10 Das will mir nicht in den Kopf gehen.

Task 10 – verbal groups and participles

The frequent use of the -ing form in English is usually overlooked by students and forgotten when translating into English. Examples in the English language items seen so far are:

the men are being held, they were being interviewed, acts of violence including manslaughter, detectives investigating the murder, a tornado tore through a rural area, ripping apart homes, six people including two children, the letter, containing the first pictures of Mr Jeremy Fisher, a number of complaints, seven out of ten relating to accuracy

Find examples in the German language news items at the beginning of this chapter (page 36/37) where you could use an -ing form for the English translation. (eg Skinheads attacked several Romanis, **killing** a 15-year-old boy.)

3.1 Quick texts

Use the following texts to practise translating short news items. Time yourself to complete each within fifteen to twenty minutes. Check your English text with other students, and against other English language examples of the genre.

**II.3
Independent
translation**

1 Tibeter demonstrieren

Neu-Dehli (AP). Mit Schlagstöcken hat die indische Polizei am Sonnabend tibetische Demonstrationen davon abgehalten, die chinesische Botschaft in Neu-Dehli zu stürmen. Rund ein Dutzend Tibeter, die gegen die chinesische Herrschaft in ihrer Heimat protestierten, wurden dabei verletzt.

(*Der Tagesspiegel* 24.5.98)

2 Getrennte Schulstunden

Düsseldorf – Jungen und Mädchen sollen in nordrheinwestfälischen Klassen-zimmern künftig in einzelnen Fächern wieder getrennt unterrichtet werden können. Während Mädchen besonders in Naturwissenschaftten, Mathematik, Technik und Informatik gefordert werden müssten, gebe es bei Jungen Aufhol-bedarf bei den sozialen Kompetenzen, sagte NRW-Schulministerin Gabriele Behler (SPD). (*Berliner Morgenpost* 23.2.98)

3 Iren stimmen ab: Klares Ja zum Friedensvertrag erwartet

Belfast – Die Volksabstimmung soll endlich den Frieden bringen. Rund 3,9 Milli-onen Wähler im unabhängigen Irland und Nordirland durften gestern über das Friedensabkommen abstimmen. Sie sollen eine Verfassungsänderung billigen, durch den beide Teile Irlands den Anspruch auf Wiedervereinigung aufgeben. Beobachter rechnen mit klarer Zustimmung, die Ergebnisse werden heute bekanntgegeben. (*B. Z.* 23.5.98)

> From the following points write a short news item in English. Beware of person and place names, they may be spelled differently in English.

4

– Während des Krieges wurden viele Kunstgegenstände, u.a. eine Gutenberg Bibel und Bilder von Rembrandt, Monet und Matisse von sowjetischen Trup-pen erbeutet und nach Moskau geschmuggelt.
– Jeltsin möchte diese Gegenstände seinem engsten europäischen Verbünde-ten zurückgeben.
– Es gibt ein Gesetz, wonach jede Restitution der Genehmigung des russi-schen Parlaments bedarf.
– Die Duma hält die Kunstgegenstände für eine legitime Siegesbeute.
– Die Bonner Regierung ist der Auffassung, dass die erbeuteten Kunstgegen-stände rechtmäßig Deutschland gehören.
– Jeltsin meint, das Gesetz stehe im Widerspruch zu internationalen Verein-barungen.
– Bonn reagiert nicht mit offenem Unmut.
– Deutschlands Hoffnungen haben einen schweren Schlag erlitten.
– Rußland blockiert die Rückgabe.

3.2 45-minute texts

> Time yourself to complete each of the following, slightly longer, texts within an hour. Consider all aspects appropriate to the English language news item text.

1 Alarmierende Zunahme der Kriminalität bei Kindern

BM/AP Hilden – Die Zahl der Straftaten in Deutschland geht nach Darstellung der Gewerkschaft der Polizei allgemein leicht zurück, jedoch nimmt die Kriminalität bei Kindern dramatisch zu. Es werden immer mehr tatverdächtige Kinder und Jugendliche ermittelt.

Der GdP-Vorsitzende Hermann Lutz erklärte gestern in Hilden, die Entwicklung bei der Kinderkriminalität sei so alarmierend wie jene bei der Rauschgift- und Gewaltkriminalität. Im vergangenen Jahr seien in diesen Bereichen die Zahlen sprunghaft angestiegen. Lutz verträt die Ansicht, daß weitere Personaleinsparungen bei Lehrern, Justiz und Polizei unverantwortlich wären.

Bei der Zahl der erstmals auffälligen Rauschgiftkonsumenten gab es 1997 nach den Worten von Lutz gegenüber dem Vorjahr einen Zuwachs von rund 20 Prozent auf 20 600. Die Gewaltkriminalität stieg im gleichen Zeitraum auf mehr als 186 000 Fälle an. *(Berliner Morgenpost 27.3.98)*

2 Moskau rehabilitiert Schauspieler Heinrich George

Moskau. Russland hat den Schauspieler Heinrich George, der 1946 in dem sowjetischen Speziallager Sachsenhausen bei Berlin gestorben ist, offiziell rehabilitiert. Das bestätigte die Generalmilitärstaatsanwaltschaft in Moskau. Den Antrag habe die deutsche Botschaft in Moskau gestellt. George, der mit Filmen wie „Berlin Alexanderplatz" und „Der Postmeister" populär wurde, aber auch bis 1944 in NS-Propagandafilmen mitwirkte, war von 1938 bis 1945 Generalintendant des Berliner Schiller-Theaters. Wie es in Moskau hieß, wurde George aus politischen Motiven von der Zentralen NKWD-Gruppe Berlin im Sommer 1945 verhaftet und später ohne Gerichtsverfahren in das Speziallager 2 des NKWD, das ehemalige Konzentrationslager Sachsenhausen eingewiesen, wo er im September 1946 starb. *(Der Tagesspiegel 21.5.98)*

3.3 Exam practice

Translate groups of any three of the following short reports within two hours, thinking very carefully about the headline, the layout and the grammatical features appropriate to an English language news item.

1 34 jähriger in Texas mit Giftspritze hingerichtet

Washington (AFP). Im US-Bundesstaat Texas ist am Montag ein 34jähriger Häftling hingerichtet worden. Robert Anthony Carter war für einen Mord zum Tode verurteilt worden, den er als Minderjähriger im Jahr 1981 begangen hätte, wie die Gefängnisbehörden mitteilten. Wie die Vollzugsanstalt am Dienstag verlauten ließ, wurde er um 18.25 Uhr Ortszeit mittels einer Giftinjektion im

Staatsgefängnis in Huntsville getötet. „Ich trete in eine bessere Welt ein", sagte er kurz vor dem Tod. Es ist bereits die zweite Exekution innerhalb eines Monats in Texas. Carter, der mehr als die Hälfte seines Lebens im Gefängnis verbrachte, hätte im Alter von 17 Jahren die Kassiererin einer Tankstelle getötet.

(Der Tagesspiegel 21.5.98)

2 USA: Erneut Blutbad in einer Schule
Springfield (AFP). Die USA sind zum vierten Mal innerhalb von acht Monaten von einem Blutbad in einer Schule erschüttert worden. Der Schütze, vermutlich ein Schüler, eröffnete das Feuer in der Kantine der Thurston High School in Springfield, einem Vorort von Eugene (Oregon). Er tötete mindestens einen Mitschüler. Vier weitere Menschen wurden lebensgefährlich verletzt.

(Der Tagesspiegel 22.5.98)

3 Studenten lieben Berlin
Berlin – in Sachen Freizeitangebot ist Berlin in Europa bei Studenten die beliebteste Stadt – ergab eine Studie von „Spiegel special". Befragt wurden 7300 Personen in 72 europäischen Städten. Platz 2 in der Beliebtheitsskala: Köln; Platz 3: Paris. *(B. Z. 28.5.98)*

4 Bayern beginnt mit regelmäßigen Mathe-Tests
Bayern hat Ende November mit regelmäßigen Mathematik-Tests der Gymnasiasten und Realschüler in den neunten Klassen begonnen. Künftig soll dieser unbenotete Test zu Beginn jeden Schuljahrs erfolgen und Aufschluß über den mathematischen Kenntnisstand der Schüler geben. Ziel der Tests ist es nach den Worten der Kultusministerin Monika Hohlmeier, aufbauendes und kontinuierliches Lernen in Mathematik und Naturwissenschaften zu sichern, nachdem die deutschen Schüler in beiden Bereichen im internationalen Vergleich nach den TIMS-Studien so durchschnittlich abgeschnitten hatten. Die Gymnasiasten mußten beispielsweise in zehn Aufgaben ihre grundlegenden Fähigkeiten in Algebra und Geometrie unter Beweis stellen. Kenntnisse im Prozent- und Bruchrechnen waren ebenso gefragt wie das richtige Deuten von Diagrammen. Die Arbeitszeit betrug 40 Minuten. *(Der Tagesspiegel 2.12.98)*

5 Mallorca schränkt Hotelbau ein
Nach dem Prinzip „Klasse statt Masse" wird der Bau neuer Hotels auf Mallorca drastisch eingeschränkt. Eine von der Regionalregierung beschlossene Neuregelung sieht vor, daß auf dem gesamten Archipel, also auch auf Menorca, Ibiza und Formentera, künftig nur noch Vier- und Fünf-Sterne-Herbergen entstehen dürfen. Sonst gelte der Grundsatz, daß ein neues Hotel nur gebaut werden darf, wenn dafür ein altes abgerissen wird. Ausgenommen sind Innenstädte.

(Der Tagesspiegel 6.12.98)

6 Mindestens 28 Tote bei Brand in Waisenhaus

Manila. Bei einem Brand in einem Waisenhaus der philippinischen Hauptstadt Manila sind gestern mindestens 23 Kinder und fünf Erwachsene ums Leben gekommen. Die Bewohner des Hauses wurden von dem Feuer im Schlaf überrascht. Die Flammen breiteten sich rasend schnell aus und schlossen die Kinder ein. In dem brennenden Haus spielten sich erschütternde Szenen ab: Verzweifelt schrien Mädchen und Jungen im ersten Stock im Hilfe, doch niemand konnte schnell genug zu ihnen kommen, da die Fenster aus Schutz vor Einbrechern vergittert waren. Ursache des Brands war vermutlich ein Kurzschluß in einer elektrischen Leitung. Unter den Trümmern des abgebrannten Hauses fand die Feuerwehr die verbrannten Leichen von Erwachsenen, Kleinkindern und Babies, verbranntes Spielzeug und die Reste der Dekoration für die Weihnachtsfeier, die am folgenden Tag stattfinden sollte.   (*Berliner Morgenpost* 4.12.98)

III Report – generalised

A "report" is a language genre for classifying and describing how things are objectively, without critique, argument or disputable interpretation. Various, indeed any, phenomena can be the subject of a report, ranging from the fauna and flora of the natural world, to social situations, to the media and methods of representation itself (such as language). This chapter focuses on the 'scientific' reports to be found in education about natural phenomena and language.

III.1 German and English examples   58
  1.1 Comparison and contrast
  1.2 Text and function
  1.3 Summary of language features

III.2 Guided translation exercises   74
  2.1 Text completion
  2.2 Evaluation and improvement
  2.3 Vocabulary extension

III.3 Independent translation   80
  3.1 Quick texts
  3.2 45-minute texts
  3.3 Exam practice

The report is a major factual genre used in the production of 'knowledge'. Reporting is used especially in writing science and education in many subject areas. In school education reporting is used mainly for the natural sciences, while recount and narrative genres dominate history and English. In tertiary education, a great deal of knowledge about both cultural and natural phenomena is constructed in information reports. They classify and describe the way things are, construct an 'objective' perspective and avoid overt evaluation. Reporting occurs in all types of higher and general public education, including textbooks and student assignments, informational brochures, newspapers and magazines. Reports might occur as one stage of a composite text, which might for example then also explain, comment on, argue about or discuss information presented. The examples below are taken from a range of sources dealing with language studies or the natural sciences.

1 Ein nahe liegendes Tätigkeitsfeld für Anglisten ist das des Übersetzers. Da die meisten belletristischen Neuerscheinungen auf dem deutschen Buchmarkt Übersetzungen aus dem Englischen sind, werden gute Übersetzer ständig gesucht. Dabei liegt die Betonung auf „gute"; denn hier zählt nur die schriftstellerische Fähigkeit in beiden Sprachen und nicht die methodische Ausbildung in der Wissenschaft. Allerdings ist ein philologisches Studium eine gute Voraussetzung, um sich als Übersetzer in Stil und Denkweise eines englischsprachigen Autors einzufühlen. Gemessen am Arbeitsaufwand werden Übersetzer von Belletristik schlecht bezahlt. Andererseits ist es eine sehr literaturnahe Tätigkeit, die vor allem Anglisten mit eigenen kreativen Neigungen befriedigt. Lukrativer ist im Allgemeinen das Übersetzen von wissenschaftlicher und technischer Fachliteratur. Doch dafür bietet das Anglistikstudium kaum die geeignete Vorbereitung. Eine besondere Qualifikation erfordert das Berufsfeld der vereidigten Übersetzer und Dolmetscher. Für sie gibt es spezielle Hochschulen, wo die spezifischen Fachsprachen der einzelnen Wirtschaftssparten und die dafür geeigneten Übersetzungstechniken gelehrt werden. Für Absolventen eines Anglistikstudiums kommt als Berufsfeld in der Regel nur das des Übersetzers von Belletristik und allgemeinen Sachtexten in Frage.

2 Mangroven wuchern in vielen Teilen der Welt an geschützten tropischen Küsten – eine Übergangswelt zwischen Meer und Land. Im Gewirr der stelzenartigen Wurzeln der Mangrovenbäume und -sträucher fangen sich die von den Flüssen angeschwemmten Pflanzenteile und alles, was von der Flut an den Strand gespült wird. Der durch diese Substanzen angereicherte Schlamm bietet einer charakteristischen und artenreichen Fauna Lebensraum und Nahrung. Die Mangroven zeigen für gewöhnlich eine klare Zonierung, denn die Bedingungen, die am unteren Rand der Gezeitenzone herrschen, wo die Pflanzen täglich von der Flut überspült werden, unterscheiden sich von denen, die weiter höher landeinwärts angetroffen werden, wo der Strand nur ein- oder zweimal im Jahr durch besonders hohe Flutwellen unter Wasser gesetzt wird. In Südostasien findet man im Allgemeinen sechs horizontale Zonen, deren jede durch eine bestimmte Art oder Artengruppe von Mangrovenbäumen charakterisiert ist.

Wichtigste Voraussetzung für das Gedeihen einer Mangrovenpflanze ist die Fähigkeit, die Überflutung des Wurzelsystems mit Seewasser zu vertragen. Die einzelnen Arten sind in unterschiedlichem Ausmaß an das Seewasser angepaßt; manche wachsen nur in den oberen Bereichen der Flußmündungen, wo der Anteil des Süßwassers hoch ist. Die hochspezialisierten Wurzelsysteme sind flach und weit verzweigt, weil der Sauerstoff und die lebenswichtigen Mineralsalze großenteils in den oberen Schlammschichten konzentriert sind. Trotzdem ist die Sauerstoffzufuhr mangelhaft, weshalb viele Mangrovengewächse Pneumatophoren entwickelt haben, Atemwurzeln, die aus den eigentlichen Wurzeln hervorwachsen und aus dem Schlamm herausragen.

An die Mangroven schließt sich oft Regenwald an, und die beiden Zonen haben manchmal einige gemeinsame Faunenelemente. Manche Tiere, die an mangrovenfreien Küsten verbreitet sind, kommen auch in diesem schlammigen Wald vor, doch mehrere Arten sind typische Mangroven-Bewohner und andernorts nicht anzutreffen. Die meisten stammen nicht von Land-, sondern von Meerestieren ab, und ihr Angepaßtsein an ein Leben halb im Wasser und halb auf dem Lande ist ein Anzeichen dafür, daß die Mangroven durchaus einen der Lebensräume gebildet haben könnten, in denen sich die Evolution vom Meeresbewohner zum Landtier vollzogen hat.

3 Wale sind Säugetiere, die vor 60 Millionen Jahren zurück ins Wasser gingen, wo sie mehr Nahrung fanden als auf dem Land. Getragen vom Element Wasser konnten sie zu den größten Lebewesen werden, die jemals diesen Planeten bewohnten. Selbst Dinosaurier erscheinen als Zwerge im Vergleich zum Blauwahl – mit 30 Metern Länge und dem Gewicht von 25 Elefanten der größte der Walfamilie.

Großwale unternehmen Wanderungen von vielen tausend Kilometern. Im Sommer halten sie sich in ihren Nahrungsgründen in arktischen und antarktischen Zonen auf, wo ihre Nahrung hauptsächlich aus Krill, winzigen Krebstierchen, besteht. Zur Paarungszeit ziehen sie dann in wärmere Gewässer; dort werden auch ihre Jungen geboren. In dieser Zeit bleiben sie ohne Nahrung. Blau- und Finnwale fasten etwa acht Monate im Jahr, Buckelwale etwa sechs Monate.

Zu den Rätseln, die uns die Wale aufgeben, gehört ihre Verständigung. Neben der sozialen Sprache, in der sie kommunizieren, haben sie Gesänge entwickelt

– berühmt sind die der Buckelwale. Ihre Lieder erklingen nur in den Paarungs-gründen, nur Männchen singen und von diesen wiederum nicht alle. Die Lieder verändern sich ständig, doch die Veränderungen werden aufgenommen, so daß alle dasselbe Lied singen.

Da Wale in einer Umwelt leben, die Wärme sehr rasch vom Körper wegführt, können sie nur überleben, wenn sie nicht mehr als ein Junges tragen, es über eine lange Periode säugen, ihm beibringen Nahrung zu finden und große Entfernungen sicher zu überwinden. Wale werden wahrscheinlich je nach Art zwischen 30 und 50 Jahre alt. Man nimmt jedoch an, daß einzelne Tiere auch älter werden können.

Wale sind friedvolle Lebewesen. Sie leiten Schiffe durch dichten Nebel zurück in die sicheren Hafen, sie retten Ertrinkende vor dem Tod und helfen sich gegenseitig – selbst in größter Not.

1 There are a number of different ways of analysing language. One common view of language, particularly in education, is to see it as a formal system of grammatical rules, and that language education has the task of imparting these rules to students. The focus of the formal, rule-based model of language is on small units – words, phrases, clauses and sentences. This traditional model is not designed to account for how language is used in different contexts.

Another approach is that of psychologically based models of language development. This approach focuses on the individual's mental capacity to acquire language, with little reference to context of use. Like the formal model, language acquisition is seen as a process of learning abstract rules. Language function is not the object of this type of study.

In a functional model, language is seen as a resource for making meaning, not as a set of rules or psychological properties. This model sees language development as a process of learning to make an ever-broadening range of meanings, of expanding one's choices in the linguistic system.

(Exploring Literacy in School English, Disadvantaged Schools Program, NSW Department of School Education, Australia, 1994.)

2 River red gums and Coolabahs line the rivers of sand right across the arid zone. These trees are analogous to a multi-storey, high-density housing development for birds. Along the Cooper, for instance, the fringing woodland has a dense crown cover and at least four well-developed levels. Species mainly confined to this habitat on the Cooper are the vocal Barking Owl, which spreads out evenly in pairs along the Creek, Mallee Ringneck Parrot, Sacred Kingfisher and Restless Flycatcher. A colourful and rich variety of other songbirds are also associated with the woodland habitat.

(Penny van OOsterzee, *The Centre: The Natural History of Australia's Desert Regions,* Reed, 1991.)

3 The Euro (*Macropus robustus erubescens*) is a subspecies of the Common Wallaroo. It differs in appearance by having shorter and redder hair. Unlike the Red Kangaroo (*Macropus rufus*) which inhabits the plains, the Euro is sedentary and solitary and lives in caves and rock piles. It leaves its shelter to graze on grasses and shrubs in the evenings. Its home range may be as much as eight kilometres radius and can include plains surrounding the rocky outcrops. In common with other kangaroos, the Euro has a ruminant-like digestive system. In a sac-like development of the alimentary tract, fibrous material is fermented by prolific bacteria and protozoan fauna. The indigestible cellulose is broken down. The bacteria need nitrogen to grow, but in the natural diet of the Euro this is very low. The Euro gets by, however, because the bacteria use recycled nitrogen from urea which would otherwise need to be flushed out with water. This is why the Euro can subsist on a diet full of fibre and low on nitrogen – it is the only mammal able to subsist on spinifex. In the Euro's home range there will normally be adequate food and water. If there is plenty of shade, and plants with sufficient water content, it can maintain itself and even breed with infrequent access to free water. During dry periods it can rely on its efficient metabolism and ability to digest poor food to survive. (see above)

1.1. Comparison and contrast

The most obvious difficulty that presents itself to the translator of such texts is that they usually include specialised vocabulary. Students tend to find, at first glance, that German text **1** would be easier to translate into English than text **2**; it has less specialised lexis, and that it does have is already from a familiar field of study. With an appropriate dictionary, translating these texts may then seem straightforward. However, even if vocabulary lists are provided to overcome the lexical hurdle, there still remain a number of grammatical obstacles. The following exercises draw attention to aspects of the texts' lexis and grammar with which beginner translators are likely to run into problems.

Task 1 – identifying lexical features

The more specialist lexis is used, the further away from the general public are the intended readers of the text, and the greater the need for a good dictionary. Lexis from the three German texts shows which is most specialised.

1 Anglisten, belletristisch, Neuerscheinung, schriftstellerisch, Ausbildung, Wissenschaft, Studium, Fachliteratur, Berufsfeld, vereidigten Übersetzer, Hochschule, Fachsprache, Absolventen, Sachtext

specialist lexis

2 Mangroven, Ubergangswelt, stelzenartige Wurzeln, Mangrovensträucher, angeschwemmte Pflanzenteile, Flut, angereicherte Schlamm, artenreichen Fauna, Lebensraum, Nahrung, Zonierung, Gezeitenzone, landeinwärts, Gedeihen, Flußmündung, Süßwasser, verzweigte Wurzelsysteme, Sauerstoff, lebenswichtige Mineralsalze, Schlammschichten, Sauerstoffzufuhr, Mangrovengewächse, Pneumatophoren, Atemwurzeln, hervorwachsen, herausragen, Regenwald, Faunenelemente, Meerestieren, Angespaßtsein, Meeresbewohner, Landtier

3 Säugetiere, Nahrung, Lebewesen, Dinosaurier, Nahrungsgründen, Krill, Krebstierchen, Paarungszeit, Finnwale, Buckelwale, Paarungsgründen, Umwelt

> Guess the original contexts of each of the three German texts – what sort of publication they have appeared in. Make lists of the specialist lexis in the English language texts also, and guess their sources.

Notice that many lexical choices in English language written reports are Latin-based; eg "indigestible / adequate / sufficient / infrequent, efficient".

written versus spoken lexis

- What words would most likely be used instead of these in spoken English?

Task 2 – identifying grammatical features

The report genre, like others, has its own characteristic grammatical features that make examples of it easily recognisable. If you were given a random pile of texts of many genres, say for example all the texts in this book, you would have little difficulty quickly putting all the recounts in one pile, all the news items in another, and all the reports in another, etc. Whether or not you can name the grammatical features that distinguish each, you can recognise them instantly. When it comes to translating texts however, it helps to be able to explicitly identify and name the various grammatical features that characterise a genre, because then you can consciously look out for them and consider their translation more carefully and systematically. Without conscious consideration, amateur translators tend to use any grammar that happens to come to mind, usually resulting in very poor translation.

One obvious grammatical feature of written reports is the complexity of Noun Groups. Examples from the first German text **1** are:

Noun Groups

- ein nahe liegendes Tätigkeitsfeld für Anglisten
- die meisten belletristischen Neuerscheinungen auf dem deutschen Buchmarkt
- Übersetzungen aus dem Englischen
- die schriftstellerische Fähigkeit in beiden Sprachen
- die methodische Ausbildung in der Wissenschaft
- Stil und Denkweise eines englischsprachigen Autors
- Übersetzer von Belletristik
- eine sehr literaturnahe Tätigkeit, die vor allem Anglisten mit eigenen kreativen Neigungen befriedigt
- das Übersetzen von wissenschaftlicher und technischer Fachliteratur
- das Berufsfeld der vereidigten Übersetzer und Dolmetscher
- die spezifischen Fachsprachen der einzelnen Wirtschaftssparten und die dafür geeigneten Übersetzungstechniken
- Absolventen eines Anglistikstudiums
- Berufsfeld des Übersetzers von Belletristik und allgemeinen Sachtexten

As most of the text's information is encoded into noun groups within a small number of clauses, the texts are said to have a high Lexical Density.

Lexical Density

List the complex Noun Groups in the other two German reports, texts **2** and **3**. Do the same with the three English language reports and judge whether there is a higher Lexical Density in one language, or about the same in both.

Many meanings encoded in report texts in noun groups and specialised lexis would be worded differently in spoken language.

- How would you say what is meant in the following?

written versus spoken English

- the natural diet of the Euro = "what the Euro usually eats"
- has a ruminant-like digestive system = "its digestive system is like a cow's"
- the Euro's home range = ?
- plants with sufficient water content = ?
- prolific bacteria and protozoan fauna = ?

There are several grammatical features that characterise reports, apart from the encoding of much information into nominal groups.

Considering the following grammatical categories (PROCESSES, PARTICIPANTS, THEMES, CIRCUMSTANCES), examine the similarities and differences between the German and English report texts.

PROCESSES

1 ist, sind, werden gesucht, liegt, zählt, ist, werden bezahlt, ist, befriedigt, ist, bietet, erfordert, gibt, gelehrt werden, kommt
2 wuchern, fangen sich, gespült wird, bietet, zeigen, herrschen, überspült werden, unterscheiden sich, angetroffen werden, gesetzt wird, findet, charakterisiert ist, ist, sind, wachsen, ist, sind, sind, ist, entwickelt haben, hervorwachsen, herausragen, schließt sich, haben, sind, kommen vor, sind, stammen ab, ist, gebildet haben könnten, sich vollzogen hat
3 sind, zurückgingen, fanden, konnten werden, bewohnten, erscheinen, unternehmen, halten sich, besteht, ziehen, werden geboren, bleiben, fasten, aufgeben, gehört, haben entwickelt, sind, erklingen, singen, verändern sich, werden aufgenommen, singen, leben, wegführt, können überleben, tragen, säugen, werden, nimmt an, werden können, sind, leiten, retten, helfen sich

1 are, is, has, is, is designed, is, focuses on, is seen, is, is seen, sees
2 line, are, has, are, spreads out, are associated with
3 is, differs, inhabits, is, lives, leaves, may be, can include, has, is fermented, is broken down, need, is, gets by, use, would need to be flushed out, is, can subsist, is, there will be, there is, can maintain itself, can breed, can rely on

Notice the verbal forms (tense) of the verbs.
They are almost all in the simple present form. This is important to remember, as students often use the -ing form in English when translating into English, which is not appropriate to the genre.

Note the types of PROCESS that are typical: mostly RELATIONAL and MATERIAL.

PARTICIPANTS

1 Tätigkeitsfeld, Neuerscheinungen, Übersetzungen, Übersetzer, Betonung, Fähigkeit, Ausbildung, Studium, Voraussetzung, Übersetzer, Tätigkeit, Anglisten, Übersetzen, Anglistikstudium, Vorbereitung, Qualifikation, Berufsfeld, Hochschulen, Fachsprachen, Übersetzungstechniken
2 Mangroven, Übergangswelt, Pflanzenteile, Schlamm, Fauna, Lebensraum, Nahrung, Mangroven, Zonierung, Bedingungen, Pflanzen, Flut, Strand, Zonen, Artengruppe, Voraussetzung, Fähigkeit, Überflutung, Arten, Anteil, Wurzel-

systeme, Sauerstoff, Mineralsalze, Sauerstoffzufuhr, Mangrovengewächse, Pneumatophoren, Atemwurzeln, Regenwald, Zonen, Faunenelemente, Tiere, Arten, Mangroven-Bewohner, Angepaßtsein, Anzeichen, Mangroven, Lebensraum, Evolution
3 Wale, Säugetiere, Nahrung, Element Wasser, Lebewesen, Dinosaurier, Zwerge, Blauwahl, der größte, Großwale, Wanderungen, Nahrung, Krill, Krebstierchen, Jungen, Nahrung. Blau- und Finnwale, Buckelwale, uns, Wale, Verständigung, Sprache, Gesänge, Lieder, Männchen, Lieder, Veränderungen, Lied singen, Wale, Wärme, Junges, Nahrung, Entfernungen, Wale, Tiere, Wale, Lebewesen, Schiffe, Ertrinkende

1 ways of analysing language, view of language, system of grammatical rules, language education, task, focus, words, phrases, clauses, sentences, model, language, approach, mental capacity, formal model, language acquisition, process, language function, object, language, resource, set of rules or psychological properties, model, language development, process of learning, range of meanings, choices
2 River red gums, Coolabahs, rivers, trees, housing development, woodland, crown cover, levels, species, Barking Owl, Mallee Ringneck Parrot, Sacred Kingfisher, Restless Flycatcher, variety of songbirds
3 Euro, Macropus robustus erubescens, subspecies, Red Kangaroo, Macropus rufus, plains, Euro, shelter, grasses, shrubs, home range, plains, Euro, digestive system, fibrous material, bacteria, protozoan fauna, cellulose, bacteria, nitrogen, Euro, bacteria, nitrogen, Euro, mammal, food, water, shade, plants, metabolism, ability

GENERIC PARTICIPANTS are typical of this genre – categories of things rather than individual examples (eg *Wale*, "fibrous material"). ABSTRACT PARTICIPANTS are also common – things that cannot be physically held but are intellectual (such as *Fähigkeit*, "linguistic system").

> List or mark those PARTICIPANTS from the German and the English language texts that are 'generic', and those that are 'abstract'.

Most new translators assume that a noun in German text should be translated as a noun in English, a verb as a verb, an adjective as an adjective, etc. Though this is usually possible, it is often very inelegant. The translator needs to carefully consider what other ways of encoding the given meanings might be available. It is also important to be aware of word order differences when translating   WORD ORDER complex noun groups, as German noun groups tend to pre-modify the head noun more than in English. The following is typical of student translation of the first German language text **1** presented in this chapter:

A closely related occupation for Anglicists is that of the translator. As most literary new releases on the German book market are translations from the English, good translators are constantly sought. Here the emphasis lies on good, as only the literary ability in both languages counts not the methodical training in science... A special qualification requires the profession of the sworn translator and interpreter. For them there are special schools...

Apart from some poor lexical choices, such as "Anglicist" and "science", there are problems with the organisation of meaning into noun groups and with the THEMATIC organisation of some clauses (what clauses begin with).

Compare and discuss the differences between the translation above and the following:

One occupation closely related to English Studies is translating. As most fiction recently released onto the German market is translated from English, good translators are always in demand. Good being the key word here, because it is not academic training that counts so much as writing talent in both languages... Professional translators and interpreters need a specialist qualification. There are special schools for them...

THEMES

Whether single words, long nominal groups or nominalisations, THEMES in English clauses are predominantly PARTICIPANTS and grammatical SUBJECT of the clause. THEMES in reports are also frequently complex, including textual elements that link the clause to other parts of the text in comparative ways. Sometimes THEMES in English language reports are CIRCUMSTANCES of place or time, but they are much less often CIRCUMSTANTIAL elements than is the case in German text.

Listed below are the THEME choices throughout the German texts.

1 Ein nahe liegendes Tätigkeitsfeld für Anglisten, da die meisten belletristi- schen Neuerscheinungen auf dem deutschen Buchmarkt, werden, dabei, denn hier, allerdings, gemessen am Arbeitsaufwand, andererseits, lukrativer, doch

66

dafür, eine besondere Qualifikation, für sie, für Absolventen eines Anglistik-studiums.

2 Mangroven, im Gewirr der stelzenatrigen Wurzeln der Mangrovenbäume und -sträucher, der durch diese Substanzen angereicherte Schlamm, die Man-groven, denn die Bedingungen, die, wo, die, wo, in Südostasien, deren jede, wichtigste Voraussetzung für das Gedeihen einer Mangrovenpflanze, die ein-zelnen Arten, manche, wo, die hochspezialisierten Wurzelsysteme, weil der Sauerstoff und die lebenswichtigen Mineralsalze, trotzdem, weshalb viele Mangrovengewächse, die, an die Mangroven, und die beiden Zonen, manche Tiere, die, doch mehrere Arten, die meisten, und ihr Angepaßtsein, daß die Mangroven, in denen.

3 Wale, die, wo, getragen vom Element Wasser, die, selbst Dinosaurier, Groß-wale, im Sommer, wo, zur Paarungszeit, dort, in dieser Zeit, Blau- und Finnwale, Buckelwale, zu den Rätseln, die uns die Wale aufgeben, neben der sozialen Sprache, berühmt, ihre Lieder, nur Männchen, die Lieder, doch die Verände-rungen, so daß alle, da Wale, die, können, wenn sie, es, ihm, Wale, man, daß einzelne Tiere, Wale, sie, sie.

> Underline those THEMES above that would not be put into first position in the English language translation of the given clauses (for example *dabei, hier*). Discuss whether there are THEME choices in the English language texts, below, that would not be put in first position in a German translation.

1 There, one common view of language, the focus of the formal, rule-based model of language, this traditional model, another approach, this approach, like the formal model language acquisition, language function, in a functional model, this model

2 River red gums and Coolabahs, these trees, along the Cooper, species mainly confined to this habitat on the Cooper, a colourful and rich variety of other songbirds

3 The Euro, it, unlike the Red Kangaroo, the Euro, it, its home range, in common with other kangaroos, the Euro, in a sac-like development of the alimentary tract, the indigestible cellulose, the bacteria, but in the natural diet of the Euro, the Euro, because the bacteria, this, it, in the Euro's home range, if there, and plants with sufficient water content, it, during dry periods, it

Compared to the other genres in this book, texts in the report genre include many CIRCUMSTANTIAL meanings. A CIRCUMSTANCE is the part of a clause that is not the Process, not the PARTICIPANT and not just a linking element to the rest of the text. CIRCUMSTANTIAL meanings

CIRCUMSTANCES

which locate the event in time, place, manner, cause, etc. Not every prepositional phrase in a clause is functioning as a CIRCUMSTANTIAL meaning – such phrases can also function as part of the PARTICIPANT. For example in the first German language text, *auf dem deutschen Buchmarkt* tells further information about *Neuerscheinungen*, and so is part of the noun group in that clause.

Some CIRCUMSTANCES from the texts are listed below.

> Look closely at the texts and mark or list all of them to complete the set.

1 in Stil und Denkweise eines englischsprachigen Autors ...
2 in vielen Teilen der Welt, an geschützten tropischen Küsten, zwischen Meer und Land ...
3 vor 60 Millionen Jahren, zurück ins Wasser, auf dem Land ...

1 in education, on small units, in different contexts ...
2 right across the arid zone, along the Cooper ...
3 in appearance, in caves and rock piles, on grasses and shrubs, in the evenings ...

Task 3 – identifying problems in English text
Only one of the following is an acceptable translation of German text 1 from the beginning of this chapter (page 58).

A An occupation for graduates of English which suggests itself is that of translation. Since most of the recently published literature in the German market are translations from the English, the demand of competent translators is continual. The stress lies on competent because it is only the quality as writer in both languages that counts here and not the education in the academic method. However, having a degree in philological studies is certainly a good prerequisite if one considers himself a translator with the style and way of thinking of a native English speaking writer. Regarding money, it can be said that compared with the amount of work literary translators are bad payed. But on the other hand, it is an occupation close to literature, which can be especially gratifying for those English language graduates who are inclined to use their own creativity. What is in general much more lucrative is the translation of academic and technical texts. The ordinary study of English is not the necessary preparation, though. A special qualification is required to work in the occupational field of sworn translators and interpreters. There are special colleges where the language specific to particular economy branches and the translation techniques which are needed for that sectors are taught. As a rule the only professional field for graduates of English is that of translating fiction or general non-fiction.

B An obvious occupation for a student of English is that of translator. There is a constant need for proficient translators, because most of the new books released on the German book market are translations of English works. The stress here lies on proficient because in these case the literary ability in both languages is important rather than the methodical education in academia. Yet, a philological training is a good prerequisite for the translators to enable them to get used to style and thinking of an English author. In comparison to the amount of work they have to do, translators of belles-lettres are poorly paid. On the other hand it is an occupation which is closely connected to literature that is satisfying especial the own creative abilities of students of English. Generally the translation of scientific and technical literature is more profitable. But the studies of English are not a suitable background for that. The occupation of a sworn in translator requires an extra qualification. There are special colleges that teach the specific scientific expressions of business and the proper techniques to translate them. Normally the only occupation possible for students of English is the translation of prose and official texts.

C One area of work closely related to English Studies is translating. Good translators are always in demand, the fiction released recently onto the German market being mostly translated from English, but the key word here is good. A talent for writing, in both languages, is essential for good literary translating, an academic training is not. A degree in language and literature does however help develop a sensibility for the style and thinking of English language writers. Translating literary texts is very poorly paid in relation to the effort involved, yet its closeness to literature is enjoyed by many graduates of English with a creative talent. Translating scientific and technical literature tends to be far more lucrative, but a degree in English is really no proper basis for that. Professional translating and interpreting requires a qualification from a specialist translation school, where the specialised languages of the various economic sectors and their appropriate translation techniques are taught. Graduates of English Studies can generally only find work translating popular fiction and non-specialist factual texts.

D Translating is an occupation that suggests itself for Anglicists. As most of the recently published novels which appear on the German book market are translations from the English, good translators are required permanently. Yet the emphasis is layed on good, for what counts here is only the literary ability in both languages and not the scientific education. However, a study in language is a good fundament for a translator to understand the style and thoughts of a native English author. In relation to their effort translators of fiction and poetry have to make, the salary is very low. On the other hand it is work that is closely connected with literature, which satisfies Anglicists with their own creative interest. Better paid in general is the translation of academic and technical literature. However, there are rarely suitable preparations during the study of Anglistics. The profession of the sworn translators and interpreters requires a special qualification. For them there are special high education colleges for learning the specific technical terms of each economical branch and for training the suitable techniques of translation. For a graduate from the study of Anglistics usually only the profession of a translator of novels and generalised texts comes into question.

Choose quickly which translation you think is most appropriate, and see if your choice agrees with others'. Explain your choice in terms of lexis and grammar, considering at least the following:

- accuracy of lexical choices as translation of German meanings
- appropriateness of lexical choices for formal written English
- grammatical relations between clauses
- LEXICAL DENSITY of NOUN GROUPS
- appropriateness to English text of THEME choices in each clause and the pattern developed through the text
- pronominal reference

1.2 Text and function

Not every text giving factual information is simply reporting. The texts below give information for slightly different purposes than the texts examined so far in this chapter. Text grammar changes when aspects of REGISTER do.

Task 4 – identifying situational context

The first text, written by a primary school student for a science class, includes features (in red) that are not appropriate to a mature report, such as personal pronouns, colloquial lexis, lack of lexical density, cause and effect relations between clauses.

1 Your food goes down a tube called the oesophagus. The oesophagus leads from the throat to the stomach. The digestive juice digests it so little that you

can't see it at all, so it can go into the blood. The white blood cells kill all the germs but if you feel sick it's because you've got too much germs in your body and the cells can't fight them all at once. You'll need to take some medicine to help them. When our blood runs out of oxygen the blood goes back to your heart and new blood goes round your body and it's more bright and clean than the old blood.

Note the grammatical features in the second text that differ from a straight report, and suggest how these differences relate to the context and purpose the text would have been written for.

2 The Long March established the leadership of Mao Zedong. Although Mao was challenged by the leader of the Fourth Route Army, Zhang Guotao, the prestige Mao acquired during the Long March assured his dominance. Mao's leadership also brought an end to the dominance of the Soviet Union in the party and made Chinese Communism more independent.
The Long March forged a tightly knit army that drew strength from its sufferings. The survivors formed the tough nucleus of the new Red Army which developed at Yanan. The policy of going north to fight the Japanese also stimulated high morale in the Red Army and inspired patriots throughout China.
As it passed through twelve provinces the Red Army brought the message of Communism to hundreds of millions of peasants, who would otherwise have never heard of Communism.

The two texts below differ from factual reports in other ways.

3 Nichts zeigt die unverkennbare Individualität, den Nuancenreichtum, die Treffsicherheit einer Sprache, aber ebenso ihren Eigensinn und ihre Grenzen deutlicher als der Versuch, sie zu übersetzen. Deswegen schwankt auch das Urteil über die Qualität der Übersetzungen so verwirrend. Denn selbst ein gerechter und umsichtiger Kritiker weiß oft nicht, ob er mehr das in die Über- tragung Hinübergerettete bewundern oder das unwiederbringlich Verloren- gegangene beklagen soll. Es gibt berühmte Übersetzungen, die buchstäblich Jahrhunderte überdauern und in der neuen Sprachumwelt Heimatrechte erworben haben, und es gibt Totgeburten, ausgeklügelte Retortenerzeugnisse, denen aber der Lebensfunke fehlt. Unter diesen wechselvollen Umständen ist es kein Wunder, daß die sprachphilosophischen Einschätzungen dessen, was Übersetzung ganz im allgemeinen zu leisten vermag, weit auseinanderliegen. Man könnte die extremen Pole des Meinungsspektrums so beschreiben: Die eine Schule, die von den Pragmatikern beherrscht wird, verkündet die Überzeugung, daß sich das, was ein Text etwa an Wertvollem enthält, auch in einer anderen Sprache werde sagen lassen. Ihre Antipoden hinwiederum, die Puristen, sind durchdrungen von der Ansicht, daß sich der Aufwand in keinem Fall lohnt, weil das Eigentliche sich dem Verpflanzen ins fremde Sprachfeld entzieht.

Ohne unbedingt Partei zu ergreifen, muß man aber zugeben, daß unter den zu derlei Urteilen Berufensten, den Dichtern und Sprachkundigen, eher die skeptische Note überwiegt.

Meine Lieblingsformel ist freilich eine italienische: *Traduttore traditore.* Hier wird die Bilanz mit Hilfe von nur zwei Wörten gezogen, kurz, bündig und – unübersetzbar. Sicher, man kann es auch auf deutsch sagen: Der Übersetzer ist ein Verräter. Aber der charmante Witz, der ganz feine Reiz ist verflogen, denn die nahezu völlige Gleichheit der beiden Vokabeln im Italienischen, die im wesentlichen durch einen einzigen Vokal voneinander unterschieden sind, ist unnachahmlich.

Unnachahmlich? Wenn es so wäre, dann gäbe es ja das Geschäft oder doch zumindest die Kunst des Übersetzens gar nicht, und jede Diskussion erwiese sich als überflüssig. Das aber ist das Geheimnis aller sprachlichen (fast möchte man hinzufügen: aller menschlichen) Bemühungen, daß man dasselbe Problem auf gelungene, überzeugende Weise erledigen kann, oder so ungeschlacht, tölpelhaft und unimaginativ, daß die Lösung einem Fehlschlag gleichkommt. Dieser Spielraum innerhalb des Unmöglichen rechtfertigt jede Anstrengung. Und so kehre ich denn, angestachelt durch meine eigene Erkenntnis, zu dem unübersetzbaren Ausspruch zurück und wage es noch einmal: Übertragen ist Unterschlagen. Das ist noch immer nicht perfekt, aber schon bedeutend besser als vorher. Dem nächsten glückt vielleicht ein weiterer Schritt. Da das Ziel unerreichbar bleibt, muß man sich mit solchen Annäherungen begnügen.

4 Es sind meines Erachtens vor allen anderen zwei Faktoren, die in diesem Jahrhundert die Geschichte der Menschheit geprägt haben: zum einen die Entwicklung der Naturwissenschaft und Technologie und zum anderen die großen ideologischen Stürme, die das Leben praktisch der gesamten Erdbevölkerung verändert haben – die russische Revolution, totalitäre Regime auf der Rechten wie auf der Linken und die Explosionen von Nationalismus und Rassismus. Interessanterweise hat keiner der großen Denker des neunzehnten Jahrhunderts sie vorausgesehen. Wenn unsere Nachkommen in zwei oder drei Jahrhunderten (falls die Menschheit bis dahin überlebt) auf unser Zeitalter zurückblicken, werden sie diese beiden Phänomene als die herausragenden Charakteristika unseres Jahrhunderts betrachten. Doch diese großen Bewegungen haben als Ideen in den Köpfen von Leuten begonnen – Ideen zum

Verhältnis der Menschen untereinander, wie es ist, wie es sein könnte und wie es sein sollte. Sie bilden die Substanz der Ethik.

Wenn wir unsere oftmals gewalttätige Welt verstehen wollen, dürfen wir die Aufmerksamkeit nicht auf die großen unpersönlichen Kräfte beschränken, die uns beeinflussen. Die Ziele und Motive, die uns leiten, müssen im Licht unseres gesamten Wissens und Verstehens untersucht werden. Ihre Wurzeln und ihr Wachsen, ihr Wesen und insbesondere ihre Gültigkeit müssen kritisch mit allen uns verfügbaren intellektuellen Mitteln geprüft werden.

• How do these texts differ from reports?
• What is their purpose?
• What context would these texts have been written for?

1.3 Summary of language features
The main grammatical features noticed in the report text, common to the German and English versions, are:

*The less popular the readership, the higher the degree of specialist lexis.

*Lexical density of clauses tends to be high, meaning a lot of information is packed into NOUN GROUPS.

*Verbal form is simple present and PROCESSES are Relational and Material.

*Grammatical relations between clauses are simple.

*Relations between clauses is expressed through textual ADJUNCTS rather than subordinating relations.

*PARTICIPANTS are generic and abstract.

*No or little MODALITY.

features in common

Though German and English report texts are similar in function, there are a couple of important differences to consider when translating them.

*The more specialist the readership for an English text, the more lexis is Latin based rather than of Germanic origin.

*THEME choices in English text are predominantly SUBJECT PARTICIPANT, whereas in German they can be object PARTICIPANT, CIRCUMSTANCE or PROCESS.

differences

Having identified the major language patterns of the report, you can now translate some examples yourself. The following exercises draw attention to lexical and grammatical choices potentially available at several points in text production, some of which are simply wrong, others possible in another context but not for the genre. An understanding of which choices are, and which are not, possible in this genre will prepare you for independent translation into English.

2.1 Text completion

The following text was part of a donor appeal to members of Potsdam University, January 1999. It reports information about the condition of the patient on whose behalf the appeal was being launched.

Menschen, die an bösartigen Erkrankungen des Blutes (z.B. Leukämie) leiden, können oft nur durch eine Knochenmarktransplantation geheilt werden. In Deutschland erkranken jährlich ca. 5000 Menschen an Leukämie. Viele können durch eine Knochenmarktransplantation gerettet werden. Dazu braucht man einen gesunden Spender, dessen Gewebe mit dem des Patienten verträglich ist. Gleiche Gewebemerkmale findet man am ehesten unter Geschwistern des Patienten. Ist kein geeigneter Geschwisterspender vorhanden, muß der Patient hoffen, daß ein nicht verwandter Spender für ihn gefunden wird. Die Wahrscheinlichkeit, daß zwei nicht verwandte Personen gleiche Gewebemerkmale besitzen, ist sehr gering. So kann nur bei einer sehr großen Anzahl zur Knochenmarkspende bereiter Menschen ein geeigneter Spender gefunden werden. Dennoch kann leider auch heute noch für viele Patienten kein passender Spender gefunden werden.   *(Aktion Knochenmarkspende Brandenburg e.V.)*

Task 5 – completing gap translation text

Complete the translation by choosing from the words offered below.

People (1) ___ from (2) ___ of the blood (eg leukaemia) can often only be cured by a bone marrow transplant. Around 5,000 people in Germany (3) ___ leukaemia every year. Many can be saved by a bone marrow transplant, (4) ___, whose tissue (5) ___ the patient's. Identical tissue features (6) ___ (7) ___ the patient's siblings, but if there is no suitable sibling the patient (8) ___ hope that a (9) ___ can be found. The likelihood (10) ___ is very small, and so a suitable donor can only be found (11) ___. Even so, suitable donors (12) ___ be found for many patients.

(1) who suffer, that suffer, suffering, with the suffering, who are suffering
(2) nasty illnesses, malignant diseases, aggressive sicknesses
(3) get, get sick with, become ill with, come down with, are affected by
(4) for which a healthy donor is needed, requiring a healthy donor, in which case a healthy donor must be found
(5) is compatible with, is bearable by, can be carried by, is acceptable to
(6) are most likely to be found, one finds first, are most quickly found
(7) under, among, in, within
(8) can only, must, has to, should
(9) donor who is not a relative, donor outside the family, unfamiliar donor, unrelated donor
(10) that two non-related people own same tissue features, of two unrelated people having the same tissue features, that unrelated people would have the same tissue features
(11) when a very large number of people are willing to donate bone marrow, from among a very large number of bone marrow donation willing people, in a very big group of people who are prepared to donate bone marrow
(12) can still not, can unfortunately also today still not, cannot still today, still cannot today

2.2 Evaluation and improvement

The following task is based on German text **3** (about whales) at the beginning of this chapter (page 59).

Task 6 – evaluating student translations

Mark every mistake and stylistic problem you can find in the following student translations of the text.

A Whales are mammals who returned in to the water 60 million years ago, where they found richer food resources than on land. The whales could grow to be the biggest animals living on this planet because of the carrying force of the element water. Even the dinosaurs seem to look like dwarfs compared to the largest whale of all – the "Blauwal", who can grow 30m in length and weights as much as 25 Elephants.

The great whales can travel for many thousands of kilometers. Usually the whales spend the summer in the arctic regions where they find their food consisting mostly of krill and tiny crayfish but during the time of copulation they travel to warmer bodies of water where they give birth to their children. During this time the whales stay without food. "Blauwale" and "Finnwale" fast 8 month per year whereas the "Buckelwal" fasts 6 month.

One of the mysteries around the whales is their communication system. Besides having a social language through which they can communicate they also developed songs that the buckelwale are especially famous for. One can hear these songs only in the warm waters in the time of copulation and only some male whales can sing them. The songs are always changed but the whales adopt the changes so that they always sing the same songs.

Whales live in a surrounding in which the warmth of their body can't be kept for a long time. To survive they can only give birth to one child which they have to feed for a long period of time, teach it how to find food and travel long distances. Depending on their species the whales can become 30 to 50 years old. But one supposes, that single whales can even become older than that.

Whales are very peaceful animals. They lead lost ships back to secure harbors through fog, rescue drowning persons or help each other even in great danger.

B Whales are mammals, that returned to the sea 60 million ago, where they found more food than on the land. Carried by the element of water they could become the largest living creature, that has ever lived on this planet. Even dinosaurs appear as dwarf in comparison to the blue-whale, who is the biggest one out of the family of whales with a length of 30 meters and a weight of 25 elephants.

Big whales move for many thousand kilometers. In the summer they live in their food grounds in the artic and antarctic zone, which offer them food, which consists mainly of krill, which are tiny organisms as crustaceans. For the mating season they move to warmer regions of the sea, there are also their babies born. During this period they have to live without food. Blue whales and finn whales are fasting for about eight months per year, buckel whales for about six months.

One of the riddles for us to understand is the communication of whales. Besides their social language in which they communicate, they have developed songs – famous are the ones of the buckelwale. Their songs are only heard in the mating grounds. Only male whale sing and on the other hand not every of them can sing. The songs are changed permanently, yet the changes are recorded by the others, so that they all sing the same song.

Since whales are living in an environment which quickly takes away warmth from the body, they can only survive, if they have not more than one intrauterine child. For the same reason they can only breastfeed one puppet for a long period of time and make it to find food and how to cross long distances on its own. Whales probably can reach an age of between 30 and 50 years which depends on the species. However, one supposes, that single animals have the ability to become older.

Whales are peaceful beings. They guide ships back through heavy fog into the save harbour. They rescue nearly drowned people from the death and they help each other – even in the biggest need.

C Whales, that belong to the mammals, returned to the water abut 60 million years ago because they found more food there. Carried by the element water they were able to become the biggest living beings that ever lived on this planet. Even dinosaurs seem to be dwarfs if compared to a blue whale, who with his 30m in length and the weight of 25 elephants, is the largest member of its group.

Big whales are wandering many thousand kilometres. In summer they stay in arctic and antarctic regions for the reason of food, which consists mainly of krill, tiny crabs. They move to warmer waters for mating season; here they also have youngs. During this period they are consuming no food. Blue whales and finnwhales are fasting approximately eight months a year; hunchback whales approximately six months.

Their communication states a mystery to us. Besides their social language whales have developed chants. The chants of the buckel whales are the most famous of these. Their songs can only be heard in the mating areas, where only some of the male whales sing. The songs keep changing continuously. These changes are integrated into the chant so that all whales are singing the same song.

Since whales are living in an environment in which warmth is quickly channelled away from their bodies, they can only survive to bear just one baby, suckle it over a long period of time, teach it how to find food and how to travel for long distances without taking harm. Differing from one species to the next, they are believed to be getting between 30 and 50 years. Yet, some individual animals might be older than that.

Whales are peaceful animals, that lead ships through fog back to a save haven, save humans from drowning and help each other, even if they are in acute danger themselves.

Task 7 – improving the translation

Write your own translation of the whale text and compare with other students.

2.3 Vocabulary extension

Use a good bilingual dictionary and a thesaurus for the following tasks.

Task 8 – words

As already stressed, translating is not just a matter of finding an English noun for a German noun, an English adjective for a German adjective, etc. It is one of the commonest errors for inexperienced translators to retain the grammar of the original text and simply substitute lexical items, though it may be a logical and manageable place to start the thinking process. It is important to consider how many possible variants might be available in the other language for a given word in the original. For example, in the first German text 1, the word *Studium*. Most students translate this as "study" and then invent words and phrases to translate *Anglistikstudium*, such as "Anglistics" or "the study of Anglistics" – neither of which are useful translations seeing "Anglistics" is not used by native English speakers.

List as many translations for the following words as you can, then discuss the most suitable for a translation of the text they come from.

Anglisten, Absolventen, Ausbildung, Hochschule, Wissenschaft, Übersetzungstechniken, vereidigten Übersetzer, Fähigkeit, Voraussetzung, Tätigkeit, Tätigkeitsfeld, Vorbereitung, Berufsfeld , Fachsprache, Fachliteratur, Sachtext, Neuerscheinung, belletristisch, schriftstellerisch

Task 9 – phrases

Find several ways of translating each of the NOUN GROUPS below, discussing the problems and merits of each version.

For example, *ein nahe liegendes Tätigkeitsfeld für Anglisten* could be translated as: "a closely lying occupational area for Anglicists", "an occupation close to English Studies", "work closely related to English Studies", "a field with close connections to the study of English" or "an activity close to the hearts of English graduates". In the given context, the second and third options seem more appropriate than the others.

– die meisten belletristischen Neuerscheinungen auf dem deutschen Buchmarkt
– die schriftstellerische Fähigkeit in beiden Sprachen
– die methodische Ausbildung in der Wissenschaft
– Stil und Denkweise eines englischsprachigen Autors

78

Task 10 – words and phrases in the other texts

Discuss the translation of the following words and phrases from the German and English language report texts presented at the beginning of the chapter. Note the etymologies of the German and English lexis used in such texts.

2 Übergangswelt, angeschwemmte Pflanzenteile, Flut, Überflutung, angereicherte Schlamm, artenreichen Fauna, Faunenelemente, Lebensraum, Nahrung, Zonen, Zonierung, Gezeitenzone, landeinwärts, Gedeihen, Flußmündung, Süßwasser, Arten, Artengruppe, Voraussetzung, Fähigkeit, Anteil, verzweigte Wurzelsysteme, lebenswichtige Mineralsalze, Schlammschichten, Sauerstoffzufuhr, Mangrovengewächse, Pneumatophoren, Atemwurzeln, hervorwachsen, herausragen, Regenwald, Meerestieren, Landtier, Angepaßtsein, Meeresbewohner

3 Säugetiere, Lebewesen, Großwale, Wanderungen, Krebstierchen, Jungen, Finnwale, Buckelwale, Verständigung, Gesänge, Männchen, Veränderungen, Entfernungen, Ertrinkende

1 ways of analysing language, view of language, system of grammatical rules, language education, task, focus, words, phrases, clauses, sentences, approach, mental capacity, formal model, language acquisition, language function, resource, set of rules, psychological properties, language development, process of learning, range of meanings, choices

2 multi-storey high-density housing development, woodland, crown cover, levels, species, variety of songbirds

3 subspecies, plains, shelter, shrubs, home range, digestive system, fibrous material, bacteria, protozoan fauna, cellulose, nitrogen, metabolism

Translating a prepositional phrase with a similar grammatical structure may be possible, but is not always the only or even the best way to encode the given meanings in the other language. For example, *in Stil und Denkweise eines englischsprachigen Autors* could be translated as "in the style and manner of thought of an English speaking writer", but this is not an elegant solution. Alternatives include at least "for the way writers in English think and express themselves", "for the style and thinking of English language writers" or "for the stylistic and expressive modes of the English language writer".

> Discuss alternatives and preferences to translate prepositional phrases from the texts. Remember that using the same grammatical structure may not be the best solution, and that some are so-called fixed phrases with no variations.

1 im Allgemeinen, in der Regel, in Frage
2 in vielen Teilen der Welt, im Gewirr der stelzenartigen Wurzeln, am unteren Rand der Gezeitenzone, im Jahr, durch besonders hohe Flutwellen, in unterschiedlichem Ausmaß, in den oberen Bereichen der Flußmündungen, in den oberen Schlammschichten, an mangrovenfreien Küsten
3 zurück ins Wasser, im Vergleich, mit 30 Metern Länge, mit dem Gewicht von 25 Elefanten, in ihren Nahrungsgründen in arktischen und antarktischen Zonen, in dieser Zeit, neben der sozialen Sprache, über eine lange Periode, nach Art, zwischen 30 und 50 Jahre, zurück in den sicheren Hafen

1 in education, with little reference, to context of use, in a functional model
2 right across the arid zone, to this habitat, on the Cooper, in pairs, with the woodland habitat
3 in appearance, on grasses and shrubs, in the evenings, in common with other kangaroos, in a sac-like development of the alimentary tract, in the natural diet of the Euro, from urea, with sufficient water content, with infrequent access to free water, during dry periods.

**III.3
Independent
translation**

3.1 Quick texts

> Practise translating the report genre with the following simple excerpts, spending no more than fifteen to twenty minutes on each.

1 Fische leben in allen Teilen der Ozeane bis hinunter in die ewige Kälte und Dunkelheit der Tiefsee. Die in den flachen, erhellten Zonen lebenden Spezies bilden oft Schwärme, wie zum Beispiel die Heringe und die Sardinen; andere, wie die Thunfische, unternehmen ausgedehnte, ja sogar transozeanische Wanderungen. Die harten Lebensbedingungen in den großen Tiefen führten zur Evolution besonders schöner und seltsamer Arten.

2 Das Knochenmark ist der Ort der Blutbildung. Im Knochenmark befinden sich die sogenannten Stammzellen. Aus diesen Zellen entstehen in mehreren Schritten die weißen und roten Blutzellen sowie die Blutplättchen. Die Blutzellen und -plättchen können ab einem gewissen Reifestadium vom Knochenmark in das Blut übertreten. Beim Gesunden ist das Knochenmark im Überfluß vorhanden und kann sich nach einer Knochenmarkspende rasch nachbilden.

3 Während das Exzerpt einen Text oder mehrere Texte unter einem ganz bestimmten Aspekt auswählend bearbeitet, also „Auszüge" herstellt, faßt der Konspekt stichwortartig die Informationen eines Sachtextes zusammen und vermittelt so eine geraffte „Übersicht". Ähnlich wie die Inhaltsangabe für erzählende Texte, stellt das Konspektieren große Anforderungen an das Abstraktionsvermögen: Das Wichtigste eines Textes ist knapp und übersichtlich – i.d.R. mit eigenen Worten – herauszuarbeiten, so daß die Gedankenführung ersichtlich wird. Nur besonders zentrale Informationen (z.B. bestimmte Fachbegriffe oder Definitionen) sind im Original als Zitat zu übernehmen.

3.2 45-minute texts

Time yourself to complete each of the following slightly longer texts within an hour.

1 Anglistik ist die Wissenschaft von der englischen Sprache und Literatur. In vielen Studienordnungen heißt das Fach auch „Englische Philologie" oder „Englisch", wobei alle drei Namen das Gleiche oder Verschiedenes bezeichnen können. Mit „Englisch" ist fast immer das Fach gemeint, das zukünftige Englischlehrer studieren müssen. Es umfasst die englische Sprache und Literatur im weitesten Sinn, d.h. unter Einschluss Irlands, des Commonwealth und der USA. Da Englischlehrer Großbritannien und Amerika im Unterricht gleich stark berücksichtigen sollen, gehören für sie die beiden Kulturräume in ein und dasselbe Studienfach. Wo das Fach „Englische Philologie" heißt, ist damit an manchen Universitäten das Gleiche gemeint, an anderen nur der britische Kulturraum unter Einschluss des Commonwealth. Auch ANGLISTIK bezog sich früher auf den gesamten englischsprachigen Kulturraum, während man heute darunter in Abgrenzung von der AMERIKANISTIK als Fach meist ausschließlich die Wissenschaft von Sprache und Kultur Großbritanniens und des Commonwealth versteht. Wer sich für das Fach entschieden hat, muss sich also zuerst vergewissern, in welcher Form es an der ins Auge gefassten Universität angeboten wird.
(Hans-Dieter Gelfert, *Einführung in das Studium, studium kompakt Anglistik · Amerikanistik*, Berlin, 1998.)

2 Die Übersetzung ist die Wiedergabe eines Textes in einer anderen Sprache.
Dabei wird oft unterschieden zwischen einer Übersetzung, die sich möglichst
wortgenau ans Original anschließt; einer Übertragung, die eine freiere sinn-
betonte Wiedergabe anstrebt unter voller Berücksichtigung der semantischen
und stilistischen Eigentümlichkeiten der Zielsprache; einer Nachdichtung, die
eine formbedachte und gehaltkonforme Nachschöpfung darstellt. Jeder Übersetzer muß sich entscheiden, ob dem Leser ein Text inhaltlich nahegebracht
oder ob der Leser zum Urtext hingeführt werden soll. Die Schwierigkeit des
Übersetzers liegt begründet in dem Problem, die verschiedenen Bedeutungs-
ebenen eines Textes in eine andere Sprache übertragen zu können; in der
Verschiedenartigkeit des Bedeutungsfeldes von Wörtern in verschiedenen
Sprachen; in den unterschiedlichen grammatischen und stilistischen Struktu-
ren; im Fehlen passender Wörter in der anderen Sprache. Als Grundregel des
Übersetzens kann gelten: Nicht aus dem Wort, sondern aus dem Sinn heraus
sollte man übersetzen.
(Peter Mettenleiten/Stephan Knoebl, Hrsg., *Blickfeld Deutsch*, Paderborn, 1991)

3.3 Exam practice
The following are examples of reports, about the length and level of
examination texts in German universities.

Translate each into English within two and a half hours.

1 Leserverhalten
Je nach dem Ziel unterscheidet man folgende Arten des Leserverhaltens: das
kursorisch-orientierende Lesen (das sog. Diagonale Lesen), um rasch einen
ersten Überblick über einen Text zu gewinnen; das intensiv-verweilende Lesen
(das statarische Lesen) als Voraussetzung für die Interpretation im Gegensatz
zum evasorischen Lesen (von lat. *evadere* = herausgehen, fliehen) für eine auf
Unterhaltung gerichtete Lektüre, bei der sich der Leser in Figuren, Situationen
und Handlungen eines fiktionalen Textes vertieft, um der Eintönigkeit des All-
tags zu entfliehen. Davon abgehoben ist das gründliche informatorische Lesen,
durch das Sachtexte exakt erschlossen werden sollen. Für das statarische
und das informatorische Lesen bieten sich vor allem zwei Methoden an:
1. Das „Lesen mit Bleistift", d.h. das Markieren eines Textes mit Farbstiften:
– Durch das Unterstreichen von Schlüsselbegriffen bzw. zentralen Aussagen
– mit Hilfe von Randmarkierungen werden optische Lesehilfen gegeben. Z.B.:
Ein senkrechter Balken zeigt eine wichtige Stelle an; ein Fragezeichen markiert
Unverstandenes oder Unklares; ein Ausrufezeichen kennzeichnet eine bemer-
kenswerte Stelle usw.
Da bei der Arbeit mit geliehenen Büchern diese Markierungen im Text nicht

möglich sind, empfiehlt sich die Einlage einer Plastikfolie in der Größe einer Buchseite, auf der dann mit wasserlöslichen Stiften die entsprechenden Kennzeichnungen für jeweils eine Seite gemacht werden können, ohne das Buch zu beschädigen.

2. Durch „auswählendes Lesen" wird das Herausschreiben zentraler Begriffe, Daten, Fakten und wörtlich zitierter Passagen möglich. Dieses Verfahren nennt man das Exzerpieren. Das Ergebnis ist das Exzerpt: Unter speziellen Fragestellungen, z.B. Hauptunterschiede zwischen „Diskussion" und „Debatte" oder „Aufgaben des Diskussionsleiters", werden aus einem Text oder mehreren Texten Informationen ausgewählt und notiert. Die Fähigkeit des Exzerpierens ist eine wichtige Arbeitstechnik zur Vorbereitung für Diskussion, Interpretationen und Referate. Wichtig ist die genaue Angabe der Fundstelle (Quelle) durch den Namen des Autors, des Titels und der Seitenzahl. Das wortwörtlich Herausgeschriebene ist als Zitat zu kennzeichnen und auf seine Genauigkeit sorgfältig zu überprüfen. (see above)

2 Der Baum: Eine Welt für sich

Die Krone eines Baumes enthält zahllose Kleinlebensräume für viele verschiedene pflanzenfressende Wirbeltiere und Wirbellose, die sich von den nahrhaften Blättern und Früchten ernähren. Raupen wie die des Eichenspinners wandern über die Blattoberfläche und beißen große Stücke heraus; andere minieren in den weicheren Teilen und bilden dabei Gänge.

Viele kleine Hautflügler und Milben legen ihre Eier auf und in Blättern ab. Die ausschlüpfenden Larven beginnen zu fressen, und die Pflanzen reagieren, in dem sie um die wachsenden Tiere herum neues Gewebe produzieren, so daß die charakteristischen Galläpfel entstehen. In manchen Gegenden gibt es allein auf Eichen 50 Arten von Galläpfel produzierenden Insekten und Milben. Andere Insekten, wie die Schild- und Blattläuse, haben lange, stilettartige Mundwerkzeuge, die sie in die Pflanze einstechen, so daß der Zellinhalt oder die flüssigen Nährstoffe durch Saugen und durch Kapillarität entnommen werden können. Diese Pflanzenfresser oder -parasiten stellen ein großes Nahrungsreservoir für räuberische Waldtiere dar – insektenfressende Vögel, Marienkäferlarven, Raubfliegen, Netzflügler, Wespen und Spinnen –, die wiederum von größeren Raubtieren gefressen werden.

Auf dem Boden leben die charakteristischen Waldstreubewohner. Manche von ihnen, wie Asseln, Tausendfüßler und bestimmte Milben und Sprungschwänze, ernähren sich direkt von den toten pflanzlichen Stoffen, andere sind Raubtiere. Unter der Streuschicht leben die echten Bodentiere, die Fadenwürme, Wenigborster und besonders die zu ihnen gehörenden Regenwürmer. Durch die Grabtätigkeit der letzteren werden tote Blätter und Blatteile in den mineralhaltigen Boden eingebracht. Sie fördern damit den Pflanzenwuchs und das

Gedeihen der Pflanzenfresser. Diese wiederum dienen räuberisch lebenden Wirbellosen und oft auch Spitzmäusen, Dachsen und insektenfressenden Vögeln als Nahrung.

All diese Tiere sind wichtig für den natürlichen Haushalt des Waldes, denn ihnen fällt die Aufgabe zu, das pflanzliche und tierische Material zu zerkleinern und es für die Bearbeitung durch Millionen von Bodenbakterien und Pilzen vorzubereiten, die zu 80% für die Atmungsaktivität des Bodens verantwortlich sind. Die Wälder sind komplexe Ökosysteme, deren zahllose Pflanzen und Tiere alle an der Erhaltung eines natürlichen Gleichgewichts mitwirken. Jeder Eingriff in diese Struktur führt zu einer Störung dieses empfindlichen Gleichgewichts.

(*Großer Atlas des Tierlebens*, Augsburg, 1995.)

IV Narrative – fictional

"Narrative" – these genres of fiction need little explanation, familiar and common as they are to any reader. This chapter focuses on the short story, illustrating with complete texts where possible, otherwise extracts. The texts range in register from stories for children to complex adult texts.

IV. 1 German and English examples   88
1.1 Comparison and contrast
1.2 Text and function
1.3 Summary of language features

IV. 2 Guided translation exercises   103
2.1 Text completion
2.2 Evaluation and improvement
2.3 Vocabulary extension

IV. 3 Independent translation   107
3.1 Quick texts
3.2 45-minute texts
3.3 Exam practice

Fictional narratives are one of the commonest of genres in the ongoing daily production of culture, being used for both entertainment and much general education. In tertiary level language studies, narrative fiction is a major object of study and has been featured in this book for that reason. Narratives construct situations in which a series of events occur, towards a goal, to solve a problem indicated at the outset. Various characters are involved, and varying degrees of description and dialogue may be used. Not all of the text examples here are complete texts, for lack of space. Text excerpts in this chapter are taken from story beginnings.

1 Einmal wollte ein Mädchen sein Fahrrad anstreichen. Es hat grüne Farbe dazu genommen. Grün hat dem Mädchen gut gefallen. Aber der große Bruder hat gesagt: „So ein grasgrünes Fahrrad habe ich noch nie gesehen. Du mußt es rot anstreichen, dann wird es schön." Rot hat dem Mädchen auch gut gefallen. Also hat es rote Farbe geholt und das Fahrrad rot gestrichen. Aber ein anderes Mädchen hat gesagt: „Rote Fahrräder haben doch alle! Warum streichst du es nicht blau an?" Das Mädchen hat sich das überlegt, und dann hat es sein Fahrrad blau gestrichen. Aber der Nachbarsjunge hat gesagt: „Blau? Das ist doch so dunkel. Gelb ist viel lustiger!" Und das Mädchen hat auch gleich gelb viel lustiger gefunden und gelbe Farbe geholt. Aber eine Frau aus dem Haus hat gesagt: „Das ist ein scheußliches Gelb! Nimm himmelblaue Farbe, das finde ich schön!" Und das Mädchen hat sein Fahrrad himmelblau gestrichen. Aber da ist der große Bruder wieder gekommen. Er hat gerufen: „Du wolltest es doch rot anstreichen! Himmelblau, das ist eine blöde Farbe. Rot mußt du nehmen. Rot!" Da hat das Mädchen gelacht und wieder den grünen Farbtopf geholt und das Fahrrad grün angestrichen, grasgrün. Und es war ihm ganz egal, was die anderen gesagt haben.

(Ursula Wölfel, *Achtundzwanzig Lachgeschichten*, Berlin, o.J.)

2 Das Telefon summte, der Polizeipräsident nahm den Hörer auf.
„Ja?"
„Hier spricht Wachtmeister Kerzig. Soeben hat ein Passant mich verächtlich angeschaut."
„Vielleicht irren Sie", gab der Polizeipräsident zu bedenken. „Fast jeder, der einem Polizisten begegnet, hat ein schlechtes Gewissen und blickt an ihm vorbei. Das nimmt sich dann wie Geringschätzung aus."
„Nein", sprach der Wachtmeister. „So war es nicht. Er hat mich verächtlich gemustert, von der Mütze bis zu den Stiefeln".
„Warum haben Sie ihn nicht verhaftet?"

„Ich war zu bestürzt. Als ich die Kränkung erkannte, war der Mann verschwunden."

„Würden Sie ihn wiedererkennen?"

„Gewiß. Er trägt einen roten Bart."

„Wie fühlen Sie sich?"

„Ziemlich elend."

„Halten Sie durch, ich lasse Sie ablösen."

Der Polizeipräsident schaltete das Mikrofon ein. Er entsandte einen Krankenwagen in Kerzigs Revier und ordnete an, daß man alle rotbärtigen Bürger verhafte.

Die Funkstreifen waren gerade im Einsatz, als der Befehl sie erreichte. Zwei von ihnen probierten aus, welcher Wagen der schnellere sei, zwei andere feierten in einer Kneipe den Geburtstag des Wirtes, drei halfen einem Kameraden beim Umzug, und die übrigen machten Einkäufe. Kaum aber hatten sie vernommen, um was es ging, preschten sie mit ihren Wagen in den Kern der Stadt.

Sie riegelten Straßen ab, eine um die andere, und kämmten sie durch. Sie liefen in die Geschäfte, in die Gaststätten, in die Häuser, und so sie einen Rotbart aufspürten, zerrten sie ihn fort. Überall stockte der Verkehr. Das Geheul der Sirenen erschreckte die Bevölkerung, und es liefen Gerüchte um, die Hetzjagd gelte einem Massenmörder…

(Kurt Kusenberg, *Ein verächtlicher Blick*. In: Benno von Wiese, Hrsg., *Deutschland erzählt*, Frankfurt a. M., 1992.)

3 Wenn wir uns, wie zwei Versteinte, zum Essen setzen oder abends an der Wohnungstür zusammentreffen, weil wir beide gleichzeitig daran denken, sie abzusperren, fühle ich unsere Trauer wie einen Bogen, der von einem Ende der Welt zum anderen reicht – also von Hanna zu mir –, und an dem gespannten Bogen einen Pfeil bereitet, der den unbewegten Himmel ins Herz treffen müßte. Wenn wir zurückgehen durch das Vorzimmer, ist sie zwei Schritte vor mir, sie geht ins Schlafzimmer, ohne „Gute Nacht" zu sagen, und ich flüchte mich in mein Zimmer, an meinen Schreibtisch, um dann vor mich hinzustarren, ihren gesenkten Kopf vor Augen und ihr Schweigen im Ohr. Ob sie sich hinlegt und zu schlafen versucht oder wach ist und wartet? Worauf? – da sie nicht auf mich wartet!

Als ich Hanna heiratete, geschah es weniger ihretwegen, als weil sie das Kind erwartete. Ich hatte keine Wahl, brauchte keinen Entschluß zu fassen. Ich war bewegt, weil sich etwas vorbereitete, das neu war und von uns kam, und weil mir die Welt zuzunehmen schien. Wie der Mond, gegen den man sich dreimal verbeugen soll, wenn er neu erscheint und zart und hauchfarben am Anfang seiner Bahn steht. Es gab Augenblicke der Abwesenheit, die ich vorher nicht gekannt hatte. Selbst im Büro – obwohl ich mehr als genug zu tun hatte – oder während einer Konferenz entrückte ich plötzlich in diesen Zustand, in dem ich mich nur dem Kind zuwandte, diesem unbekannten, schemenhaften Wesen, und ihm entgegenging mit all meinen Gedanken bis in den warmen lichtlosen Leib, in dem es gefangen lag.

Das Kind, das wir erwarteten, veränderte uns. Wir gingen kaum mehr aus und vernachlässigten unsere Freunde; wir suchten eine größere Wohnung und richteten uns besser und endgültiger ein. Aber des Kindes wegen, auf das ich wartete, begann alles sich für mich zu verändern; ich kam auf Gedanken, unvermutet, wie man auf Minen kommt, von solcher Sprengkraft, daß ich hätte zurückschrecken müssen, aber ich ging weiter, ohne Sinn für die Gefahr.

Hanna missverstand mich. Weil ich nicht zu entscheiden wußte, ob der Kinderwagen große oder kleine Räder haben solle, schien ich gleichgültig. (Ich weiß wirklich nicht. Ganz wie du willst. Doch, ich höre.) Wenn ich mit ihr in Geschäften herumstand, wo sie Hauben, Jäckchen und Windeln aussuchte, zwischen Rosa und Blau, Kunstwolle und echter Wolle schwankte, warf sie mir vor, daß ich nicht bei der Sache sei. Aber ich war es nur zu sehr ...

(Ingeborg Bachmann, *Alles*. In: Benno von Wiese, Hrsg., *Deutschland erzählt*, Frankfurt a. M, 1992.)

1 Once upon a time, but not very long ago, deep in the Australian bush lived two possums. Their names were Hush and Grandma Poss. Grandma Poss made bush magic. She made wombats blue and kookaburras pink. She made dingoes smile and emus shrink. But the best magic of all was the magic that made Hush invisible.

What adventures Hush had!

Because she couldn't be seen she could be squashed by koalas.

Because she couldn't be seen she could slide down kangaroos.

Because she couldn't be seen she was safe from snakes, which is why Grandma Poss had made her invisible in the first place.

But one day, quite unexpectedly, Hush said, "Grandma, I want to know what I look like. Please could you make me visible again."

"Of course I can", said Grandma Poss, and she began to look through her magic books.

She looked into this book and she looked into that. There was magic for thin and magic for fat, magic for tall and magic for small, but the magic she was looking for wasn't there at all.

Grandma Poss looked miserable.

"Don't worry Grandma", said Hush. "I don't mind."

But in her hear of hearts she did.

All night long Grandma Poss thought and thought. The next morning, just before breakfast, she shouted, "It's something to do with food. People food –

not possum food. But I can't remember what. We'll just have to try and find it."
So later that day, they left the bush where they'd always been to find what it was that would make Hush seen. They ate Anzac biscuits in Adelaide, mornay and Minties in Melbourne, steak and salad in Sydney and pumpkin scones in Brisbane. Hush remained invisible.

"Don't lose heart!" said Grandma Poss.

"Let's see what we can find in Darwin."

It was there, in the far north of Australia, that they found a vegemite sand-wich. Hush breathed deeply and began to eat.

"A tail! A tail!" shouted both possums at once.

For there it was. A brand new, visible tail.

Later, on a beach in Perth, they ate a piece of pavlova. Hush's legs appeared. So did her body.

"You look wonderful you precious possum!" said Grandma Poss.

"Next stop – Tasmania."

And over the sea they went.

In Hobart, late one night, in the kitchens of the casino, they saw a lamington on a plate.

Hush closed her eyes and nibbled. Grandma Poss held her breath and waited.

"It's worked! It's worked!" she cried.

And she was right. Hush could be seen from head to tail. Grandma Poss hugged Hush, and they both danced "Here We Go Round the Lamington Plate" till early in the morning.

From that time onwards Hush was visible. But once a year, on her birthday, she and Grandma Poss ate a vegemite sandwich, a piece of pavlova and a half a lamington, just to make sure that Hush stayed visible forever. And she did.

(Mem Fox, *Possum Magic*, Norwood, South Australia, 1993.)

2 It's midnight in a free country a week before Christmas with the war receding like the tide, and the celebrations already forgotten. A dray-load of men trundles down the limestone road. There's been two-up and boxes of home brew tonight, and plenty of talk, too much of it. A bottle of whisky does the rounds on the decline toward the solitary light by the sea. Two horses shiver and shake their steamy manes and the moon hovers in the treetops. Somewhere a mopoke calls with some hesitation. Pipes flare and glow. Two figures do not smoke. They are rigid and wide-eyed, the only sober passengers aboard. The ocean growls down there. A light down there. A shack down there. A man appears with a lantern and the dray rolls to a stop outside the tin shack.

"Gentlemen."

"Ah, Hanford."

The man called Hanford holds the lantern high and sees the farmers on the dray. He sees the boys with them, sees their eyes, their naked limbs, their hands over their balls. In the lamplight they are the colour of Keen's curry powder. He tries to think quickly.

"What's this, then, Mister Buckridge?"

"Oh, just some unfinished business."

Hanford looks at the boys, smells the booze, sees the shotgun broken across a farmer's lap.

"The war's over, Mister Buckridge."

"It'll be over tonight, that's a fact."

"I know about your boy."

"Well, then you know."

"He was a soldier. They're kids."

"An eye for an eye, Hanford"

"They've got nothing to do with it, and you know it. Why don't you leave 'em here with me."

Buckridge laughs. Already Hanford sees there'll be no stopping this. This is something he could not have imagined in his direst sleep. He has fought fires with these men, kicked a football with them, ruffled their children's hair. Outside the glow of the lamp there is only darkness, and in it the moon. Inside the shack his own son sleeps...

(Tim Winton, *Wire*. In: Dee Mitchell, ed., *Amnesty*, Port Melbourne, 1993.)

3 The Rev. Joseph Simmondsen had been appointed by his Bishop to a cure of souls in the Far North, in the days when Queensland was an ungodly and unsanctified place. Naturally, the Rev. J., who was young, green, and zealous, saw a direct mission in front of him. His predecessor had never gone twenty miles outside the little seaport that formed the commercial outlet of the district; but this did not suit Joseph's eager temperament. Once he felt his footing and gained a little experience, he determined on a lengthened tour that should embrace the uttermost limits of his fold.

Now, although beset with the conceit and priggishness inseparable from the early stages of parsonhood, Simmondsen was not a bad fellow, and glimpses of his manly nature would at times peep out in spite of himself. This, without his knowledge, ensured him a decent welcome; and he got a good distance inland under most favourable auspices, for, the weather being fine, everybody was willing to lend him a horse or drive him along to the next station upon his route. The Rev. Joseph began to think that the roughness of the back country had been much exaggerated...

(Ernest Favenc, *The Parson's Blackboy*. In: *Australian Short Stories*, Melbourne, 1951.)

1.1. Comparison and contrast

Narratives such as children's stories seem easy to translate, while more sophisticated description, narrative technique and dialogue might pose more obvious obstacles. Even simple children's narratives, however, are challenging for the untrained translator. Their lexical and grammatical qualities must be maintained in the second language, or they will not function well as stories for small children. Similarly, an adult narrative must be suited to its readership. Careful consideration has to be given to lexis (whether it is colloquial and everyday), and to the grammatical relations within and between clauses. Narratives usually combine features typical of speech with features of written language, and the wrong features in the wrong part of a narrative make for a poor translation. The following exercises draw attention to aspects of the texts' lexis and grammar with which beginner translators are likely to run into problems.

Task 1 – identifying grammatical features

The story genre has its own characteristic grammar, making each example of the genre easily recognisable as a story. The generic sructure is well-known and often described in education: orientation or scene setting, indication of a problem which the plots events will eventually resolve, a climax and resolution and a final coda or evaluation of events. Explicitly identifying the **grammatical** features that characterise a genre helps students avoid the random and careless choices that are the hallmark of amateur translators.

Stories typically feature Material, Mental and Verbal PROCESSES, human and individual PARTICIPANTS and many CIRCUMSTANCES. They do not package information into the sort of complex noun groups typical of reporting, and they include many colloquial and idiomatic wordings, especially within dialogue. They do not use a great deal of unusual or specialist vocabulary, though the range of vocabulary is often wide, and difficult to translate for the second language learner.

Notice the forms (tense) of the verbs below, taken from the text examples given above.

1 wollte anstreichen, hat genommen, hat gefallen, hat gesagt, habe gesehen, mußt anstreichen, wird schön, hat gefallen, hat geholt und gestrichen, hat gesagt, haben, streichst an, hat überlegt, hat gestrichen, hat gesagt, ist, ist, hat gefunden und geholt, hat gesagt, ist, nimm, finde, hat gestrichen, ist   PROCESSES

gekommen, hat gerufen, wolltest anstreichen, ist, mußt nehmen, hat gelacht und geholt und angestrichen, war, gesagt haben

2 summte, nahm auf, spricht, hat angeschaut, irren, gab zu bedenken, begegnet, hat, blickt, nimmt sich aus, sprach, war, hat gemustert, haben verhaftet, war, erkannte, war verschwunden, würden wiedererkennen, trägt, fühlen sich, halten durch, lasse ablösen, schaltete ein, entsandte, ordnete an, verhafte, waren, erreichte, probierten aus, sei, feierten, halfen, machten, hatten vernommen, ging, preschten, riegelten ab, kämmten durch, liefen, aufspürten, zerrten fort, stockte, erschreckte, liefen um, gelte

3 setzen, zusammentreffen, denken, abzusperren, fühle, reicht, bereitet, treffen müßte, zurückgehen, ist, geht, zu sagen, flüchte, hinzustarren, sich hinlegt, zu schlafen versucht, ist, wartet, wartet, heiratete, geschah, erwartete, hatte, brauchte zu fassen, war, vorbereitete, war, kam, zuzunehmen schien, verbeugen soll, erscheint, steht, gab, gekannt hatte, zu tun hatte, entrückte, zuwandte, entgegenging, lag, erwarteten, veränderte, gingen aus, vernachlässigten, suchten, richteten ein, wartete, begann zu verändern, kam, kommt, hätte zurückschrecken müssen, ging, missverstand, zu entscheiden wußte, haben solle, schien, weiß, willst, höre, herumstand, aussuchte, schwankte, warf vor, sei, war

1 lived, were, made, made, made, was, made, had, couldn't be seen, could be squashed, couldn't be seen, could slide down, couldn't be seen, was, is, had made, said, want to know, look like, could make, can, said, began to look through, looked, looked, there was, was looking for, wasn't, looked, don't worry, said, don't mind, did, thought, and thought, shouted, is to do with, can't remember, will have to try and find, left, they'd been, to find, was, would make seen, ate, remained, don't lose heart, said, let see, can find, was, found, breathed, began to eat, shouted, was, ate, appeared, did, look, said, went, saw, closed, nibbled, held, waited, worked, worked, cried, was,could be seen, hugged, danced, was, ate, to make sure, stayed, did

2 is, trundles, there's been, does the rounds, shiver, shake, hovers, calls, flare, glow, do not smoke, are, growls, appears, rolls, holds, sees, sees, sees, are, tries to think, is, looks, smells, sees, is, will be, is, know, know, was, are, have got, know, leave, laughs, sees, there'll be no stopping, is, could not have imagined, has fought, kicked, ruffled, there is, sleeps

3 had been appointed, was, was, saw, had never gone, formed, did not suit, felt, gained, determined on, should embrace, was not, would peep out, ensured, got, being, was willing to lend, drive, began to think, had been exaggerated

Specific and concrete PARTICIPANTS are typical of this genre, rather than categories of things or abstractions – individual people and touchable objects (eg "the Rev. Simmondsen/ Hanford/ a bottle of whisky/ a vegemite sandwich", *ein Fahrrad/ das Kind/ Hanna/ das Telefon*). PARTICIPANTS of the first text are listed below, as are some from the remaining texts.

PARTICIPANTS

> Complete the lists of PARTICIPANTS from each of the story texts given.

1 Mädchen, Fahrrad, grüne Farbe, Mädchen, große Bruder, grasgrünes Fahrrad, es, es, Mädchen, es, rote Farbe, Fahrrad, Mädchen, rote Fahrräder, alle, es, Mädchen, es, Fahrrad, Nachbarsjunge, Mädchen, gelbe Farbe, Frau aus dem Haus, scheußliches Gelb, himmelblaue Farbe, ich, Mädchen, Fahrrad, große Bruder, er, du, es, blöde Farbe, Mädchen, grünen Farbtopf, Fahrrad, ihm, anderen

2 Telefon, Polizeipräsident, Hörer, Wachtmeister, Passant, mich, Sie, Polizeipräsident, jeder, Polizisten, schlechtes Gewissen, ihm, Geringschätzung, Wachtmeister, er, mich, Mütze, Stiefeln, Sie, ihn, ich, ich, Kränkung, Mann, Sie, ihn, er, roten Bart, Sie, Sie, ich, Sie, Polizeipräsident, Mikrofon, er, Krankenwagen

3 wir, zwei Versteinte, wir beide, sie, ich, Trauer, Bogen, Pfeil, unbewegten Himmel, wir, sie, sie, ich, ihren gesenkten Kopf, ihr Schweigen, sie, sie, ich, Hanna, sie, das Kind, ich, Wahl, Entschluß, ich, etwas, Welt, Mond, ...

1 possums, names, Hush, Grandma Poss, Grandma Poss, bush magic, she, wombats, kookaburras, she, dingoes, emus, best magic, magic, adventures, Hush, she, she, she, she, she, she, Grandma Poss, her, Hush, I, I, you, me, I, Grandma Poss, she, she, she, magic, magic, magic, she, Grandma Poss, Hush, I, she, Grandma Poss, she, something, I, we, they, bush, ...

2 midnight, dray-load of men, two-up, boxes of home brew, talk, bottle of whisky, horses, steamy manes, moon, mopoke, pipes, figures, they, sober passengers, ocean, light, shack, man, dray, man, lantern, farmers, he, boys, eyes, naked limbs, hands, they, he, unfinished business, ...

3 Rev. Joseph Simmondsen, Queensland, ungodly and unsanctified place, Rev. J., direct mission, predecessor, ...

The PARTICIPANTS you will have listed are clearly everyday (in the context of their target audience), specific, and of a relatively small number. The action is also clearly centred around one or a small group of human PARTICIPANTS (or humanised in the case of the animal story for children), as the most frequently repeated PARTICIPANTS are those referred to by 'personal pronoun'.

CIRCUMSTANCES

Narratives also include many CIRCUMSTANTIAL meanings. A CIRCUMSTANCE locates a clause event in time, place, manner, cause, etc. If you mark the CIRCUMSTANCES in the narrative sections of the story texts (not the dialogue) you will see clearly that there are significantly more such meanings in narrative texts than in most of the other genres examined in this book. More significant in terms of translating such texts, however, is the position of such meanings within clauses. As we have seen in the other chapters, word order in English text can differ markedly from German word order.

THEME

The first element in each English clause, the THEME, is usually a PARTICIPANT, and usually the grammatical SUBJECT of the clause. THEME in stories are also very frequently complex, including textual and interpersonal elements. Textual elements in the THEME link the clause to other parts of the text in coordinating, subordinating, temporal or comparative ways (such as *aber/ und/ dann/ als/ so/ weil/ wie*, "and/ but/ or/ because/ so/ for/ then/ now/ once"). Interpersonal elements give commentary (such as *vielleicht*, "naturally"). In terms of how German and English texts compare, we have seen in other chapters that THEMES in English are much less often CIRCUMSTANCES than is the case in German. In narrative fiction texts, however, it is interesting to notice that CIRCUMSTANCES (time and place) in THEME position in English are common, and that PARTICIPANTS are dominant as THEME in German stories. Listed below are the THEME choices throughout the German texts.

1 einmal, es, Grün, aber, so ein grasgrünes Fahrrad, du, dann, Rot, also, und das Fahrrad, aber ein anderes Mädchen, rote Fahrräder, warum, das Mädchen, und dann, aber der Nachbarsjunge, Blau, Gelb, und das Mädchen, und gelbe Farbe, aber eine Frau aus dem Haus, das, nimm, das, und das Mädchen, aber da, er, du, Himmelblau, rot, da, und wieder den grünen Farbtopf, und das Fahrrad, und es

2 Das Telefon, der Polizeipräsident, ja, hier, soeben, vielleicht irren, gab, fast jeder, das, nein, so, er, warum, ich, als ich, war, würden Sie, gewiß, er, wie, ziemlich elend, halten Sie, ich, der Polizeipräsident, er, die Funkstreifen, als der Befehl, zwei von ihnen, zwei andere, drei, und die übrigen, kaum aber, Sie, und, Sie, und so sie, überall, das Geheul der Sirenen, und es, die Hetzjagd

3 wenn wir, weil wir beide, fühle, und an dem gespannten Bogen, wenn wir, ist, sie, und ich, um dann, ihren gesenkten Kopf, und ihr Schweigen im Ohr, ob sie, oder wach, worauf, da sie, als ich, geschah, weil sie, ich, ich, weil sich etwas, und weil, wie der Mond, es gab Augenblicke der Abwesenheit, selbst im Büro, oder während einer Konferenz, und ihm entgegenging, das Kind, wir, wir, aber des Kindes wegen, ich, aber ich, Hanna, weil ich, ich, ganz wie, doch ich, wenn ich, warf, daß ich, aber ich

> Underline those THEMES that would NOT be put into first position in the English language translation of the given clauses. (eg PARTICIPANTS which are the grammatical object of the clause and adverbs).

> Discuss whether there are THEME choices from the English language texts listed below that would NOT be put in first position in a German translation of the texts.

1 Once upon a time, their names, Grandma Poss, she, she, but the best magic of all, what adventures, because she, she, because she, she, because she, she, but one day I, please, of course, and she, she, and she, there, but the magic she was looking for, Grandma Poss, don't worry, I, but in her hear of hearts, all night long, the next morning, just before breakfast, it, people food, but I, we, so later that day, they, Hush, don't lose heart, let, it, in the far north of Australia, Hush, a tail, for there, a brand new visible tail, later, Hush's legs, so, you, next stop, and over the sea, in Hobart, Hush, Grandma Poss, it, and she, Hush, Grandma Poss, and they both, from that time onwards, but once a year, and she

2 It, a dray-load of men, there, a bottle of whisky, two horses, and the moon, somewhere, pipes, two figures, they, the ocean, a light, a shack, a man, and the dray, gentlemen, ah Hanford, the man called Hanford, he, in the lamplight, he, what, oh, Hanford, the war, it, I, well then, he, they, an eye for an eye, they, and you, why, Buckridge, already, this, he, outside the glow of the lamp, and in it, inside the shack

3 The Rev. Joseph Simmondsen, naturally the Rev. J. who was young green and zealous, his predecessor, but this, once he, he, now although beset with the conceit and priggishness inseparable from the early stages of parsonhood Simmondsen, and glimpses of his manly nature, this, and he, for the weather, the Rev. Joseph

Task 2 – identifying problems in English text
Only one of the following is an acceptable translation of German text **1**.

A Once upon a time there was a girl who wanted to paint her bike. She took green paint, because green colour had always been her favourite. But her elder brother told her: "I never saw such a grass-green bike before. It would be nice, if you would paint it red." Red was also a pleasing colour to the girl, and so she bought red paint and painted the bike red. But there was another girl saying: "Everyone has a red bike! Why don't you paint it blue?" The girl thought about it, and in the end painted her bike blue. But her neighbour said: "Blue? It's such a dark colour. Yellow is a lot more lively!" The girl thought yellow more lively as well and bought yellow paint. But again her elder brother came and shouted: "You wanted to paint it red! Yellow is a stupid colour. You have to take red. Red!" The girl laughed and took the can with the green paint again, and she painted the bike green, grass-green. And she did not care about what the others had said.

B There was once a little girl who wanted to paint her bicycle. She got some green paint, because she liked green. But her big brother said: "I've never seen a bike that was as green as grass. You have to paint it red, that'll look good". The little girl liked red too, so she got some red paint and painted the bike red. But then another girl said: "Everybody's got a red bike! Why don't you paint it blue?" The little girl thought about this for a while and then she painted her bike blue. But then the boy next door said: "Blue? But that's so dull! Yellow's much more fun!" And then she thought straight away that yellow was much more fun too and got some yellow paint. But then a lady from the apartment block said: "That's a yucky yellow! Get some light blue, I think that'd be lovely!" And so the little girl painted her bike sky blue. But then her big brother came back and he yelled: "But you were going to paint it red! Light blue's a silly colour. You have to use red, red!" At that the little girl burst out laughing and she got the tin of green paint again and painted her bike green as grass. And she didn't care one bit what the others said.

C Once upon a time a girl wanted to paint her bicycle and used green paint in order to do it. The girl liked the colour green very much but her brother said: "I never saw a bicycle as green like grass before. You have to paint it red, then it becomes pretty". The girl liked the colour red as well therefore she fetched red paint and painted her bicycle red. Then another girl came and said: "Everybody has red bicycles – why don't you paint your bike blue?" The girl thought about it for a while and then painted her bicycle again, with blue colour. A boy living next door came and said: "Blue is too dark. Yellow looks much happier!" After that the girl thought that yellow is much happier too and fetched yellow paint, but then her brother returned and shouted: "I thought you intended to paint it red! Yellow that is a stupid colour. Red, you have to paint it red!" Then the girl laughed and she fetched the tin of green paint again and she painted her bicycle green – like grass – and she didn't care anymore about what the others said.

D A girl once wanted to paint her bicycle. She used green colour. Green was a colour that the girl liked very much. But her older brother said: "I have never seen such a grass green bicycle. You should paint it red, that would be nice." Red was a colour that the girl liked very much, too. So it got red paint and painted the bicycle red. However, another girl said: "Everybody has a red bicycle! Why don't you paint it blue?" The girl was thinking about it and eventually painted her bicycle blue. Nevertheless, a boy from the neighbourhood said: "Blue? That's so dark. Yellow is much more delighting." And immediately the girl really found yellow more delighting and got yellow paint. But the older brother came back and called: "You said, you wanted to paint it red! Yellow! What a stupid colour! Red! You must take red!" That made the girl laugh and she went to get the green paint again and painted her bike green. Grass green. And she didn't care at all what the others said.

E A girl wanted to paint her bike and she chose green, a colour which she liked much. Her older brother said to her: "I have never seen such a greenish bike, its like grass! You should better paint it red, and it will be nice!" The girl found red nice as well, so she went for a red colour and she painted her bike red. Another girl said to her: "Everybody has a red bike, why don't you paint it blue?". The girl thought a while about it and then she painted her bike blue. The boy next door said: "Blue? That's too dark! Yellow is a nice bright colour!" The girl found yellow nice and bright as well, and she went for a yellow colour. A lady in the same house said: "Oh what a horrible yellow colour! Why don't you take pale blue, it' s a nice colour! So the girl painted her bike pale blue. Her brother came along again and cried: "You wanted to paint your bike red! This pale blue is a horrible colour. You should take red, definitely!" By that moment the girl started to laugh and she took her old green colour again, and she painted her bike green, green like grass. By now she did not bother any more what the other people said.

> Choose quickly which translation you think is best as an English language text for children, and see if your choice agrees with others'. Explain your choice in terms of lexis and grammar, considering at least the following:

- accuracy of lexical choices as translation of German meanings
- appropriateness of lexical choices for a children's story
- grammatical relations between clauses
- LEXICAL DENSITY of NOUN GROUPS
- appropriateness to English text of THEME choices in each clause

1.2 Text and function

Not every narrative text is telling a fictional story. The texts below tell stories for slightly different purposes than the texts examined so far in this chapter, though they draw on many of the same grammatical resources. Distinguishing between 'fiction' and 'history' is thus largely made on the basis of factors outside the individual text.

Task 3 – identifying situational context

The two texts below feature grammatical and lexical choices typical of all narratives, though they are not intended to be read as fictional within the cultures that produced them.

1 One day towards the middle of the seventeenth century John Aubrey, a young law student at the Middle Temple, set out to explore the countryside around his fathers estate in Wiltshire. Near the village of Avebury he came upon an extraordinary circle of huge stones which seemed to him to comprise an ancient monument "as much surpassing Stonehenge as a cathedral doth a parish church". Remarkable as the monument was and long as it had stood there, however, Aubrey's was the first detailed account of it. Even so, it aroused little interest...

2 In the Dreamtime all the earth lay sleeping. Nothing grew. Nothing moved. Everything was quiet and still. The animals, birds and reptiles lay sleeping under the earths crust. Then one day the Rainbow Serpent awoke from her slumber and pushed her way through the earths crust, moving the stones that lay in her way. When she emerged, she looked about her and then travelled over the land, going in all directions. She travelled far and wide, and when she grew tired she curled herself into a heap and slept. Upon the earth she left her winding tracks and the imprint of her sleeping body. When she had travelled all the earth, she returned to the place where she had first appeared and called to the frogs, "Come out!"

The frogs were very slow to come from below the earths crust, for their bellies were heavy with water which they had stored in their sleep. The Rainbow Serpent tickled their stomachs, and when the frogs laughed, the water ran all over the earth to fill the tracks of the Rainbow Serpents wanderings – and that is how the lakes and rivers were formed. Then the grass began to grow, and trees sprang up, and so life began on earth. All the animals, birds and reptiles awoke and followed the Rainbow Serpent, the Mother of Life, across the land. They were happy on earth, and each lived and hunted for food with his own tribe. The kangaroo, wallaby and emu tribes lived on the plains. The reptile tribes lived among the rocks and stones, and the bird tribes flew through the air and lived in the trees...

(*The Beginning of Life*. In: *Stradbroke Dreamtime*, Sydney, 1993.)

The text below differs from fictional narratives in other ways.

3 I was born at Daly River in the Northern Territory. I lived there two and a half years – before the authorities came and took me away, put me on Croker Island, a Methodist Mission for Half Caste Children. My brother and sister, twins two years older than I, were taken at the same time. I was there about eight years, had some good times and some sad. I remember that I forgot my mother.

Actually, we were told she was dead – so it would be acceptable to my sister, brother and I that we should forget her and that the most important influence in our lives should be God (and the missionaries).

When I was 11, there was a big event. The Superintendent on the island actually told me I'd been chosen by God to go down south and become the sister of a white family. I remember being absolutely elated that God had chosen me out of all the other girls on the island. There was a big Christian farewell for me: all the other girls said prayers and the missionaries took me to the church and blessed me in preparation for the event. I was to leave my brother and sister there, unaware that I'd be 38 years old by the next time I found my brother.

The day of my departure is fixed in my mind. I remember I had a little pleated yellow skirt, a brown and yellow cardigan, yellow socks, brown shoes. I remember exactly how I looked and exactly how I felt. I'd never been out of the tropical north, so the chill of the southern winds as I came off the plane went right through my bones. I remember walking towards this lady who had something in her hands, she threw it towards me to wrap it around me. It was a fur coat but I had never seen one – I thought it was a dead dog she was throwing on me and I screamed, pushed it off me and ran under the aeroplane and off up the tarmac, yelling and crying, with airport officials all running behind me. That was my introduction to civilised society!

> Related to the sort of context and purpose these texts would have been written for, suggest why they would not be not read as fictional stories.

• What context would these texts have been written for?

1.3 Summary of language features
Grammatical features of narrative fiction in both German and English are:

features in common

> *Use of Material and Verbal PROCESSES
> *Variety of verbal forms
> *Extensive CIRCUMSTANTIAL meanings
> *Dominance of human PARTICIPANTS and use of pronouns

Though German and English story texts are similar in function, there are differences to consider when translating them.

grammatical differences between English and German

> *In English language narratives, either the simple past tense of verbs, or the simple present dominates text. Present simple is of course also featured in dialogue sections.
> *In German narratives set in past time, the present perfect dominates, though the simple past is also very frequently used. The use of the present perfect in German brings qualities of spoken language into the text. Hence children's stories will almost exclusively be in this form, while more sophisticated adult narratives will use both forms. The less like everyday speech the text is intended to sound, the less it will use the present perfect tense.
> *The use of the *Konjunktiv* in German to report speech and thought is of course not available in English, where other grammatical resources do the job.

Having identified the major language patterns of simple stories, you can now make some translation choices. An understanding of which lexical and grammatical choices are, and which are not, possible in this genre will prepare you for independent translation into English.

2.1 Text completion

The following text is from *Achtundzwanzig Lachgeschichten*, a book for small children by Ursula Wölfel.

IV.2
Guided
translation
exercises

Einmal waren zwei Stiere auf einer Wiese. Sie wollten den Kühen zeigen, wie stark sie waren. Der eine hat gebrüllt: „Ich bin stärker als du! Ich kann dich umrennen, wenn ich will!" Und der andere hat gebrühlt: „Nein, ich bin stärker! Ich kann dich mit den Hörnen in die Luft werfen, wenn ich will!" Und die Kühe haben am Zaun gestanden und gestaunt, und die Stiere haben weitergebrüllt. Der eine hat gebrüllt: „Ich kann dich zu Brei stampfen, wenn ich will!" Und der andere hat gebrüllt: „Ich kann dich anschnauben, daß dir dein Fell verbrennt, wenn ich will!" Und die Kühe am Zaun haben gemuht und sich gewundert. Die Stiere haben gebrüllt, bis sie heiser waren. Sie konnten nur noch piepsen und quietschen. Da haben die Kühe sich gelangweilt über das dumme Gebrüll. Sie haben den Stieren den Rücken zugedreht und sie allein weiterschreien lassen.

Task 4 – completing gap translation text

Complete the translation of the above text by choosing from the words offered in the box below.

There were once two bulls in a field. They ___ (1). ___ (2) ___ (3): "I'm stronger ___ (4)!
I ___ (5)!" And ___ (6) ___ (7): "No way, I'm stronger! I ___ (8)!" And the cows ___ (9) at the fence and ___ (10), and the bulls ___ (11). One ___ (12): "I ___ (13) !" And ___ (14) ___ (15) : "I ___ (16)!" And the cows at the fence ___ (17). The bulls ___ (18) and they ___ (19). Then the cows ___ (20). They ___ (21) and ___ (22).

(1) wanted, that the cows saw, how tough they were / wanted to show the cows how tough they were / wanted to show the cows, how tough they were / wanted the cows seeing how tough they were
(2) the one of them, one of them, the one, one
(3) cried, had cried, has cried, was crying
(4) as you are, than you, as you
(5) can run around you, when I please / could run the pants of you, if I wanted to / can outdo you whenever I want
(6) the other one, the other, another,

(7) cried, had cried, has cried, was crying

(8) could toss you in the air with my horns, if I wanted to can chuck you into the sky with my horns, should I wish am able to throw you high in the sky with my horns, when I want

(9) have stood, have been standing, had stood, stood

(10) have stared, have watched, stared, watched, were staring, were watching, were amazed, have been astonished

(11) went on crying out / continued to cry out / kept up the crying out / have cried out further

(12) cried, had cried, has cried, was crying

(13) can pump you into porridge, if I so please / would be able to stomp you into stew, were I of a mind to / could stomp you into porridge if I wanted to / could mash you into mush, when I wish

(14) the other one, the other, another,

(15) cried, had cried, has cried, was crying

(16) could pummel you til your skin burned, if I wanted to / can pound you until your fur fumes, should I wish to do so / would be able to stomp you til your skin would scorch, when I want it

(17) mooed and wondered / have been mooing and wondering to themselves / have mooed and wondered themselves

(18) cried out til they were hoarse / cried until their voices broke / have cried until such time as they lost their voice / were crying until they were no longer able to speak

(19) have only been able to squeak and to squeal / could only squeak and squeal / were only able to be squeaking and squealing

(20) got bored with all the silly yelling / were feeling boring after the stupid bellowing / have bored themselves over the dumb bawling / have been bored over the stupid shouting

(21) have the bulls the back turned / were turning the back at the bulls / turned their backs on the bulls
did turn their back at the bulls

(22) let them go on shouting on their own / them alone further cry have let / did allow them further crying alone

2.2 Evaluation and improvement

The following task is based on German text **2** at the beginning of this chapter (page 86).

Task 5 – evaluating student translations

Translating is not just a matter of finding an English noun for a German noun, an English adjective for a German adjective, etc. It is one of the commonest errors for inexperienced translators to retain the grammar of the original text and simply substitute lexical items with the aid of a dictionary, though it may be a logical and manageable place to start. Student translators should consider many possible variations available in the other language for a given word, phrase or sentence in the original.

The following translation was done by a software programme on the Internet (AltaVista), but such programmes are clearly still far from capable of proper text translation!

Mark every lexical, idiomatic and stylistic problem you can find.

The telephone hummed, the policepresident took up the listener.
Yes?
Here speaks watchmaster Kerzig. Just a passant looked at me despicably.
Perhaps you err, gave the policepresident to consider. Almost everyone, which meets a police, has a bad conscience and looks at it past. That takes itself then like depreciating out.
No, spoke the watchmaster. Like that was not it. It had examined me despicably, from the cap to the boots.
Why didn't you arrest it?
I was too alarmed. When I detected the offense, the man had disappeared.
Would you recognise it?
Certain. He carries a red beard.
As you feel?
Rather miserablly.
Stops you through, I let you replace.
The policepresident switched the microphone on. It sent an ambulance in Kerzigs province and arranged, that one arrests all redbearded citizens.
The radio patrols were even in the use, when the instruction achieved them. Two of them tries out, which car the faster be, two others celebrated in a bar the birthday of the landlord, three helped a comerade with the removal, and the remaining ones made shopping. Hardly but had they heard, about what it went, they dashed with their cars in the core of the city. They bolted the streets off, one after the other, and combed them through. They ran in the shops, in the pubs, in the houses, and so they tracked down a redbeard, they dragged it away. Everywhere the traffic stopped. The howling of the sirens scared the population, and it ran rumours about, the hunting applied to a massmurderer.

Task 6 – improving the translation

List as many translations for each sentence of this text as you can, and decide on the most suitable for the genre. Write your own complete translation of the text and compare with other students.

2.3 Vocabulary extension

Use a good bilingual dictionary and a thesaurus to translate the following.

Task 7 – German text 3

Translating a prepositional phrase with a similar grammatical structure may be possible, but is not always the only or even the best way to encode the given meanings in the other language. For example, *Der Mond am Anfang seiner Bahn* would NOT be translated into English as "the moon at the beginning of its course".

Discuss alternatives and preferences, and translate the following noun groups and prepositional phrases to suit the context.

Remember that using the same grammatical structure may not be the best solution, and that there may be 'fixed phrases' and frequent collocations to consider.

- zwei Versteinte
- ihren gesenkten Kopf vor Augen und ihr Schweigen im Ohr
- Der Mond am Anfang seiner Bahn
- eine größere Wohnung
- ich kam **auf Gedanken**, wie man auf Minen kommt
- Sprengkraft
- ohne Sinn für die Gefahr
- nicht bei der Sache

Task 8 – German text 3

Translate the following verbal groups and clauses from the same text to suit the context, considering carefully the grammatical options and collocational tendencies of English.

- ohne „Gute Nacht" zu sagen
- ich flüchte mich in mein Zimmer

- Ob sie sich hinlegt und zu schlafen versucht oder wach ist und wartet?
- wir richteten uns besser und endgültiger ein
- ich hätte zurückschrecken müssen
- weil ich nicht zu entscheiden wußte
- ganz wie du willst
- doch, ich höre
- sie warf mir vor, daß ich nicht bei der Sache sei aber ich war es nur zu sehr

3.1 Quick texts

Practise translating the story genre with the following excerpts, spending no more than fifteen to twenty minutes on each, and maintaining their style.

IV.3
Independent
translation

1 Es war einmal ein bildhübsches Bauernmädchen, deren Mutter und vor allem Großmutter völlig in sie vernarrt waren. Die gute alte Dame ließ ihr ein rotes Käppchen machen, das ihr so gut stand, daß man sie überall nur noch Rotkäppchen nannte. Eines Tages sagte ihre Mutter, die gerade Kuchen gebacken hatte, zu ihr: „Ich habe gehört, daß deine Großmutter krank ist. Geh doch einmal zu ihr und bring ihr einen Kuchen sowie dieses Töpfchen Butter". Das Rotkäppchen machte sich sofort zu seiner Großmutter, die in einem anderen Dorf wohnte, auf den Weg. Beim Durchqueren des Waldes begegnete sie Meister Wolf, der große Lust verspürte, sie zu fressen, sich aber wegen einiger Holzfäller, die in der Nähe waren, nicht traute. Er fragte sie, wohin sie ginge ...
(Charles Perrault, *Das Rotkäppchen*. In: Jack Zipes, Hrsg., *Rotkäppchen und Leid*, Köln, 1982.)

2 In dieser Story gehts um sonen reichen Zahn, der wohl mords knackig aussah, aber durch die feine Family total out war. Jede Menge Klamotten und sonen Plunder, aber dafür immer auf liebes Mädchen machen und sonen Scheiß. Die fuhr da aber entweder voll drauf ab oder blickte überhaupt nich durch, jedenfalls machte se nie Rabbatz sondern lief auch noch mit soner affigen roten Samtmütze rum, die ihr die Großmutter mal verpaßt hatte ...
(Uta Claus/Rolf Kutschera, *Total Tote Hose: 12 Bockstarke Märchen*, Frankfurt a. M. 1986.)

3 Ich kam ein paar Minuten zu spät zum Bahnhof, und während ich den Groschen in den Automaten für die Bahnsteigskarte warf, versuchte ich, mich an das Mädchen zu erinnern. Ich stellte mich an die Treppe zum Bahnsteig und dachte: blond, zwanzig Jahre, kommt in die Stadt, um Lehrerin zu werden; als ich die Leute, die an mir vorübergingen, musterte, schien es mir, als sei die Welt voller blonder zwanzigjähriger Mädchen – so viele kamen von diesem Zug her, und sie hatten alle Koffer in der Hand und sahen aus, als kämen sie in die Stadt, um Lehrerin zu werden. Ich steckte eine Zigarette an und ging auf die andere Seite des Augangs, und ich sah, daß hinter dem Geländer ein Mädchen auf einem Koffer hockte ... (Heinrich Böll, *Das Brot der Frühen Jahre*, Köln, 1955.)

3.2 45-minute texts

Time yourself to complete each of the following slightly longer children's texts within an hour.

1 Einmal ist eine Bachstelze über die Wiese gelaufen. Sie hat hier ein bißchen gepickt und da ein bißchen gepickt und mit dem Schwanz gewippt und gezwitschert. Aber der Kater ist durchs Gras geschlichen. Gerade wollte er auf die Bachstelze losspringen, da ist sie aufgeflogen, und der Kater ist auf seine Pfoten gefallen. Die Bachstelze hat sich auf einen Stein im Bach gesetzt und gezwitschert und mit dem Schwanz gewippt und ein Tröpfchen Wasser getrunken. Wieder ist der Kater herangeschlichen. Gerade wollte er wieder losspringen, da ist die Bachstelze aufgeflogen, und der Kater ist ins Wasser geplumpst. Die Bachstelze hat sich auf einen Baum gesetzt und mit dem Schwanz gewippt und gezwitschert und zugesehen, wie der Kater niesen mußte. Der wollte jetzt auf den Baum springen. Er hat sich schon geduckt und die Pfoten eingestemmt und die Krallen ausgestreckt. Dat hat ihm die Bachstelze – plitsch! – ein Häufchen auf den Kopf gemacht. Der Kater hat geschrien und ist nach Hause gerannt und hat sich drei Stunden lang geputzt. Und die Bachstelze ist wieder über die Wiese gelaufen und hat gepickt und mit dem Schwanz gewippt und gezwitschert. (Ursula Wölfel, *Achtundzwanzig Lachgeschichten*, Berlin, o.J.)

2 Das Bäuerlein im Himmel

Es war einmal ein armes, frommes Bäuerlein. Es wurde krank und starb, und nun kam es vor die Himmelspforte. Zusammen mit ihm ist auch ein reicher, reicher Herr da gewesen und hat auch in den Himmel gewollt. Da kommt der heilige Petrus mit dem Schlüssel, macht auf und läßt den Herrn herein. Das Bäuerlein hat er aber, wie es scheint, nicht gesehen und machte also die Pforte wieder zu. Da hat das Bäuerlein von außen gehört, wie der Herr mit aller Freude im Himmel aufgenommen worden ist und wie sie drinnen musiziert und gesungen haben. Endlich ist es da drinnen wieder still geworden, und der heilige Petrus kommt, macht die Himmelspforte auf und läßt das Bäuerlein ein. Da hat das Bäuerlein gemeint, es werde jetzt auch musiziert und gesungen, wenn er käme; aber da ist alles still gewesen. Man hat es freilich mit aller Liebe aufgenommen, und die Engel sind ihm entgegengegangen – aber gesungen hat niemand. Da fragt das Bäuerlein den heiligen Petrus, warum man bei ihm nicht singt wie bei dem reichen Herrn; es ginge da, scheint es, im Himmel genauso ungerecht zu wie auf der Erde.

Da sagt der heilige Petrus: „Aber gewiß nicht, du bist uns so lieb wie alle anderen und darfst alle himmlischen Freuden genießen wie der reiche Herr; aber schau, so arme Bäuerlein, wie du eines bist, kommen alle Tage in den Himmel; so ein reicher Herr aber – da kommt alle hundert Jahre nur etwa einer."

(Gebrüder Grimm, *Das Bäuerlein im Himmel*. In: *Grimms Märchen*, Hamburg, 1988.)

3.3 Exam practice

The following are examples of stories of about the length and level of examination texts in German universities. Translate each into English within two and a half hours.

1 Vogelgezwitscher

„Diese selten blöde Kuh", grummelte Jasmin vor sich hin. Sie meinte ihre Lehrerin, die die Kinder mal wieder mit Hausaufgaben belästigt hatte. Dabei lachte die Sonne vom ansichtskartenblauen Himmel. Im Schwimmbad wäre es jetzt viel amüsanter gewesen, als durch den Stadtpark zu stolzieren. „Diese doofe Frau Schlingbein", sagte Jasmin noch eine Spur zorniger.

Sie packte den Kassettenrecorder aus ihrem Rucksack, steckte das Microfon in die Buchse, drückte die Aufnahmetaste. Eine seltsame Idee von Frau Schlingbein – Vogelstimmen aufnehmen...! Jasmin schaute sich ratlos um. Auf dem Rasen aalten sich die Menschen in der Sonne. Im Teich schwamm ein einsamer Schwan. Auf einmal lachte Jasmin laut. Sie stellte den Recorder auf einer Bank ab und schlug vor Freude einen Purzelbaum – einmal vorwärts und einmal rückwärts, so begeistert war sie von ihrer Idee. Sie flitzte quer über die Wiese, blieb vor einer Reihe Ahornbäume stehen, die den Park umzäunten. Zum Glück war sie eine gute Turnerin. Es kostete sie keine große Mühe, auf einen der Bäume zu klettern. Sie plazierte das Kassettengerät auf einem breiten Ast, versteckte das Microfon zwischen Zweigen.

„So, ihr Vöglein, jetzt zwitschert mal schön. Ciao..."

Im Freibad vergaß sie bald den Recorder und die Vogelstimmen. Erst als sie am Abendbrottisch saß, erinnerte sie sich wieder an die Hausaufgabe. Ehe die Eltern sie ausfragen konnten, war sie schon aus der Wohnung. Der Abend dämmerte. Der Wind machte die Bäume flüstern. Die Angst machte Jasmin Beine. Vogelfederleicht holte sie den Recorder aus dem Geäst und sauste nach Hause.

Die Eltern empfingen sie mit Vorwürfen. Jasmin murmelte eine Entschuldigung, setzte sich an den Tisch und ließ das Band zurückspulen.

„Ich mußte doch für die Schlingbein Vogelstimmen aufnehmen".

Die Mutter runzelte die Stirn. Vogelgezwitscher war es wirklich nicht, was sie hörten.

„Es geht ganz leicht", sagte eine Krächzstimme. „Nach Ladenschluß warten wir am Hinterausgang. Der Filialleiter bringt das Geld meistens persönlich zur Bank, und wir..." Ein fieses Lachen dröhnte aus dem Lautsprecher, dann zischte jemand: "Morgen abend... Schubertstraße... Hinterausgang."

„Mensch...!" entfuhr es Jasmin.

Ihr Vater telefonierte mit der Polizei, aber der Beamte glaubte ihm nicht, und sie mußten Kassette und Recorder zur Wache bringen. Am nächsten Abend wartete die Polizei auf die beiden Ganoven.

Der Leiter des Supermarktes schenkte Jasmin einen Einkaufsgutschein.

Frau Schlingbein war auch freigebig: Sie brummte Jasmin eine Strafarbeit auf, weil sie die Hausaufgaben nicht gemacht hatte.

(Herbert Friedmann, *Vogelgezwitscher*. In: Hannelore Westhoff, Hrsg., *Die schönsten Schulgeschichten*, Ravensburg, 1990.)

2 Bevorzugte Landschaft

Mira packte auf der gegenüberliegenden Straßenseite. Es war nach sechs, und vor ihrem Haus war kein Platz mehr frei. Sie nahm die Notenhefte vom Beifahrersitz und stieg aus. Es war windig. Der Wind, der aus der Richtung von Randmeer kam und einen schweren, unangenehmen Geruch in die Stadt trieb, erfaßte den Saum ihrer Regenjacke. Instinktiv drückte sie sich den wollenen Schal gegen den Hals. Als sie genau gegenüber von den erleuchteten Fenstern ihres Hauses die Fahrbahn überqueren wollte, sah sie ihre Familie am Tisch sitzen. Wie angewurzelt blieb sie stehen.

Auf seinem gewohnten Platz mit dem Rücken zur offenen Küche war ihr Mann gerade dabei, etwas anzuschneiden oder auf dem Teller ihrer siebenjährigen Tochter Jeanne, die wie immer neben ihm saß, etwas zu zerkleinern. Das Kind achtete überhaupt nicht auf das Essen, sondern hörte mit offenem Mund der Frau zu, die auf der anderen Seite des Tisches saß und lachend und gestikulierend etwas erzählte. Nun deutete die Frau mit einer knappen Bewegung auf etwas. Mira reckte sich und sah, daß Jeanne fragend die Arme hob und sie, als die Frau nickte, voll Vertrauen ausstreckte. Die Frau rollte die zu langen Ärmel von Jeannes Bluse hoch, was beim Essen vernünftig war; Mira sah, wie die rührenden weißen, immer noch molligen Kinderarme zum Vorschein kamen.

Für einen Moment schloß sie die Augen und schaute dann wieder hin.

Auf ihrem Platz saß eine fremde Frau.

Mira war klein, aber sehr stolz und aufrecht, mit runden Schultern und großen runden Brüsten – der Wind blies die Jacke gegen ihren Körper –, sie hatte dunkles Haar – der Wind wehte ihre kurzen Locken in alle Richtungen, aber sie waren so dicht, daß die Kopfhaut nirgends zu sehen war – und blasse Haut. Die Frau am Eßtisch sah anders aus. Schulterlanges weißblondes Haar stach gegen die sehr rosige Gesichtsfarbe ab; sie hatte eckige Backenknochen, und als sie sich halb von ihrem Stuhl erhob, um die Herbstastern, die auf der Fensterbank neben ihr standen, wieder auf den Tisch zu stellen, konnte man bemerken, daß sich diese Eckigkeit in ihren Schultern, Armen und Hüften fortsetzte. Sie trug eine elfenbeinfarbene Jacke …

(Margriet de Moor, *Bevorzugte Landschaft*, München, 1994.)

3 Zum ersten Mal

Sie ist noch nicht dreizehn, er ist vierzehn Jahre alt. Er heißt Peter und sie Franziska. Und die Sonne scheint. Franziska hat noch die leise einander berührenden kindlichen Knie, aber manchmal, wenn sie lächelt oder ihn anschaut, dann ist es, als wäre sie schon eine Frau.

Man ist sehr ernst in diesem Alter. Man fühlt, wie etwas Unbekanntes aufsteigt in einem und den Atem hemmt; die Luft ist ganz besonders leuchtend, und das Keinem der Blätter hat zum ersten Mal seine ganz eigene Bedeutung. „Eigentlich sind wir doch schon richtig erwachsen", sagt Peter. „Lächerlich, wie die andern herumtoben im Schulhof oder sich um Fußballresultate streiten – ich muß dann immer still daneben stehen, ich habe den Kontakt dazu verloren. Aber ich kann nicht sagen, daß ich mich deshalb unglücklich fühle, im Gegenteil, diese große Einsamkeit, die um mich herum wächst…"

„Ja ja –" antwortete Franziska. Und dann laufen sie nebeneinander her und sind ganz still, und das ist sehr schön, zu wissen, daß jemand neben einem ist, der einen versteht. Es ist Vormittag, und im Park sind nicht allzu viele Menschen, man setzt sich auf eine Bank. Links an der Ecke hockt schon ein Landstreicher in abgeschabtem Mantel, er scheint fast zu schlafen, mitunter aber gleiten seine Blicke seitlich auf die beiden Kinder, und dann verzieht sich ein wenig sein Mund.

„Früher müssen es die Menschen schwer gehabt haben", bemerkt Franziska und spielt an einer kleinen Kette, die um ihren noch dünnen Hals liegt. „Aber wir – wir wissen doch, was mit uns los ist–"

„Ach – ich wünschte, mir wäre alles so klar wie dir", seufzt Peter. „Ich weiß nur, daß ich alles mit einem Male anders sehe, als wären meine Augen plötzlich größer geworden oder tiefer. Früher war alles einfach, jetzt ist es verworren. Ich verstehe beinah, wenn die Großen nach den guten alten Zeiten stöhnen. Das muß wohl so gewesen sein wie damals, als ich noch ein Kind war und nur spielte. Schön und gerade und gut und voll Selbstverständlichkeit."

„Aber das ist doch ganz einfach – Pubertät!" Franziska trompetet das Wort fast stolz und aufgeklärt. Und sie beginnt Peter ihre Gedanken auseinanderzusetzen.

Peter nickt. Gut und schön. Und teilweise weiß er ja auch um die Dinge. Aber trotzdem, es bleiben ein paar Mysterien. „Und dann – vielleicht will ich, daß dies und jenes dunkel bleibt? Vielleicht ist es gut, wenn ich mich quäle?"

„Nein", sagt Franziska, „diese Selbstquälerei sei auf alle Fälle dumm und unrationell. Eines Tages lege man eben die Puppen weg, weil sie einem keinen Spaß mehr machen. Das sei naturgesetzlich und erfordere kein Kopfzerbrechen. Nein, sie, Franziska, stehe auch nachts nie an den Brücken, die über den dunklen Fluß führen. Einmal, weil es die Eltern nie erlauben würden, und dann finde sie den Fluß auch sehr gewöhnlich und absolut nicht anziehend oder poetisch."

„Kannst du verstehen", bohrt er wieder. „Manchmal bin ich so grundlos unglücklich, so überflüssig – oder ich glaube es wenigstens – und dann möchte ich mich auslöschen – "

„Unsinn! Ich habe dich für vernünftiger gehalten."

Peter bewundert Franziska sehr. Tolles, kluges Mädchen. Viel reifer zu sein als er. Der Landstreicher lacht plötzlich unvermittelt auf, zieht aus seiner schmierigen Tasche Zorra-Zigaretten und bietet Peter eine an. Peter lehnt verlegen ab. Der Landstreicher raucht und bläst philosophische Ringe in die Luft. Peter und Franziska sehen sich unsicher um und stehen auf.

In der Nähe ist ein Rummelplatz. Sie gehen hin. Peter möchte gern Franziskas Arm umfassen, aber wagt es nicht. Er hat plötzlich Angst. Er kommt sich ganz klein vor neben diesem Mädchen.

Und dann sind sie vor einer Schießbude. Peter bekommt es mit der Männlichkeit. Er zieht eine Krone aus der Tasche, er schmeißt sie auf den Tisch, der Schießbudenmann drückt ihm ein schweres Gewehr in die Hand – voller Spannung blickt Franziska auf Peter. Er ist ganz kaltblütig.

Visier, Korn und Ziel müssen eine Linie bilden, etwas unterhalb des schwarzen Zielpunktes anvisieren! Er schießt. Trifft. Eine plumpe, hölzerne Seiltänzerin kippt vom Seil, reckt hilflos die Beine in die Luft – dumme, hölzerne, dicke Frauenbeine. Wie alles seine Bedeutung hat! denkt er. Wie alles kreist um den einen, schwarzen Zielpunkt!

Franziska ist stolz auf Peter. Wie gut er schießt! Wir sind ja schon richtig erwachsen. Ein Mann muß schießen können. Diesmal nimmt Franziska seinen Arm, und in Peters Brust steigt unvermittelt eine Hitzewelle auf.

Links beginnen die Felder. Es ist Frühling, die Sonne scheint. Das Getreide steckt vorsichtig seine grünen Köpfchen aus der schweren, krumigen Erde. Sie sind ganz allein. Die Wege sich etwas staubig. Von fernher orgelt ein Leierkasten herüber, eine süße, schmalzige Melodie. Und dann kommt ein kleiner, dürrer, verkrüppelter Wald. Sie bleiben stehen. Franziska schaut auf Peters

Gesicht. Er hustet trocken auf, vor seinen Augen schwimmt alles. „Du" – sagt Franziska. Und noch einmal „Du" –. Pause. Wenn jetzt nicht geschieht! denkt Peter krampfhaft. Ja, wenn... Und er blickt auf die Sonnenstrahlen, die zwischen den Zweigen zittern.

Und dann nimmt er ganz zart Franziskas Kinderköpfchen. Überdeutlich sieht er die angedeuteten Sommersprossen auf ihrer Nase, den sanften Schwung der Augenbrauen, sieht, wie ihre Augen sich schließen, wie ihr Mund sich unbeholfen öffnet –

Er küßt sie. Dann stößt sie ihn von sich. Nicht unwillig, aber doch. Und sie gehen miteinander wieder der Stadt zu, und zwischen ihnen ist die Luft wie eine Wand aus Glas. Und sie schämen sich sehr.

(Stefan Heym, *Zum ersten Mal*. In: *Junge Liebe. Eine Anthologie*, München, 1985.)

V   Procedure – constructional

The term "procedure", as used in functional grammars, describes a genre that sets out the steps to be followed in order to do or make something. Procedure texts can instruct the reader how to make just about anything, or how to behave in a given situation, how to use a machine, how to get from one place to another or how to carry out a complex intellectual process – anything that requires a number of steps to complete in a chronological order.

V.1   German and English examples   114
1.1   Comparison and contrast
1.2   Text and function
1.3   Summary of language features

V.2   Guided translation exercises   124
2.1   Text completion
2.2   Evaluation and improvement
2.3   Vocabulary extension

V.3   Independent translation   131
3.1   Quick texts
3.2   45-minute texts
3.3   Exam practice

The constructional procedure is a common instructional genre. Instruction texts come in various forms (procedures, directions, check lists, tips, recommendations, rules, regulations, statutes) but basically all tell people what to do or how to behave. What distinguishes the procedure from other forms of instruction is that the instructions are presented as a strictly chronological sequence of steps to be taken, one after the other, to reach a specific aim or goal. Typical text examples of this genre are cookery recipes, do-it-yourself and handicraft instructions and appliance operating instructions. Though the contexts and aims may be similar, the grammar of the German and the English texts realising instructions may be quite different.

1 Brathähnchen

1 Brathähnchen, küchenfertig (ca 100 g)	Cayennepfeffer
Salz, Pfeffer	Thymian
120 g Tatar, Rohgewicht	1 Bund Petersilie, gehackt
30 g Brötchen, altbacken	2 TL Pflanzenmargarine
1 Ei	125 ml Hühnerbrühe
100 g Joghurt, bis 1,5% Fett	2 TL Mehl
50 g Zwiebeln	7 TL saure Sahne

Hähnchen häuten, rundherum mit Salz und Pfeffer einreiben. Tatar mit eingeweichtem und ausgedrücktem Brötchen, Ei, Joghurt und den gehackten Zwiebeln vermischen. Mit Salz, Pfeffer, etwas Cayennepfeffer, Thymian und Petersilie abschmecken. Füllung in das Hähnchen drücken und die Öffnung schließen. In eine ausgefettete Auflaufform geben und im vorgeheizten Backofen bei 220 °C 60 Minuten braten. Ab und zu eßlöffelweise die Hälfte der Brühe darübergießen. Hähnchen herausnehmen und warm stellen. Bratensatz mit der restlichen Brühe loskochen. Mehl mit der Sahne verrühren und die Sauce damit binden. Pro Portion 90 g Hähnchenfleisch und ein Viertel der Füllung abwiegen.

(*Weight Watchers. Das neue 365-Tage-Kochbuch*, München 1989.)

2 Bügelbild

Geeignet für alle Textilien, die aus Baumwolle oder Leinen sind (z.B. T-shirts und Hemden).

Das Bügelbild – auf der Rückseite dieser Anleitung – auf die gewünschte Stelle des Kleidungsstückes legen. Bügeleisen auf Baumwolle-Leinen stellen (Stufe 3). 20 Sekunden fest aufdrücken und etwas hin und her bewegen.

2 Minuten abkühlen lassen, dann Papier abziehen.

Achtung: überbügeln – auch nach dem Waschen – nur noch von der Rückseite.

(*Nutella*, Bügelbild, Ferrero GmbH)

3 Zopf für Zopf

Haare in der Mitte scheiteln, unterschiedlich dicke Strähnen abteilen, flechten und an den Enden mit einem Faden zusammenbinden. Zöpfe links und rechts zusammennehmen, zu je einer kleinen Schnecke drehen und mit Haarklammern feststecken. Blüten mit kleinen Haarnadeln ins Haar stecken.

(*Brigitte, Young Miss*, 6/97.)

4 Aufbau eines Vortrages/Referats

EINLEITUNG Thema vorstellen und motivieren (Literatur zum Thema ebenfalls vorstellen!).

Vorwissen der Zuhörer aktivieren.

HAUPTTEIL gut strukturieren und die Struktur den Zuhörern immer wieder verdeutlichen.

Unterpunkte zusammenfassen, zwischen Themen überleiten.

Verständlich vortragen.

Beispiele geben, ungenaue Begriffe vermeiden (fast, ziemlich, irgendwie, ungefähr).

Verwendung rhetorischer Mittel (Metaphern, Gleichnisse, Übertreibung, Ironie, Steigerung).

Aufrechterhaltung der Aufmerksamkeit durch engagiertes Vortragen.

Medien verwenden (Dias, Folien, Bilder, Filme, Tafelbild), Humor und Enthusiasmus zeigen.

SCHLUSSTEIL wesentliche Inhalte zusammenfassen.

Schlußfolgerungen darstellen.

Schlußsatz geben.

(http://134.176.76.159lehre/ws199798/stumk/infos/praesent.htm)

1 Thai Grilled Chicken

1 medium red chilli, deseeded
2 garlic cloves, skinned
5 spring onions, trimmed and roughly chopped
10 ml (2 level tsp) sugar
125 g (4oz) creamed coconut, roughly chopped
10 ml (2 tsp) Thai-style fish sauce
15 ml (1 level tsp) chopped fresh coriander
4 skinless chicken breast fillets, about 125 g (4oz) each

1 Put all the ingredients, except the chicken, in a food processor with 150 ml (1/4 pint) warm water. Blend until almost smooth.
2 Cut four slashes in each chicken breast, then place in a non-metallic dish and

spoon the marinade over. Turn to coat, then cover and leave to marinate for 1 hour.

3 Place the chicken on a foil-lined grill pan with half the marinade. Grill for 6 minutes on each side (spread the remaining marinade over the second side) or until cooked.   (*Good Food in 30 Minutes*, London 1998.)

2 Transfer Know-How

1 Wash the fabrics thoroughly in order to remove any fabric dressing. Press well.

2 Place iron-on transfer ink side down onto the right side of fabric. Pin or tack carefully in position.

3 Heat iron to a hot setting (don't use steam) and press lightly over the transfer for a few seconds. Don't let the iron glide. Lift, then reposition the iron until all the motif has been transferred onto the fabric.

4 Lift corner of transfer to ensure a good print has been left. If not, repeat procedure, keeping the transfer in the same position to avoid smudging.

(from a British women's magazine)

3 How to create the loose-ringletted, seventies inspired style

Dampen hair with hairspray, then twist 2 inch sections of it around rags and tie the ends of each section to the top. Leave for as long as possible. Alternatively, use heated bendy rollers or curling tongs. When your hair is ready, don't brush it, just add finishing gloss or serum and rake your fingers through. Add some fixing spray, then leave it alone.   (*Woman*, Sept. 7/98.)

4 How to Write an Essay

One of the most important abilities needed to master essay writing in the humanities and social sciences is the ability to ask questions of the essay topic itself as well as of the books you will read. If you can develop a facility in asking questions and in reflecting on likely answers to those questions, it is possible for a general shape for your essay to become evident to you even before you have begun on any detailed reading. The procedure is something like this:

1 Choose an essay topic because it interests you, one about which you perhaps already have some questions or ideas.

2 Ask questions of the topic: try to work out what it is driving at, what is meant by various words or phrases in it, and what kinds of connection there may be between the various issues it raises. Do no more reading than is necessary to suggest possible answers to your questions.

3 Propose to yourself a few likely answers to the question raised by the topic, write them down in no more than a sentence or two. Then choose which seems to be the best. Discuss the topic with friends at this stage, if possible.

4 Develop this answer into a short paragraph, aiming to list the reasons for your answer or some of the facts and ideas that might support it.

5 Regard this paragraph as no more than a hypothesis about, a proposal for, or a forecast of, your eventual answer. It might well lay the foundations of the opening paragraph of your essay, but it will need to be tested out by your detailed reading – which should not begin until now.

(Gordon Taylor, *The Student's Writing Guide for the Arts and Social Sciences*, Cambridge 1989.)

1.1 Comparison and contrast

Whether written for the general or specialist reader, such procedural instructions are designed for a specific audience and aim to be quickly and easily understood by their intended readers. Instructions may number the steps, use italics, bold type or graphics to make the chronological sequence of the steps clearer. Sentences tend to be short and simple, not involving any or much clause coordination or subordination. The typical Mood choices of clauses to realise the steps are not however always the same in English and German.

Task 1 – identifying grammatical features

Looking back at the examples, one of the most obvious differences between the German and English text is what is in Theme position. In English almost all the sentences begin with the Process, and this realises the imperative Mood. Less frequently, a conditional ("if") or temporal ("when/ after/ before/ while") clause may be in Theme position of a clause complex. In German, procedures tend to use the 'infinitive' form of the verb, so that the Process to be carried out is at the end of the clause. What the German clauses have in Theme position is generally the affected Participant or a Circumstantial element of time, manner or place.

Theme

Mood

> Check this by underlining the Themes of the clauses in all text examples.

The more quickly a procedure text needs to be followed, the more likely it is to use devices to create conciseness. Many clauses in English procedures leave out Subject and Finite ("if necessary/ if not, when ready/ until soft"), affected Participant ("cut and place in a dish"/ "cover and leave to marinate") and sometimes Determiners ("right side of fabric"/ "heat iron"). English also uses non-finite clauses to omit elements ("keeping the transfer in position"). The German

conciseness

texts also create conciseness by ellipsis. Nominalisation, however, plays a greater role in condensing German procedure texts than in English (*nach dem Waschen/ Verwendung rhetorischer Mittel/ Aufrechterhaltung der Aufmerksamkeit durch engagiertes Vortragen*). German also makes perhaps more extensive use of noun groups in which PROCESSES are not spelled out but summarised into modifiers of nouns (*eingeweichtem und ausgedrücktem Brötchen/ gehackten Zwiebeln*).

> Highlight or underline all the cases of ellipsis and other devices for condensing text in each of the four examples in each language.

REGISTER

An important aspect of the context each text represents is its REGISTER. This can be described as made up of the MODE, FIELD, and TENOR of the communication. MODE is basically the coding of the text as either written or spoken language. The examples given are all written for silent reading, but if such instructions were given orally, the change would be indicated in the lexicogrammar of the spoken text produced. There would be less ellipsis and greater clause complexity. FIELD refers essentially to the activity going on and is realised mainly in lexical choices (nouns, adjectives, verbs). The constructional procedures exemplified use vocabularies (for cooking, hairdressing, etc) which form quite restricted sets and are easily learned. TENOR refers to the relationship represented in the language between text writer and reader. The procedure texts usually address a "you" reader implicitly, and one who is unknown and universalised. When a second person pronoun is explicit, this indicates a type of REGISTER shift.

> Imagine you are telling a friend how to put transfers onto fabric and rewrite English text **2** (Transfer Know-How) as you would actually say the message.

Task 2 – identifying stylistic problems in German texts

The following examples in German illustrate the strange effect produced when the conventions of a genre are confused. The texts may be grammatically possible in a sense, and there are instructional genres which use some of the grammatical devices illustrated here (see section **1.2**), but such usage is not suited to the register of the average recipe.

A Waschen Sie die Putenschnitzel und tupfen Sie sie trocken. Würzen Sie sie mit Salz und Pfeffer. Legen Sie sie in eine mit 1 El Rapsöl eingefettete Auflaufform oder auf ein Backblech. Pürieren Sie frische Kräuter, Kerne, Knoblauchzehe, 2/3 Rapsöl und Käse. Verteilen Sie die Paste auf Putenschnitzeln und bestreuen Sie sie mit dem restlichen Käse. Backen Sie sie im auf 200 °C vorgeheizten Backofen. Überbacken Sie sie dann 5 Minuten mit dem Grill. Putzen Sie und waschen Sie das Gemüse und schneiden Sie sie in mundgerechte Stücke. Waschen Sie den Rosmarin. Zupfen Sie die Nadeln ab, hacken Sie sie. Würfeln Sie die Zwiebel und dünsten Sie sie in 2 El Rapsöl in einem Topf oder einer hohen Pfanne. Geben Sie das Gemüse und den Rosmarin hinzu. Fügen Sie den Gemüsefond hinzu und dünsten Sie ihn ca 10 Minuten. Schmecken Sie ihn mit Salz und Pfeffer ab. Rühren Sie Crème fraîche darunter. Richten Sie die Putenschnitzel auf Gemüse.

B Man häutet das Hähnchen und reibt es rundherum mit Salz und Pfeffer ein. Danach vermischt man Tatar mit einem Brötchen, das man vorher eingeweicht und ausgedrückt hat, mit Ei, Joghurt und den gehackten Zwiebeln. Man schmeckt das Hähnchen mit Salz, Pfeffer und etwas Cayenne pfeffer, Thymian und Petersilie ab. Danach drückt man die Füllung in das Hähnchen und schließt die Öffnung. Man gibt das Hähnchen in eine Auflaufform, die man vorher ausgefettet hat, und brät es 60 Minuten lang bei 220 °C in einem Backofen, der schon vorgeheizt ist. Man gießt ab und zu mit einem Eßlöffel die Hälfte der Brühe darüber. Nun nimmt man das Hähnchen heraus und stellt es warm. Man kocht den Bratensatz mit der restlichen Brühe, verrührt Mehl mit der Sahne und bindet damit die Sauce. Pro Portion wiegt man 90g Hähnchenfleisch und ein Viertel der Füllung ab.

> Identify the grammatical features that make these texts 'sound strange'.

Text **A** follows grammatical patterns of English language cookery recipes. A recipe in German is unlikely to use the finite imperative form or the explicit person reference. Other types of procedure may, such as in women's and teenagers' magazines. The use of direct personal reference in *Sie* or *Du* form however indicate a shift in TENOR from the less personalised, universalising recipe genre to the more intimate, friendly, conversational tone of the 'women's magazine'. Such shifts in TENOR occur in spoken instructions also, which are inherently personalised (eg giving directions, *gehen Sie bis zur nächsten Ampel, dann biegen Sie rechts ab*). It would be extremely unusual to find a written recipe in German with such grammar.

Text **B** uses grammatical choices typical of other types of instructional text (such as are exemplified in section **1.2** below). It also makes little use of grammatical conciseness, with its many clause complexes (sentences of more than one clause, linked by coordinating or subordinating conjunctions).

Task 3 – identifying stylistic problems in English text
Students generally have little difficulty with MOOD choice, translating German infinitive forms into English imperative forms. There are still however a number of stylistic problems in other parts of the grammar that are very typically made by the novice translator. The examples below are student translations of German text **3** (page 115) into English.

A Part the hair in the middle, part strands of different size, plait it and with a string put it together at the end. Take the plaits together from right and left, twist them together to a coiled plait and stick it with hairpins. With the help of little hairgrips put flowers in the hair.

B Part your hair in the middle, then divide it in different strands, and then plait them and then tie them together with a rubber band at the ends. When this has been done, take the plaits together on the left and right and twist each plait into a coil, then fasten them with hairgrips. Finally, decorate the plaits by pinning little flowers into the hair by the use of little hairgrips.

C First you part your hair in the middle and form strands of varied thickness, then you plait them and hold the ends together with a hairband. Next you roll up the plaits on either side, like a little snail and then you fix them with pins. Then you add flowers for decoration, also with pins.

> Identify the problems and write a better translation, so that the English text sounds convincingly like a procedural instruction text.

1.2 Text and function
The constructional, or practical, procedure texts exemplified so far show some clear grammatical differences in their realisations in English and German – particularly in the grammatical expression of imperative function and the grammatical devices used to achieve conciseness. Not every text giving instructions, however, stipulates a sequenced procedure to be followed for the instructions. The range of instruction types is wide, and the context and the purpose determine

the appropriate grammatical choices, whether for example 'person' is explicit, ellipsis is used and 'Mood' is imperative. When aspects of the Register change, so does the text grammar.

Task 4 – identifying situational context

The two texts below instruct according to a sequential procedure, but differ from the previous examples.

1 Mau Mau

From three to five players each receive 5 cards from a 32-card pack, the next is turned as a starter, and the rest are stacked face down. Each in turn must match the previous card by rank or suit, or play a Jack. A Jack entitles its player to name the suit to be followed, which need not be that of the Jack itself. A player unable to follow may draw one card from stock (so long as any remain). If he still cannot follow, the turn passes to the left. The first to play out all his cards ends the round by announcing "Mau Mau". The others are then penalized by the total face value of cards left in their hands, counting Ace 11, Ten 10, King 4, Queen 3, Jack 2 (or 20), others zero (or face value). The whole game ends when someone reaches 100 penalty points.

(David Parlett, *A Dictionary of Card Games*, Oxford 1992.)

2 Mau Mau

Mau Mau spielt man mit Skatkarten zu zweit, zu dritt, zu viert oder zu fünft. Jeder Spieler erhält fünf Karten, eine Karte wird offen als Anfang des Abwurf-stoßes ausgelegt, die restlichen Karten kommen verdeckt in die Tischmitte. Der Reihenfolge nach legt jeder Spieler jeweils eine Karte auf den Abwurfstoß und zwar entweder eine Karte der gleichen Farbe wie die der vorangegangenen (z. B. Karo auf Karo oder Herz auf Herz), wobei ihr Zahlenwert ohne Bedeutung ist, oder eine Karte des gleichen Wertes (z. B. Dame auf Dame oder Acht auf Acht), wobei die Farbe keine Rolle spielt. Besitzt er keine in Farbe und Wert passende Karte, so kann er mit einem Buben eine neue Farbe ansagen. Kann der Spieler weder mit Farbe oder Wert bedienen, noch mit einem Buben eine neue Farbe ansagen, so nimmt er eine Karte vom verdeckten Kartenstapel und versucht es damit. Geht es auch jetzt noch nicht, kommt der nächste Spieler dran. Wer zuerst alle Karten abgelegt hat, sagt „Mau Mau" und hat die Runde gewonnen. Bei den übrigen Spielern werden die in der Hand verbliebenen Kar-ten ihrem Zahlenwert nach ausgezählt und als Minuspunkte angeschrieben. Dabei zählen: As = 11, König = 4, Dame =3, Bube, alle übrigen Karten zählen das, was darauf steht, also Zehn = 10 usw. Ein Spiel ist zu Ende, wenn einer der Spieler nach beliebig vielen Runden 100 Minuspunkte erreicht hat. Gesamt-sieger ist, wer zu diesem Zeitpunkt die wenigsten Minuspunkte hat.

(German pack of cards)

> Note down grammatical features in these two texts, describing for example person, pronouns, MOOD, voice, MODALITY, ellipsis and the complexity of clauses and clause relations.

• How does the context (MODE and TENOR) motivate the grammatical differences you notice between these and the texts beginning this chapter?

In relation to pronouns, note that the German *man* would NOT be translated appropriately by "one" in English.

The third person is also commonly used in topographic procedures, as the following example shows:

3 Stadtbesichtigung von Valencia

An der Nordspitze der Plaza del Caudillo kreuzt man bei einem 63m hohen Geschäftshaus die Calle de San Vicente, die besonders in ihrem nördlichen Teil sehr beliebte Hauptstraße der Stadt – von der obigen Kreuzung gelangt man halblinks durch die neuangelegte Calle de Maria Christina zu der sehr belebten langgestreckten Plaza del Mercado, die früher Schauplatz von Turnieren und Festen war.

(*Baedeckers Autoführer Spanien und Portugal*, Stuttgart 1969/70.)

Rather than being tempted to translate *man* as "one", note the grammatical options used in the following topographical procedure in English.

4 Singapore

...If you continue up Coleman St from the Padang, you pass the American Church and come to Fort Canning Hill, a good viewpoint over Singapore.(....) Further along the waterfront,you'll find large office blocks, airline offices and ore ships.

Note that the "will" modal in the last clause of text **4** would NOT be translated into German with *werden*.

Below is an instructional text in which chronological sequence is of little consequence: the 'rules' could be given in another order. These instructions do not assist in the practical construction of an object but give personal tips for the reader.

5 Diät Regeln

1 Hungern Sie nicht tagsüber, um abends „zuschlagen" zu können. Essen Sie das, was Sie normalerweise auch zu sich nehmen.

2 Fragen Sie den Gastgeber, was es zu essen gibt. Das ist nicht unhöflich, wenn Sie erklären, warum Sie das wissen wollen. Planen Sie dann, was Sie gerne essen möchten. Bitten Sie gegebenenfalls um kleine Änderungen.

3 Halten Sie sich möglichst auf Distanz zum Buffet. Lenken Sie sich durch Unterhaltung ab.

4 Wählen Sie als Getränk Mineralwasser oder Weinschorle, Tomaten- oder Orangensaft.

(*Weight Watchers. Das neue 365-Tage-Kochbuch*, München 1989.)

• Why does text **3** use the imperative form, like an English instructional text, while the previous, authentic, German instructions realised the imperative function with the infinitive?

1.3 Summary of language features

The main grammatical features noticed in the constructional procedure are:

> *Sequence of instructions is chronological.
> *Steps are often numbered, in bold, etc. Abbreviations and diagrams are often used.
> *Sentences are simple and short with little subordination.
> *Subordination is restricted mostly to temporal or conditional clauses.
> *ELLIPSIS is used to achieve conciseness.
> *PROCESSES are Material.
> *Most procedures do not address the readers explicitly with a 2nd person pronoun.

features in common

Though German and English procedure texts are similar in function, there are differences and specificities to consider when translating them, such as the person reference, use of pronouns, the grammatical mood, the use of passive voice, devices used to make the text concise, and the lexis and directional prepositions typical in each language.

> *English uses imperative MOOD, so that the PROCESS is in THEME position.
> *THEME in German is usually an affected PARTICIPANT or a

grammatical differences between English and German

CIRCUMSTANCE, a shift in TENOR being indicated when the FINITE imperative is used.
* Conciseness is achieved in English by ELLIPSIS of SUBJECT, affected PARTICIPANT and perhaps DETERMINERS, and by the use of non-finite clauses which omit SUBJECT and avoid clause conjunction.
* German achieves conciseness by NOMINALISATION, complex NOUN GROUPS and ELLIPSIS.

**V.2
Guided
translation
exercises**

Having identified the major language patterns of a type of procedure, you have some preparation for translating some yourself. The following exercises draw attention to lexical and grammatical choices at several points in text production, some of which are simply wrong, other possible in some contexts but not for this genre. An understanding of which choices are and which are not possible in this genre will prepare you for independent translation into English.

2.1 Text completion

The following text was introduced at the beginning of the chapter (page 115).

Aufbau eines Vortrages/Referats

EINLEITUNG Thema vorstellen und motivieren. Literatur ebenfalls vorstellen! Vorwissen der Zuhörer aktivieren.

HAUPTTEIL Gut strukturieren und die Struktur den Zuhörern immer wieder verdeutlichen.

Unterpunkte zusammenfassen, zwischen Themen überleiten. Verständlich vortragen. Beispiele geben, ungenaue Begriffe vermeiden (fast, ziemlich, irgendwie, ungefähr) Verwendung rhetorischer Mittel (Metaphern, Gleichnisse, Übertreibung, Ironie, Steigerung). Aufrechterhaltung der Aufmerksamkeit durch engagiertes Vortragen. Medien verwenden (Dias, Folien, Bilder, Filme, Tafelbild), Humor und Enthusiasmus zeigen.

SCHLUSSTEIL Wesentliche Inhalte zusammenfassen. Schlussfolgerungen darstellen. Schlusssatz geben.

Task 5 – completing gap translation text

At each gap, choose one of the three suggestions given below to complete the English translation.

(1) ___ a (2) ___ / (3) ___.
(4) ___. Introduce the (5) ___ and (6) ___ it. Also present (7) ___. Activate your (8) ___ (9) ___.
(10) ___. Structure well and (11) ___ to your (12) ___. (13) ___ (14) ___, (15) ___ (16) ___. (17) ___ (18) ___, give examples, avoid (19) ___ (20) ___ such as almost, fairly, somehow, approximately.
(21) ___ rhetorical (22) ___ such as metaphors, similes, hyperbole, irony, intensification. Keep your audience's attention by speaking in a (23) ___ manner. (24) ___ media, such as slides, transparencies, pictures, films, blackboard. Be humorous and enthusiastic.
(25) ___. (26) ___ essential (27) ___.
(28) ___ (29) ___. (30) Give a good ___.

(1) assembling, construction of, how to organise
(2) talk, lecture, recital
(3) paper, presentation, report
(4) introduction, opening, preliminaries
(5) theme, subject, topic
(6) motivate, give reasons for, arouse interest in
(7) a bibliography, secondary literature, the readings
(8) hearers', listeners', audience's
(9) pre-knowledge, foreknowledge, prior knowledge
(10) main part, body, major section
(11) make the structure clear again and again, keep making the structure clear, always make the structure clear again
(12) audience, listenters, hearers
(13) put together, summarise, recapitulate
(14) sub-points, under-points, minor points
(15) form a transition between, lead over between, link
(16) themes, topics, subjects
(17) lecture, report, speak
(18) comprehensibly, clearly, intelligibly
(19) vague, inexact, inaccurate
(20) concepts, notions, terms
(21) application of, use, employ
(22) means, resources, devices
(23) engaged, lively, committed
(24) use, make use of, utilise
(25) ending, closing remarks, conclusion
(26) put together, condense, summarise
(27) contents, subject matter, information

(28) portray, represent, present

(29) deductions, conclusions, inferences

(30) final sentence, last line, closing speech.

2.2 Evaluation and improvement

The following procedure text accompanies the yellow *Packsets* you can buy from the Post Offices in Germany.

Zusammenbau des PackSets

1. Karton komplett entfalten (gelbe Seite nach unten)

2. Seitenteile aufrichten

3. Die vier Schmalseiten **Ⓐ** nach innen klappen

4. Seite **Ⓑ** über die kurzen **Ⓐ**-Teile ganz nach innen klappen

5. Ausschnitte „Hier drücken!" mit dem Daumen nach innen knicken

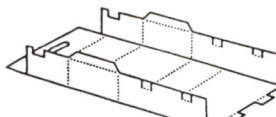
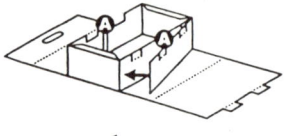
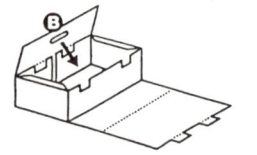

6. **Vor dem Schließen:** Adressdoppel ausfüllen und einlegen

7. **Nach dem Schließen:** Zukleben mit den beigefügten Klebestreifen an den Stellen „Hier zukleben!"

Bitte Hohlräume mit Holzwolle, Papier oder ähnlichem füllen und Karton vor Nässe schützen.

Besondere Verpackungsbestimmungen für Auslandspakete und -päckchen bitte am Schalter erfragen.

Bitte immer alle Klebestreifen verwenden, dies erhöht die Stabilität.

Task 6 – evaluating student translations

Mark every mistake and stylistic problem you can see in the following student translations of the *Packset* text.

A How to fold a package box

1 Unfold the box completely (yellow side upside down)

2 Put the side part up

3 Put the four small sides into the middle

4 Fold the B sides over the A sides, turn it into the middle

5 With your thumbs, press the parts "press here" into the middle

6 Before you finish closing the paper box: do not forget to fill in the address-doublette and put it into the box

7 When you have closed the box, fix it with the sellotape enclosed where it says "fix here"

Please fill out the empty space with woodwool, paper or anything alike. Protect the paper box from getting wet. For special package restrictions concerning international packages please request at the post office counter. Please use all the sellotape to give it more stability.

B To make a packet set

1 Flatten the carton completely (yellow part below)
2 Erect sides as shown in the picture
3 Fold the four small sides A to inside
4 Bend side B backwards over the short A piece
5 Press the sign "press here" with your thumb inside
6 Before you close the package: Fill out the adress-double and lay it inside
7 After you closed the package: Close it with the enclosed stripes where it's written: "stick here"

Please fill the empty room with wool, paper or so and cover the box of getting wet. Special package's advice for packets to other countries and small foreign packages can you get at the post office box office. Please use always stripes because they guaranteed a higher stability

C Construction of Pack Sets

1 Completely unfold the cardboard box (with yellow side pointing downwards)
2 Lift up the side pieces
3 Turn the four narrow sides inwardly
4 Put side B over the short A pieces completely to the inside
5 Fold with the thumb inwardly the piece with "to press here"
6 Before closure: Fill in the double form for the address and enclose
7 After closing: Tape it with the enclosed tesa film at the points where it is marked "tape together here" together

It is recommended to fill hollow space with wooden wool, paper or similar things and avoid wetness. Please ask at your local post office at the counter for special wrapping regularities for packets to be sent abroad. Please use all tapes provided for stability.

D Assemblance of a package-set

1 Completely unfold cartonage (yellow side face down)
2 Fold side pieces upwards
3 Fold the four narrow sides marked with A to the centre
4 Fold side B so that it overlaps sides A and enclosures them

5 Push perforation "push here" and fold them to the inside
6 Before closing it: fill out the second adressform and put it inside the box
7 After closing: glue together at the "glue here"-labeled areas with the with added glue stripes

Please fill in the empty areas with fine wood shavings, paper or similar material and keep the package safe from moisture. Ask for special regulations concerning sending packages abroad at the counter. Please use all the tapes, this will increase the stability of the package.

Task 7 – improving the translation

Write your own, improved translation of the *Packset* text.

2.3 Vocabulary extension

Task 8 – recipe vocabulary
A variety of verbs in cookery recipes refer to some kind of cutting.

Using a good dictionary and any cookery book in English, answer the following:

• Which ingredients do these verbs typically collocate with?

split, slice, dice, mince, hack, halve, chop, scrape, trim, shred, strip, slash, score, carve, skin

• Adding to the list below, what other verbs are typically used in cookbooks?

mix, simmer, boil, add, garnish, spoon, cut, arrange, stir, garnish, fold, cube, shred, take, serve ....

Using the list of cooking verbs above you now have, complete the following recipe.

Luxury potato salad
450 g potato salad with chives
100 g marinated sun-dried tomato salad
10 cm piece of cucumber
300 g ham
2 little gem lettuces
8 chive sprigs

(1) ___ together the potato and tomato salads. (2)___ the cucumber into fine strips. (3)___ the ham. (4) ___ both into the salad mixture. (5) ___ the larger leaves from both lettuces and (6) ___ four on each serving plate, (7) ___ the remaining lettuce and (8) ___ seperately. (9) ___ the potato salad onto the leaves and (10) ___ with chives.

Task 9 – translating *man*

Some procedure texts in German use *man*, but "one" will NOT be used in English in similar circumstances. *Man* is frequently translated by students with the pronoun "one" as they assume that this word must fulfil all the purposes for which *man* is used in German. Unfortunately, different strategies must be used to translate *man* depending on the context. Possibilities are: "one/ you/ people/ they/ we/ anyone/ everyone" passive forms and imperative forms.

- one = people in general, i.e. it expresses a general truth, but it is also a rather formal word and is nowadays usually replaced by 'you'
- you = people in general
- people = people other than yourself; some of a group
- they = people in general excluding yourself (as in 'they say'), or specific groups of people such as the government, police, authorities, doctors, scientists, etc.
- we = people in general including yourself; you and the person(s) you are speaking to
- anyone = any single person in a group or in the world
- everyone = every single person in a group or in the world
- passives = often used to translate *man*, particularly in phrases like *man sagt, man weiß, man nimmt an, man erwartet*
- imperatives = used to translate *man* in certain kinds of instructions/directions

Bearing this in mind, determine the best way of translating *man* in the following:

1 Man könnte heute abend ins Kino gehen.
2 Man wird reden.
3 Hat man das Recht, die Umwelt so zu zerstören?
4 Man nimmt an, dass Kinder aus zerrütteten Familien im Leben mehr Probleme haben.
5 Man soll den Tag nicht vor dem Abend loben.
6 Man kann sich auf sein Wort verlassen.

7 Hat man den Verbrecher schon gefasst?
8 Von hier kommt man sehr gut mit dem Bus hin.
9 Heute weiß man, dass ein Baby schon im Mutterleib hören kann.
10 Wie kann man so unsensibel sein!
11 Man muss in Betracht ziehen, dass berühmte Kritiker sich in diesem Punkt uneinig sind (formal essay).
12 In der Firma weiß man, dass er immer so reagiert.
13 Man munkelt, dass sie ein Verhältnis mit dem Chef hat.
14 Man muss zugeben, dass er ein Lebenskünstler ist.
15 Man hat halt zu tun.

Translate the following passage into English:

Gesprächshaltung

Wenn man sich mit jemandem unterhält, sollte man gewissen Regeln folgen, die dem Gesprächspartner signalisieren, daß man ihm oder ihr wirklich zugewandt ist, daß man also zuhört. Das beginnt mit der Haltung: Man steht aufrecht und gesammelt da, dem Gesprächspartner schon körperlich zugewandt. Man schaut ihm beim Sprechen an. Man unterläßt es, während des Gesprächs nach anderen oder anderem Ausschau zu halten.

(Sybil Gräfin Schönfeldt, *Gutes Benehmen gefragt*, München, 1977.)

Task 10 – translating *wer*

Students often have problems translating the pronoun *wer*. Unlike in German, "who" in English can only introduce questions and relative clauses later in the sentence. Statements cannot begin with this pronoun in English.

Compare the following:

– Wer zuerst alle Karten abgelegt hat, sagt „Mau Mau".
– The first to play out all his cards ends the round by announcing "Mau Mau".

One way of translating *wer* in such contexts is to use a suitable noun, as in "the woman who marries him", for *wer ihn heiratet*. Another way is to use "whoever/ anyone who/ he/she/they who", or even an if-clause. However, proverbs beginning like this may have a very different translation that can only be learned.

Translate the following:

1 Wer zum ersten Mal in New York ist, staunt über die vielen Obdachlosen.
2 Wer zuerst kommt, mahlt zuerst.
3 Wer im Beruf weiterkommen möchte, muss mehrere Fremdsprachen beherrschen.
4 Wer es möchte, kann an dem Wettbewerb teilnehmen.
5 Wer die Prüfung im Sommer ablegen möchte, muss sich jetzt anmelden.
6 Wer fragt, bekommt viele Antworten.
7 Wer es auch getan hat, muss bestraft werden.
8 Wer einmal lügt, dem glaubt man nicht, und wenn er auch die Wahrheit spricht.
9 Wer es glaubt, wird selig.
10 Wer diese Übung gemacht hat, weiß jetzt, dass man bei der Übersetzung von Sätzen, die mit „wer" anfangen, aufpassen muss.

3.1. Quick texts

Practise translating the procedure genre with the following simple texts, spending no more than twenty minutes on each. Remember to keep sentences short.

**V.3
Independent
translation**

1 Chicoreesalat

150 g Sauerkraut kleinschneiden, die Blätter einer Staude Chicoree und einen großen geschälten Apfel in feine Streifen schneiden. Einen TL gehackte Haselnüsse dazugeben. Aus zwei EL Zitronensaft, Salz und ggf. einer Prise Zucker, einem TL gehackter Petersilie, einem TL gehacktem Schnittlauch eine Marinade bereiten und über den Salat geben. Gut durchmischen und den Salat ca. 1 Std. ziehen lassen.
(Broschüre *Abnehmen mit Sauerkraut*, CMA Deutschland, Bonn, o.J.)

2 Party time

Hast du Lust, deine Augen mal kräftig zu betonen? Dunkelgrünen Lidschatten auf das obere Lid bis über die Lidfalte und am unteren Lid entlang der Wimpern auftragen und weich verwischen. Am unteren Lidrand innen mit schwarzem Kajal eine Linie ziehen. Mach auf dem oberen und unteren Lid noch einen feinen Lidstrich mit glitzerndem Lidschatten. Wimpern oben und unten schwarz tuschen. Für die Lippen reicht farbloses Gloss.
(*Brigitte, Young Miss*, 3/97.)

3 Brötchen backen ganz einfach

Backanleitung: 1. Backofen ca. 10 Minuten vorheizen (Umluft 200 °C, E-Herd 220 °C). 2. Brötchen aus dem Beutel nehmen. 3. Brötchen auf den Rost legen und in die Mitte der Backofens schieben. 4. Je nach gewünschter Bräunung ca. 7–9 Minuten backen, bei Tiefkühlung ca. 3 Minuten länger.

Guten Appetit! (Aufbackbrötchen, *Golden Toast*.)

3.2 45-minute texts

Time yourself to complete each of the following longer texts within an hour.

1 Kellogs Bügelbild

Und so wirds gemacht.

1 Bügelbild an der Markierung abschneiden.

2 Bügeleisen auf Stufe 3 (Baumwolle-Leinen) erhitzen. (Unbedingt ohne Dampfeinstellung!)

3 T-Shirt auf dem Bügelbrett faltenlos auflegen. Bügelbild mit Motiv nach unten auflegen. (Anleitung ist lesbar)

4 Jetzt das Bügeleisen vorsichtig etwa 50 Sekunden auf dem Trägerpapier mit Druck hin und her bewegen, dabei auch die Ecken sorgfältig aufbügeln.

5 Bügeleisen herunternehmen und abschalten.

6 Trägerpapier noch ca. 6 Minuten abkühlen lassen, erst dann vorsichtig abziehen.

7 Eventuell zum Fixieren ein dünnes Baumwolltuch auflegen und noch einmal kurz über die Ecken bügeln.

8 Nach dem Aufbügeln nicht mehr über das festige Motiv bügeln. Das T-Shirt mit dem Bügelbild läßt sich bei 30-Grad waschen. Dazu und zum Bügeln auf links drehen.

Achtung: auf keinen Fall mit dem Bügeleisen auf das Motiv kommen!

Viel Spaß wünscht Kelloggs.

2 TRIOMINO

1 TRIOMINO wird mit 56 Steinen gespielt, welche die Werte von 0 bis 5 Punkte aufweisen.

Die Steine werden verdeckt gemischt, jeder Spieler zieht sich seine Steine: bei 2 Spielern = je 9 Steine, bei 3–4 Spielern = je 7 Steine, bei 5–6 Spielern = je 6 Steine.

Die restlichen Steine bilden den Vorrat.

2 Die Spieler stellen ihre Steine so vor sich hin, daß sie von den Mitspielern nicht eingesehen werden können. Der Spieler mit dem höchsten TRIOMINO-Stein legt diesen in die Tischmitte und eröffnet das Spiel. Er erhält den Gesamtwert dieses Steines sowie einen Bonus von 10 Punkten gutgeschrieben.

3 Der nächste Spieler kann jetzt an diesen Stein anlegen, wenn er einen Stein mit dem passenden Werten hat. Auch er erhält den Wert seines Steines gutgeschrieben.

4 Wer keinen passenden Stein hat, nimmt sich bis zu 3 Steine aus dem Vorrat. Kann er auch dann nicht ablegen, muß er passen. Für jeden gezogenen Stein erhält er 10 Minuspunkte.

5 Ziel einer Runde ist es, möglichst als erster Spieler alle Steine loszuwerden bzw. die höchsten Werte abgelegt zu haben, wenn ein anderer Spieler Schluß macht.

6 Gewinner einer Runde ist, wer als erster alle seine TRIOMINO-Steine verbraucht hat. Er erhält 25 Sonderpunkte plus die Gesamtpunktezahl aller TRIOMINO-Steine, die noch in den Händen der anderen Spieler sind.

7 Wenn alle Spieler passen müssen, ist das Spiel gesperrt. Es gewinnt dann der Spieler mit der geringsten Gesamtpunktezahl auf seinen restlichen Steinen. Diese Summe zieht er jeweils von der Punktezahl der verbliebenen Steine seiner Mitspieler ab und schreibt sich die entsprechenden Ergebnisse (ohne Bonus) gut. (Peri-Spiele GmbH, Nürnberg.)

3.3 Exam practice

Translate each of the following instructional texts into English within two and a half hours.

1 Sieben Etappen der Entstehung einer wissenschaftlichen Arbeit

Hier werden Ihnen Hinweise darauf gegeben, wie Sie Ihr Arbeiten sinnvoll organisieren können.

Etappe 1: Sich orientieren

Bevor Sie mit einer wissenschaftlichen Arbeit beginnen, werden und müssen Sie sich orientieren und ein geeignetes Thema ins Auge fassen. Sie sollten es dadurch auf seine Tauglichkeit überprüfen, daß Sie es genau definieren. Lesen Sie dazu Handbucharartikel und Zeitschriftenaufsätze. Bestimmen Sie ein konkretes Forschungsziel, und entwickeln Sie einen Arbeitsplan. Sie sollten das ruhig schriftlich, in Form eines Exposés, tun, selbst wenn Sie später von Ihrem Plan, insbesondere dem Zeitplan, abweichen. Also sind die folgenden Arbeitsschritte erforderlich:

1 eine geeignete Themenstellung suchen,
2 Literatur sichten,
3 das Thema eingrenzen,
4 die Vorgehensweise festlegen,
5 einen Zeitplan aufstellen,
6 ein Exposé schreiben.

Etappe 2: Recherchieren

Wenn Sie Ihr Thema umrissen haben, können Sie sich in die Tiefe arbeiten: Sie beginnen, systematisch nach Schlagwörtern, Stichwörtern, gängiger Literatur und Literaturhinweisen zu suchen. Dazu sollten Sie:

1 bibliographieren,
2 lesen,
3 exzerpieren und paraphrasieren,
4 ggf. Daten sammeln,
5 Nachdem Sie im Anschluß an eine ausgiebige Lesephase alle Facetten Ihres Themas kennen, ist es wichtig, die Gedanken und Positionen zu ordnen.

Etappe 3: Strukturieren

Häufig gibt es verschiedene Möglichkeiten, das Erarbeitete zu strukturieren, Argumente in eine logische Folge zu bringen. Sie sollten das tun; sebst wenn Sie keine argumentatorische Arbeit verfassen wollen, ist es hilfreich, sich Argumente und Gegenargumente klar zu machen. Auf dieser Grundlage können Sie Ihr Material leichter ordnen. Folgende Arbeitsschritte sind dazu erforderlich:

1 Material analysieren,
2 Begriffe klären,
3 logische Beziehungen herstellen,
4 differenzieren.

Problematisch ist in der Regel, daß komplexe logische Zusammenhänge im Text in einer linearen Folge angeordnet werden müssen. Daher besteht die nächste Etappe darin, nach einem für Ihr Anliegen, für Ihre Aussageabsicht geeigneten roten Faden zu suchen.

Etappe 4: Gliedern

Auch für die Gliederung Ihrer Arbeit stehen Ihnen verschiedene Möglichkeiten offen. Sie können gliedern in:

1 chronologischer Anordnung,
2 hierarchischer Anordnung oder,
3 logischer Anordnung, die sich aus dem Thema ergibt.

Erst jetzt sollten Sie sich Gedanken über das Schreiben machen.

Etappe 5: Formulieren

Klären Sie die Begriffe, die Sie verwenden wollen, und vergleichen Sie Ihre Verwendungsweise mit der in Zitaten. Auf dieser Grundlage sollten Sie zunächst schreiben, ohne sich viele Gedanken über den sprachlichen Ausdruck zu machen. Halten Sie sich an die grobe Richtlinie: Wissenschaftlicher Stil ist vor allem präzise. Achten Sie darauf, deutlich zu argumentieren und auch kritisch zu beurteilen. Bringen Sie Überflüssiges möglichst gar nicht erst zu Papier.

1 Begriffe definieren
2 Formate festlegen

3 Schreiben

4 Pointieren

5 Kritisieren

6 Weglassen

7 Gegebenfalls Gliederung ändern

Der nächste Schritt ist nicht unwesentlich: Trennen Sie sich von Ballast.

Etappe 6: Edieren

Prüfen Sie Ihren Text in bezug auf inhaltliche Geschlossenheit, machen Sie ihn gut lesbar. Jetzt sollten Sie einige Techniken des Formulierens anwenden. Achten Sie darauf, daß Ihre Überlegungen und Begründungen nachvollziehbar sind, daß Ihre Zitate richtig gekennzeichnet sind. Jetzt ist die Gelegenheit, den sprachlichen Ausdruck zu überprüfen und zu verbessern.

1 Abfolge, Logik des Textes nachvollziehen

2 Überflüssiges streichen

3 Wiederholungen eliminieren

4 Satzlänge und Wortwahl überprüfen

5 Überleitungen und Zusammenfassungen einfügen

6 Tabellen, Grafiken, Abbildungen durchnumerieren

7 Zitate überprüfen

8 Quellenangaben vereinheitlichen

9 Literaturverzeichnis vervollständigen

10 Formate überprüfen

Nun sind Sie fast fertig. Bevor Sie Ihrem Text den letzten Schlif geben, sollten Sie ihn einige Tage nicht gesehen haben: Solange Sie ihren Text allzugut kennen, sind Sie „textblind", sehen vor allem in bezug auf Rechtschreibung und Zeichensetzung das, was Sie schreiben wollten, und nicht das, was Sie tatsächlich geschrieben haben.

Etappe 7: Redigieren

Achten Sie in dieser Phase ausschließlich auf die Form, ändern Sie nichts mehr an Ausdruck oder Inhalt. Wenn Sie jemanden für das Korrekturlesen gewinnen können, ist das sehr hilfreich.

1 Tippfehler korrigieren

2 Layout gestalten

(K.-D. Bünting / A. Bitterlich/ U. Tospiech, *Schreiben im Studium. Ein Trainingsprogramm*, Berlin 1996.)

2 Ratschläge für einen schlechten Redner

Fange nie mit dem Anfang an, sondern immer drei Meilen vor dem Anfang! Etwa so: „Meine Damen und Herren! bevor ich zum Thema des heutigen Abends komme, lassen Sie mich Ihnen kurz ..."

Hier hast du schon ziemlich alles, was einen schönen Anfang ausmacht, eine steife Anrede; der Anfang vorm Anfang, die Ankündigung, daß und was du zu sprechen beabsichtigst und das Wörtchen „kurz". So gewinnst du im Nu Herzen und Ohren der Zuhörer. (...)

Sprich nicht frei – das macht einen so unruhigen Eindruck. Am besten ist es, du liest deine Rede ab. Das ist sicher, zuverläßig, auch freut es jedermann, wenn der lesende Redner nach jedem viertel Satz mißtrauisch hochblickt, ob auch noch alle da sind. (...)

Sprich wie du schreibst. Und ich weiß, wie du schreibst. Sprich mit langen, langen Sätzen – solchen, bei denen du, der du dich zu Hause, wo du ja die Ruhe, deren du so sehr benötigst, deiner Kinder ungeachtet, hast, vorbereitest, genau weißt, wie das Ende ist, die Nebensätze schön ineinandergeschachtelt, so daß der Hörer ungeduldig auf seinem Sitz träumend, sich in einem Kolleg wähnend, in dem er früher so gern geschlummert hat, auf das Ende einer solchen Periode wartet ... nun, ich habe dir eben ein Beispiel gegeben. So mußt du sprechen. Fang immer bei den alten Römern an und gib stets, wovon du auch sprichst, die geschichtlichen Hintergründe der Sache. Das ist nicht nur deutsch – das tun alle Brillenmenschen. Ich habe einmal an der Sorbonne einen chinesischen Studenten sprechen hören, der sprach glatt und gut französisch, aber er begann zu allgemeiner Freude so: „Lassen Sie mich Ihnen in aller Kürze die Entwicklungsgeschichte meiner chinesischen Heimat seit dem Jahre 2000 vor Christi Geburt ..." Er blickte ganz erstaunt auf, weil die Leute so lachten.

So mußt du es auch machen. Du hast ganz recht: man versteht es ja sonst nicht, wer kann denn das alles verstehen, ohne die geschichtlichen Hintergründe ... sehr richtig! (...)

Kümmere dich nicht darum, ob die Wellen, die von dir ins Publikum laufen, auch zurückkommen – das sind Kinkerlitzchen. Sprich unbekümmert um die Wirkung, um die Leute, um die Luft im Saale: immer sprich, mein Guter, Gott wird es dir lohnen.

(Kurt Tucholsky, *Ratschläge für einen schlechten Redner*, Reinbeck, 1995.)

VI   Advertising – product

"Advertising" means to promote products or services, aiming to entice potential consumers to buy. Advertisements might employ a wide range of rhetorical strategies and styles to do so, often borrowed from other genres such as poetry, narrative or reporting.

VI.1   German and English examples   **138**
1.1 Comparison and contrast
1.2 Text and function
1.3 Summary of language features

VI.2   Guided translation exercises   **159**
2.1 Text completion
2.2 Evaluation and comparison
2.3 Vocabulary extension

VI.3   Independent translation   **165**
3.1 Quick texts
3.2 45-minute texts
3.3 Exam practice

Advertising pervades all areas of life in contemporary Western culture and takes on many shapes and forms. The largest category is commercial consumer advertising, using a short message to persuade people to buy a certain product. Texts of this kind of advertising can be spoken or written, accompanied by music or pictures. Though displaying great variation, such texts still share common features that make them recognisable, first and foremost, as "ads". The language of advertisements plays an essential role in getting the consumer to remember the name of a product, however much techniques change and trends increase the importance of visual impact. Language features include distinctive lexis, grammar and rhetorical devices. Written product advertisements are the focus of this chapter because of their ubiquity, the language learning opportunities they offer, the creativity their translation demands, and because advertisements can provide linguistic enjoyment. The examples below illustrate some of the typical features of German and English ads.

1

Eine gute suppe braucht eine gute Brühe.

Jetzt ganz frisch auf dem Markt: die neuen flüssigen Brühen von Erasco.
Natürlich nur aus besten Zutaten und ohne jegliche Zusatzstoffe.
Denn echter Geschmack ist durch nichts zu ersetzen. Probieren Sie mal!
Feine Brühen von Erasco. Das Herz feiner Suppen und Eintöpfe.

Erasco

Das Gute daran ist das Gute darin.

2

WIEDER FREI...
ATMEN
Gelomyrtol® löst den Schleim bei Bronchitis

WIEDER FREI...
RIECHEN
Gelomyrtol® befreit Nase und Nebenhöhlen

WIEDER FREI...
SCHMECKEN
Gelomyrtol® wirkt tief von innen heraus

Gelomyrtol®
Wieder frei atmen!

3

CORDOBA.
NIX STINKNORMALES.
NIX LANGWEILIGES.
NIX ALLERWELTS- MÄSSIGES.

ZEIGEN SIE'S.

4

JEDERZEIT IST WALNUSSZEIT
Gute-Nacht-Nuß.

Lassen Sie den Tag doch mal gesund ausklingen – mit kalifornischen Walnüssen!

Echte Kracher für Ihre Gesundheit!

In dem knackigen Knabberspaß steckt nämlich alles, was der Körper gut gebrauchen kann: Viele Vitamine, Mineralien – und keine Spur von Cholesterin.

5

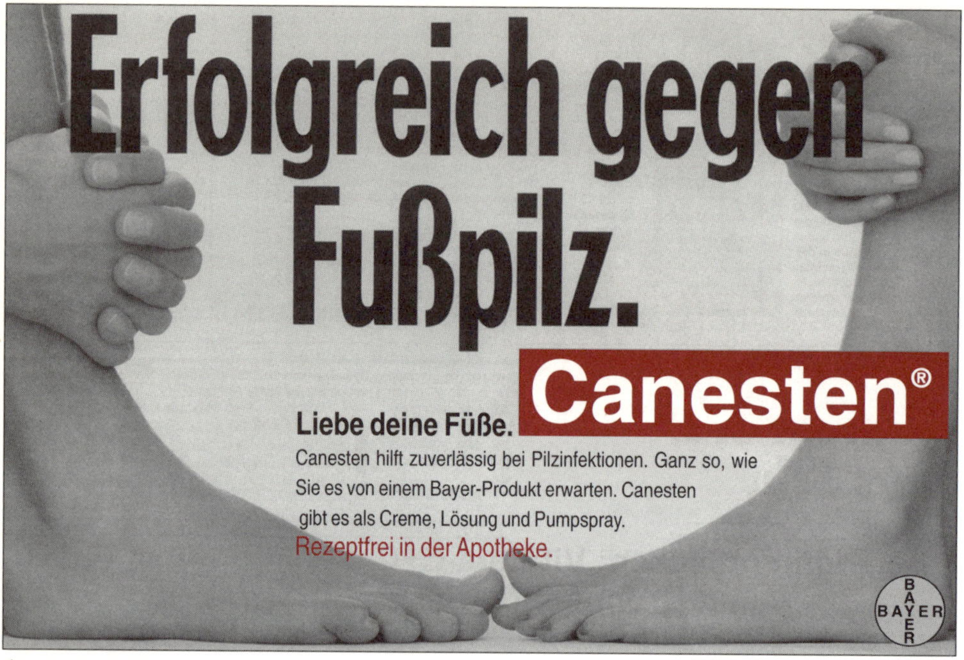

Erfolgreich gegen Fußpilz.
Canesten®
Liebe deine Füße.
Canesten hilft zuverlässig bei Pilzinfektionen. Ganz so, wie Sie es von einem Bayer-Produkt erwarten. Canesten gibt es als Creme, Lösung und Pumpspray.
Rezeptfrei in der Apotheke.
BAYER

6

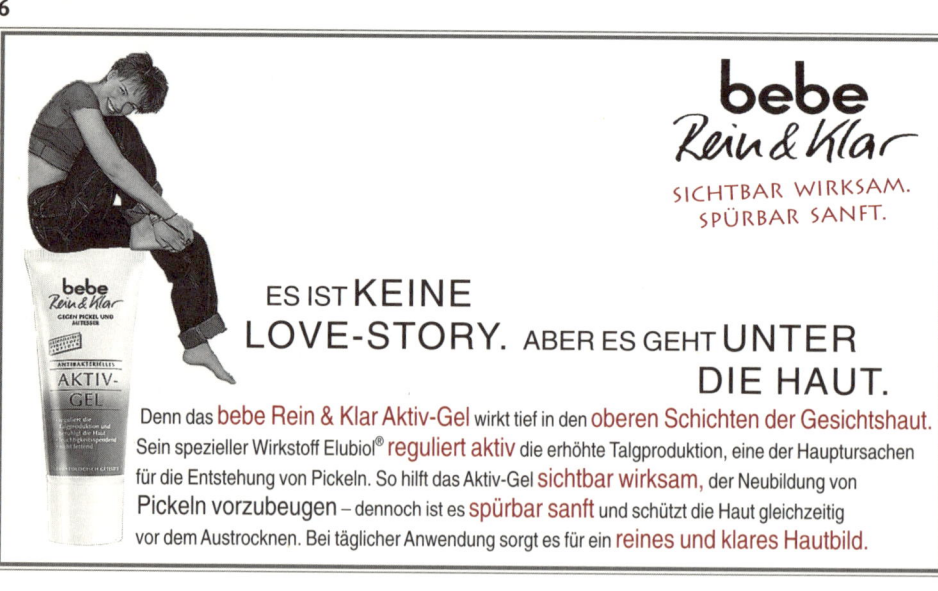

bebe
Rein & Klar
SICHTBAR WIRKSAM.
SPÜRBAR SANFT.
ES IST KEINE LOVE-STORY. ABER ES GEHT UNTER DIE HAUT.
Denn das bebe Rein & Klar Aktiv-Gel wirkt tief in den oberen Schichten der Gesichtshaut. Sein spezieller Wirkstoff Elubiol® reguliert aktiv die erhöhte Talgproduktion, eine der Hauptursachen für die Entstehung von Pickeln. So hilft das Aktiv-Gel sichtbar wirksam, der Neubildung von Pickeln vorzubeugen – dennoch ist es spürbar sanft und schützt die Haut gleichzeitig vor dem Austrocknen. Bei täglicher Anwendung sorgt es für ein reines und klares Hautbild.
bebe
Rein & Klar
AKTIV-GEL

Bekömmlichkeit
sagt der Verstand.

Volles Aroma
sagt das Gefühl.

„Idee Kaffee"
sagt Albert Darboven.

„Unser einzigartiges Herstellungsverfahren macht Idee Kaffee so bekömmlich – und erhält dabei das volle Aroma".

Albert Darboven
IDEE KAFFEE-HERSTELLER

„Du kleines Luder. Komm her, du knuspriges Ding. Ich pack'dich jetzt. Du machst mich ganz verrückt mit deiner braunen Haut und deine zarten Rundungen. Oh jaa, ich will dich haben, ich will dich anknabbern. Darf ich zufassen"?

„Mein Gott, John, kannst du nicht einmal 1.2.3 PomPoms von McCain essen wie jeder andere auch?"

Wer weniger darüber redet, hat mehr davon.

WER, WIE, WAS – SO MACHT DAS BADEN SPASS.
WIESO, WESHALB, WARUM – NIVEA *schützt* RUNDUM.

NEU!
Speziell **FÜR KINDER.**

Jetzt wird Baden zum Kinderspiel – mit dem neuen
NIVEA BATH CARE FOR KIDS: *Extra* **MILD**, *damit es*
KEINE TRÄNEN *und* **KEIN ZIEPEN** *gibt. Extra pflegend, damit die*
zarte Kinderhaut **NICHT AUSTROCKNET**. *Extra sicher, weil dermatologisch*
und augenärtzlich getestet. Und dazu mit tollem **APRIKOSENDUFT**.

MILDE BADPFLEGE FÜR KINDER.

Was macht das
neue Tempo bloß so
durchschnupfsicher?

Im neuen Tempo
sind die Fasern
fest miteinander
verbunden – wie mit
Mikrobrücken.
So wird Ihr Schnupfen
besser aufgenommen
als von irgendeinem
anderen Taschentuch.
Das neue Tempo:
nicht nur reißfest,
sondern
durchschnupfsicher.

Verlass dich drauf.

9

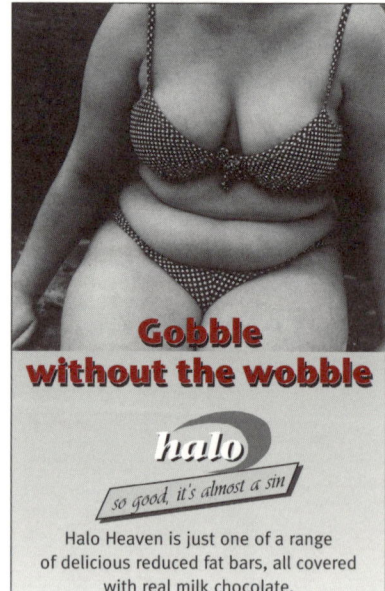

Gobble
without the wobble

halo

so good, it's almost a sin

Halo Heaven is just one of a range
of delicious reduced fat bars, all covered
with real milk chocolate.

1

Max ice creams contain real fruit and dairy goodness. But what they don't know won't hurt them.

It's every mum's dilemma; do you let the kids have their ice cream treat or choose something more nourishing and suffer the long faces? Not any more

The Max ice cream range, from Wall's, is full of dairy goodness and real fruit juice so that the kids can have their treat yet your conscience will be clear.

And the individual Max ice creams come in child-size portions which could save on washing powder too.

But don't tell the children all these interesting facts. You know what they're like.

3

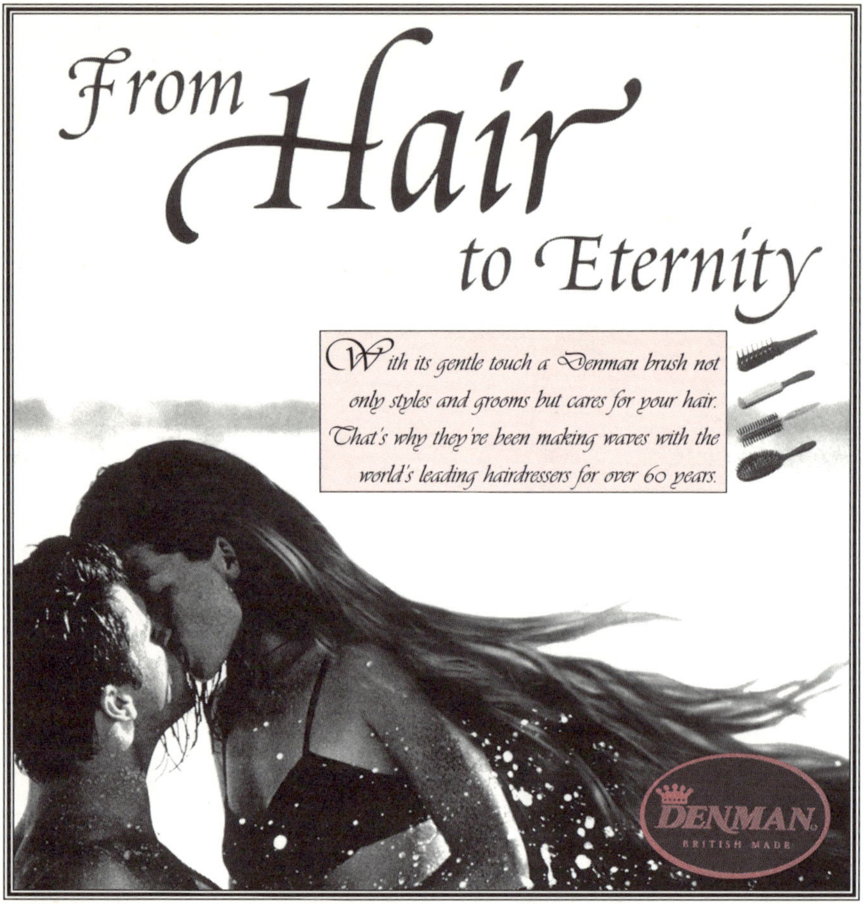
From Hair to Eternity
With its gentle touch a Denman brush not only styles and grooms but cares for your hair. That's why they've been making waves with the world's leading hairdressers for over 60 years.
DENMAN
BRITISH MADE

4

With its unique active formula, there isn't a more effective way to shift stubborn stains than Bio-tex.

No doubt you're familiar with our powder and liquid versions for soaking. Well, now there are two new developments. A handy Super Spray for larger stains and an ingeniously shaped Super Soap for spot-on accuracy.

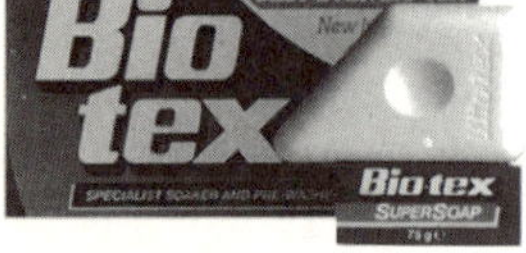
Bio tex
BEST EVER BIO-TEX
Bio-tex
SUPERSOAP

So, whether it's gravy, grass, grime or grease you want to get rid of, we've got it covered.

STAINS EXIT WHEN YOU BIO-TEX IT.

NO MARKS FOR SPOTTING OUR NEW STAIN REMOVERS.

NEW
Bio tex
SUPERSPRAY

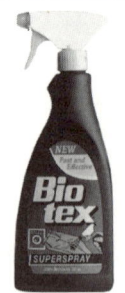

5

You've got the shoes. The dress. And the perfect shade of lipstick.

But without soft, smooth legs,

are you ready?

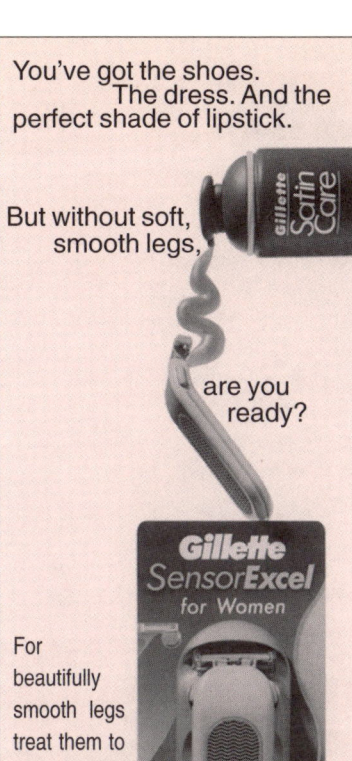

For beautifully smooth legs treat them to the **Gillette for Women** collection of products.

Start your beauty routine with the **Sensor Excel® for Women** razor, with soft, protective microfins that give you a safe, smooth, shave. And try **Satin Care** moisture-rich products that enhance, pamper and revitalise your skin. It's your moment. So be ready.

Gillette® for Women
Are you ready?

6

NEW CANESTAN AF. PUT YOUR ATHLETE'S FOOT DOWN.

ATHLETE'S FOOT: IRRITATING ISN'T IT? IT'S ITCHY, SORE, PAINFUL, AND A PERSISTENT LITTLE ROTTER TOO. JUST WHEN YOU THINK IT'S GONE FOR GOOD IT RETURNS WITH A VENGEANCE. CANESTAN AF IS A CREAM THAT CAN GET TO THE ROOT OF THE PROBLEM. IT HAS A PROVEN ACTIVE INGREDIENT CALLED CLOTRIMAZOLE which doesn't just soothe the symptoms, it treats the actual infection. Doctors have been prescribing Clotrimazole for athlete's foot for the last twenty years. But it is now available to you as Canesten AF, from your chemist. So put your foot down and ask your pharmacist for new Canesten AF.

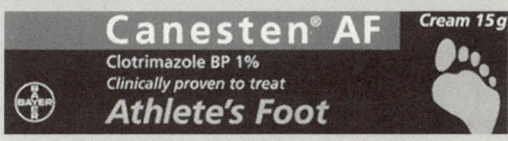

Canesten® AF
Clotrimazole BP 1%
Clinically proven to treat
Athlete's Foot
Cream 15g

7

9

146

10

NO MORE TEARS.
NO MORE TANTRUMS.
NO MORE TANGLES!

NEW JOHNSON'S KIDS DETANGLING SPRAY

That dreaded daily tangle wrangle is over.
And it's as simple as new Johnson's Kids Detangling Spray. With its easy to use pump action, you apply it to wet or dry, straight or curly hair and then just comb through.
Magic! Not a knot. Tangles totally disentangled.
All achieved in a fraction of the usual time, with none of the usual anguish.
And with Johnson's No More Tears formula, the spray is so mild on the hair (and eyes) that you can use it every day.
Which is good news for you. And even better news for your daughter.

1.1 Comparison and contrast

Whether targeted at a mass audience or a specific group, the function of advertisements is to attract attention in order to inform, persuade or to do both simultaneously. Although in recent years advertisements with emotive images have become more popular, many containing little or no text, there are innumerable advertisements whose effect relies on language or the connection between image and language. The need to translate such consumer advertisements has increased greatly due to global marketing. To keep the high costs of advertising campaigns down photo material is often kept and the text translated, adapted or revised to appeal to the target culture. Cultural specifics must be kept in mind when translating advertising messages.

Task 1 – identifying lexical features

> Looking at the examples, list and discuss which lexis seems typical of advertisements. Discuss any similarities or differences between the English and the German texts.

There are obviously many parallels between advertisements in English and in German. One of the most striking features is the laudatory, often hyperbolic descriptions used. Adjectives abound emphasising the goodness, the newness, the freshness and the uniqueness of the products advertised. Yet, studies of both languages have shown that a comparatively small set of such adjectives is used, the most popular being 'new' and 'good'. Exotic and foreign vocabulary is also frequent. Cosmetics and perfumes often have French names, and English being popular all over the world, slogans are often in 'English' in non-English speaking countries.

> Collect more advertisements in English and list the most frequent adjectives.

Few negatives will be found in consumer advertising. Negative forms are occasionally used to stress a favourable comparison, such as "no other", "nothing like", "no more", etc, and this is similar in German

comparatives

ads. Unqualified comparatives and superlatives, such as "the whitest whites" or "a brighter shine" are extremely common. Direct comparison of products is forbidden by advertising codes in most European countries, so that incomplete comparisons, the use of a definite article or 'probably' are ways of comparing vaguely.

compounds

Both German and English use unusual or invented compounds. In the Gillette advertisement (English text **5**), examples include "moisture-rich products", "satin-soft skin" and "creamy-mild soap".

German can make much greater use of this compounding feature, not only to pre-modify nouns with compound adjectives, but also to form new noun compounds, such as *Knabberspaß* or *Walnusszeit*. In fact, many of the compound nouns, adjectives or even verbs now used in everyday speech in German originated in advertisements. Examples include *Meeresfrische*, *Schmusewolle*, *ofenfrisch*, *nikotinarm*, *geruch-tilgend* or *weichspülen*. This device is extremely useful for keeping text short, intensifying meanings and packing a lot of information into a small space. When translating, however, it needs to be borne in mind that such compounds are easier to achieve grammatically in German than in English.

neologisms

New words are coined in advertising in a variety of ways apart from compounding – by shifting word class for example. Oranges may be recommended for their "peelability" or chocolates praised as "temptational". In the examples at the beginning of the chapter, *Tempo* tissues are supposedly *durchschnupfsicher*. (You might like to try to think of a translation for this useful word). Some coinages will be forgotten again but some will remain in the language.

colloquial language

Advertising also imitates some aspects of everyday speech, by using colloquial lexis and short or fragmented sentences. Ellipsis and sentence fragments, apart from making text sound conversational, are used to reduce a message to its key words and to create special focus. Examples include *Natürlich nur aus besten Zutaten und ohne jegliche Zusatzstoffe* or "Which is good news for you". The attempt to reproduce colloquial speech often also results in deviant punctuation, paragraphing and spelling, eg *nix* from the Cordoba ad (ad **3**). Deviant spellings are also common in English. Using non-mainstream spelling is often used in British advertisements for bread, dairy products and beer to indicate rural accents and thereby emphasise tradition and create a superficial sense of "the good old days". It is important that student translators understand the function of summarised text and any lexical or grammatical deviations, and find ways to transfer the flavour of colloquialism and creativity of the original ads.

Task 2 – identifying grammatical and poetic features
Deviant grammar can also be found in many ads. For example, adverbs may be used as adjectives, as in "the now cigarette".

> Look at the examples again and note any grammatical deviations or novelties which seem typical of advertising. Discuss any similarities or differences between the English and the German texts.

In advertising, the passive voice is avoided. The most usual verbal form is the simple present (unless another genre is being imitated,

such as a narrative). Past tense choices are used to stress the long tradition and reliability of a product. Imperative Mood is one of the most noticeable features of advertising. Consumers are often told or advised to "get X" or "try Y". Such instructions are often presented as the solution to a problem posed in the interrogative, such as in the Gillette ad.

An extremely effective device used in advertising, as in poetry, is repetition. Words, particularly the name of the product, parallel structures and even series of ads in slightly different form, repeat the key message. Parallel structures in English language ads are frequently participles, as in "relaxing, soothing, calming, comforting...zzz...Pure Flowers of Camomile. There's more to tea with Twining's". English makes extensive use of participial constructions, a feature that does not work well in German.

Another device also used in advertising and in a lot of poetry is an eye-catching layout. Ad text is nearly always set in more than one kind of typeface and size, the graphological variety drawing attention to key words or just separating body text from heading and slogan. Other visual features distinctive of ads, such as images, colour, handwriting and comic strips are not considered here, as they tend to be easily transferable between cultures. The focus of this chapter is the meanings made in and through language, which are more difficult to translate between cultures.

Many of the above lexical, grammatical and poetic features are used in both English and German language advertisements, and do not necessarily pose major obstacles for the translator. However, to catch attention, please and persuade, advertising also makes use of numerous poetic devices which are problematic or impossible to

translate, such as alliteration, assonance, phonetic effects, rhythm, rhyme, grammatical parallelism, culturally-specific metaphors and word play reliant on proverbs, catch-phrases, idioms, quotations from and allusions to literature, films, and song titles. Ads often exploit ambiguity or rely on knowledge of other ads and slogans. A recent German washing powder ad, for example, began *Zu Clementines Hochzeiten...* It was obviously addressed to a certain generation, as many young people would not remember the *Clementine* of former washing powder ads. Similarly, the Heineken ads in English "Heineken reaches the pirates other beers cannot reach" and "Heineken reaches the parrots other beers cannot reach" only make sense if one knows the original: "Heineken reaches the parts other beers cannot reach".

The connotation of many words, vitally important to advertising, is usually difficult to translate, placing great demands on the creativity of a translator. When connotations cannot be transferred through the same lexical or intertextual means as the original, other linguistic means must be found. The original English language slogan for Mars Bars echoes a proverb: "A Mars a day helps you work, rest and play" reminds the audience of "an apple a day keeps the doctor away". Though the German slogan *Mars macht mobil bei Sport, Spaß und Spiel* does not similarly echo a proverb, it is memorable and successful through its use of rhyme and alliteration. Word play seems to be a hallmark of advertising in much of the English speaking world, and although it is also used in German advertising, it is not as common.

| Find examples of word play in the examples at the beginning of the chapter. | word play |

Punning is particularly prevalent, and probably easier, in English. (It has been shown statistically that English has more ambiguous, double-entendre lexis than German). Native English speakers also seem to enjoy witty and humorous advertising more than the Germans. Word play can also quickly lead to the limits of translatability. Consider the following hoarding ads for light bulbs; "Ohm and Away" and "Ohmward Bound". They are very clever, but hardly translatable. Similarly, the IBM ad "I think therefore IBM" and the inter-language Perrier ad "H2Eau". `puns`

| Explain why these ads (Ohm, IBM and Perrier) cannot be translated. Find some German language ads you consider untranslatable and ask another translation student to try and render it into English. |

Task 3 - Slogans
Many ads rely for their effect on entertaining one-liners that can be memorised easily. These slogans sometimes become so well-known that they enter into the language and become modern 'proverbs'. Examples in English include:

"Have a break, have a KitKat"/ "Wot a lot I got"/ "Drinka pinta milka day"/ "Players please"/ "Put a tiger in your tank"/ "Guiness is good for you"/ "Been there. Done that"/ "Once driven, forever smitten"/ "A Mars a day helps you work, rest and play" and "Don't be vague – ask for Haig".

German examples include:

Mach mal Pause/ Mercedes der gute Stern auf allen Straßen/ Wer wird denn gleich in die Luft gehen/ Der Duft der großen weiten Welt/ Keine Feier ohne Meyer/ Nicht immer aber immer öfter/ Milch von glücklichen Kühen/ Kaba, Kaba, hält dich gesund/ Man gönnt sich ja sonst nichts!

Try translating the following slogans:

1 Go to work on an egg
2 Only ours lasts hours (toothpaste)
3 Polo: the mint with the h(©)le
4 Elegant but not stuck up (Organics hair spray)
5 It's not only coughs and sneezes that spread diseases (toothbrush)

6 Milch macht müde Männer munter (Milch)
7 Du sollst keine fremden Biere neben mir haben (Bier)
8 Genießen auf gut deutsch! (Butter)
9 Ein Schaum wird wahr (Haartönungsmittel)
10 Sie brauchen nur Köpfchen (Wechselkopf-Zahnbürste)

Task 4 - Brand Names

Brand names are often chosen for their idiomatic quality. Product names, however, can be risky in foreign culture markets, as a name might have unpleasant or obscene associations in another country. Snickers was originally not sold in Britain under this name, sounding perhaps too much like knickers. A car called Nova isn't likely to sell well in Spain where it would mean "no go". Sugar Puffs became Sugar Smacks in Germany for obvious reasons. Real products, which English speakers are hardly likely to buy, include:

BONKER   (Spanish coffee)
KRAPP   (Swedish toilet paper)
PSCHITT   (French lemonade)
SKUM   (Skandanavian sweets)
SKINABABE (Japanese baby powder)
SOD   (Chinese face cream)

Sometimes humorous slogans are used to counteract the negative connotations some brand names have. Two examples given by Guy Cook in his book on advertising, are:

SCHMUCKERS – with a name like that, it's gotta be good. (mustard)
MILKA LILA PAUSE – hate the name, love the chocolate.

Task 5 – identifying stylistic problems in German text
If it's raining but neither of you notice
It's love
If it's a night in and it feels like a night out
It's love
If it's knowing you'd do it all again
It's love
If it's Match of the Day and you're watching
It's love
& if it's love, it's L'Aimant

Below is a student translation of the above advertisement for L'Aimant perfume, one of the text examples at the beginning of the chapter:

Wenn es regnet, und ihr merkt es nicht
Dann ist es Liebe
Wenn ihr zu Hause bleibt und doch die ganze Welt habt
Dann ist es Liebe
Wenn ihr wißt, daß ihr es wieder tut
Dann ist es Liebe
Wenn das Spiel des Tages läuft und du mitschaust
Dann ist es Liebe
Und wenn es Liebe ist, dann ist es L'Aimant

The original advertisement was obviously directed at a British audience. A cultural reference not understood by the student was "Match of the Day", so this was just translated literally. "Match of the

Day" refers to the best football match of a particular Saturday. It is televised late Saturday evening on BBC 1, at approximately the same time as the *Sportschau*, and so *Sportschau* might be a better translation, if the connotations are similar. Is *Sportschau* as important for German males as "Match of the Day" is for British males? The reference might amuse British women, but is a similar reference likely to go down well with German females in a perfume ad? Amongst young people in Britain, Saturday night is **the** night out. To stay in on this night is generally regarded as a special sacrifice. It is also difficult to convey the word play in "night in" and "night out".

The English advertisement has five parallel structures at the beginning of the five sentences ("If it's..."). The student has not succeeded in repeating this parallelism. It might be a good idea to find a solution that makes five parallel structures possible. One way would be to begin with *Liebe ist/heißt*...The rhythm of the English advertisement is not completely regular but the German is less so. Particularly the rendering of the second sentence is too long.

Try to write a better German translation of this ad.

Task 6 – Identifying stylistic problems in English text
bebe
Rein&Klar
Sichtbar wirksam, spürbar sanft
Es ist keine Love-Story
Aber es geht unter die Haut
Denn das bebe Rein&Klar Aktiv-Gel wirkt tief in den oberen Schichten der Gesichtshaut. Sein spezieller Wirkstoff Elubiol reguliert aktiv die erhöhte Talg-produktion, eine der Hauptursachen für die Entstehung von Pickeln. So hilft das Aktiv-Gel sichtbar wirksam, der Neubildung von Pickeln vorzubeugen – denoch ist es spürbar sanft und schützt die Haut gleichzeitig vor dem Austrock-nen. Bei täglicher Anwendung sorgt es für ein reines und klares Hautbild.

Examine the following student's English version of the **bebe** ad above, noting any problems you can see with it, lexical, grammatical, idiomatic, etc.

bebe
Pure and clear
Visibly effective, sensuously soft
Its not a love story
But it's more than skin deep
The bebe Pure&Clear Active-Gel goes deep into the upper layers of your facial skin. Its special ingredient Elubiol actively regulates the heightened production of grease, a major cause for the growth of spots. The active gel visibly helps to prevent the return of the spot – yet it is sensuously soft and at the same time protects the skin from dehydration. Use it daily, and it will keep your skin looking peachy clean.

The ad appeared in a magazine for teenagers (*Sugar*). The student's attempt is quite good but still has several weaknesses. "Pure and clear" does not collocate well in English. The product might be more successfully marketed with "clean and clear", a collocation often used in ads of this kind. The parallelism of the German *sichtbar* and *spürbar* has not been kept, and part of the alliteration has been lost. "Sensuously soft" is nice, but in choosing "visibly effective", the student has ignored the fact that the structures in this part of the ad must be repeatable later in the body copy. "Visibly helps" does not repeat "visibly effective". Also, the phrase "peachy clean" does not repeat the name of the product at the end of the ad, which *reines und klares Hautbild* does, and which most ads do.

An attempt at word play has been made to translate *es geht unter die Haut*, but "skin deep" in this context does not unfortunately work very well. "Skin deep" means shallow or superficial, so "more than skin deep" would be not bad. On the other hand, the gel **is** skin deep – it penetrates under the skin. Perhaps the addition of "deeper" would improve it: "not a love story, but it goes deeper than skin deep".
The English phrase "to get under ones skin" unfortunately means "to irritate", and so is not the best choice for skin cream. Another possibility would be to use the phrase "to go deep", which also has two meanings. The translation would then be "not a love story, but it still goes deep".

The nominal structures of the German text (*Neubildung, Entstehung, Talgproduktion*) have been taken over too often in this student translation. Only with *Anwendung* was a verb used. Though the

German text does not address the reader directly, most ads for this kind of product in English teenage magazines do use direct address.

Some expressions used in this translation sound strange to native speakers of English: "the upper layers of the facial skin", "the heightened production of grease" and "the growth of spots". Also, "dehydration" is the wrong translation of *austrocknen* in this context.

Compare the following good translation:

bebe
Clean&Clear.
Spot the difference. Sense the softness.
Not a love story yet deeper than skin deep.
bebe Clean&Clear Active-Gel goes deep under your skin to treat your complexion from within. Its special active ingredient elubiol regulates the excess oil that can cause spots and acne. You can spot the difference as Active-Gel helps keep your skin clear of acne – and you can sense the softness as it helps protect your skin from dryness and damage. Use Active-Gel daily to keep your skin looking clean and clear.

1.2 Text and function

Advertisements very often mix genres, appropriating functions and features of other genres, such as narrative or report. Attitudes, strategies and trends change more quickly in this area of cultural expression than in many others, and text patterns change accordingly. The earlier 'hard-sell' technique, in which consumers are told to "buy X because it is cheaper and better", is being replaced by more subtle 'soft-sell' advertising techniques, in which the persuasive function is not immediately recognisable. There are ads that sound like reports, look like diary entries or personal letters or popular narrative fiction. Features of narrative, such as the typical 'setting-problem-solution-evaluation' structure and characterisation, as well as lexical and grammatical features typical of narrative fiction, are increasingly to be found in advertising. On the next page are two advertisements that imitate the patterns of children's stories:

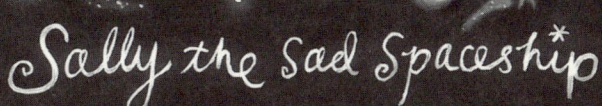

Sally the sad Spaceship*

Once upon a time there was a little spaceship called Sally. All the other spaceships were bright and colourful and would show off around the solar system, but they wouldn't let Sally play. They would say 'Silly Sally hasn't got any lights, she's too boring to play with us.' Now also in the solar system was a big, dark black hole which scared everybody, but one day Sally felt so sad she decided to fly into it anyway and hide. But when she got inside the black hole Sally was so surprised.

It was filled with New Angel Delight Topples. Not just Angel Delight but lots of lovely, brightly coloured jelly beans too. 'These jelly beans are perfect for me!' cried Sally. And with that she flew out flashing her big, colourful lights.

The End

Despite the narrative structure, the second example is more obviously an advertisement than the first.

> Discuss the features that make it recognisable as an ad, and identify any aspects that would make a translation into English difficult.

1.3 Summary of language features
Among the many parallels between product advertisements in English and German are:

features in common

> *laudatory, inflated, hyberbolic lexis
> *colloquial lexis
> *unqualified comparatives and superlatives
> *strings of adjectives, often in compound form
> *neologisms
> *"scientific" language for medical or health products, cars and technical equipment
> *extensive use of imperative Mood
> *lack of negative expressions
> *avoidance of passive
> *use of deviant spellings, punctuation, grammar
> *poetic devices, such as repetition, word play, layout

The main areas of difference are:

grammatical differences

> *more extensive use of compounding in German, to form adjectives, nouns and verbs
> *use of participial constructions in English
> *language-specific use of poetic devices, such as word play and punning (more in English)
> *culture-specific metaphors
> *culture-specific inter-textual references

Having identified some features of advertising, you can now translate more examples yourself. The following exercises draw attention to lexical and grammatical choices potentially available at several points in text production.

2.1 Text completion

The following text, promoting French cheeses, was printed in a women's magazine.

Frankreichs erstes Käserezept
oder
die göttliche Eingebung

Vor 1.000 Jahren wurden in Frankreichs Klöstern die ersten Käserezepte aufgeschrieben, und schon bald gaben die Mönche ihr Wissen an Landfrauen weiter. Bis heute verraten die Namen vieler Käsesorten ihren klösterlichen Ursprung, wie etwa der Citeaux aus der Burgund. Mit 500 Spezialitäten ist Frankreich das Paradies für Käsekenner. Ob cremiger Camembert, aromatischer Roquefort oder würziger Comté – die göttlichste Erfindung auf Erden ist gewiß Käse aus Frankreich.

KÄSE AUS LEIDENSCHAFT

Task 7 – multiple choice translation

From the following options, choose those that render the best translation.

1 (a) the first French cheese recipe/ (b) the original cheese recipe from France/ (c) France's original cheese recipe

2 (a) or divine inspiration/ (b) or divine revelation/ (c) or heavenly insight

3 (a) the first cheese recipes were written down in the monasteries of France a thousand years ago/ (b) it was 1000 years ago that the first cheese recipes were written down in France's monasteries/ (c) in France's monasteries the first cheese recipes were written down a 1000 years ago

4 (a) and soon the monks passed on their knowledge to the country women/ (b) and soon knowledge of them was passed on to the country women by the monks/ (c) and soon the monks were passing on their knowledge to country women

5 (a) until today the names of many kinds of cheese bear witness to their monasterial origins/ (b) until today the names of many sorts of cheese betray their monkish origins/ (c) the names of many French cheeses still reveal their monastic origins

6 (a) like, for instance, Burgundy's Citeaux/ (b) like, for example, the Citeaux from Burgundy/ (c) such as Citeaux from Burgundy

7 (a) with 500 specialities, France is the paradise for cheese experts/ (b) with its 500 specialities, France is a paradise for cheese connoisseurs/ (c) France, with 500 specialities, is a paradise for cheese lovers

8 (a) whether creamy Camembert, aromatic Roquefort or spicy Comté/ (b) whether creamy-textured Camembert, pleasantly pungent Roquefort or full-flavoured Comté/ (c) whether creamy-soft Camembert, strong-smelling Roquefort or peppery Comté

9 (a) the most heavenly thing on earth is certainly cheese from France/ (b) the most divine concoction on earth is doubtlessly French cheese/ (c) the heavenliest invention on earth is without doubt cheese from France

10 (a) cheese from passion/ (b) for the love of cheese/ (c) cheese is my passion

2.2 Evaluation and comparison

The following advertisement (page 161) for cleansing strips appeared simultaneously in English and German magazines, using the same photo material.

Task 8 – free translation

Write your own German translation of the English version before reading the published German version.

Task 9 – comparing student and professional translations

Now compare your work with that done by a professional translator, discussing any difference and the possible reasons for those changes the professional translator has made to the text.

The quick fix for pores.

VISIBLE
DIFFERENCE
PORE-FIX C

The only cleansing
strip that **cleans**
and **treats**
with **Vitamin C**

New double action
Pore Cleansing Strips
peel away dirt, oil and
blackheads, leave behind
visibly clean, clear,
healthy-looking pores.
Plus an extra treat,
antioxidant **Vitamin C.**

Seeing is Believing.

Elizabeth Arden

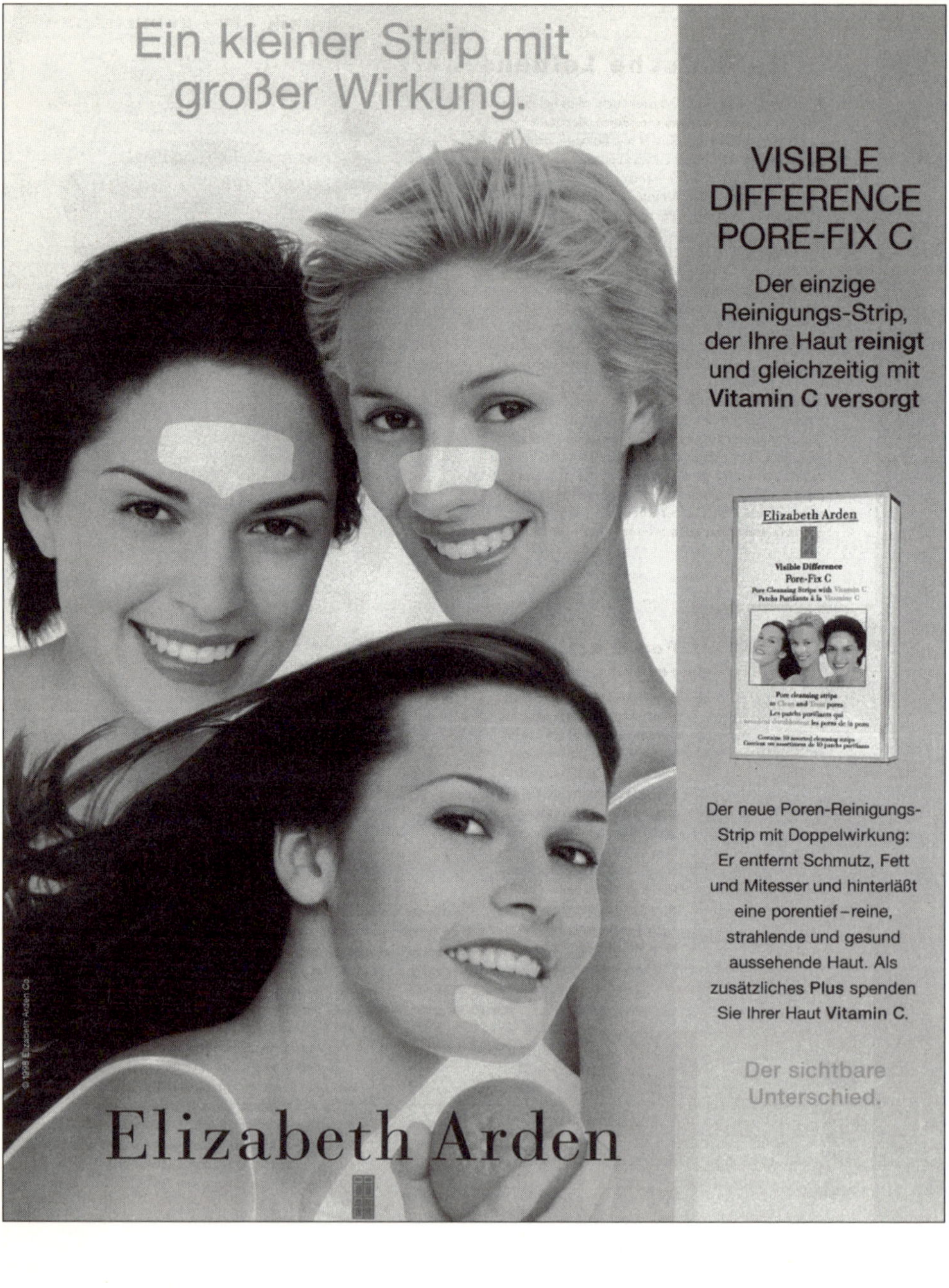

Ein kleiner Strip mit großer Wirkung.

VISIBLE DIFFERENCE PORE-FIX C

Der einzige Reinigungs-Strip, der Ihre Haut **reinigt** und gleichzeitig mit **Vitamin C versorgt**

Der neue Poren-Reinigungs-Strip mit Doppelwirkung: Er entfernt Schmutz, Fett und Mitesser und hinterläßt eine porentief – reine, strahlende und gesund aussehende Haut. Als zusätzliches Plus spenden Sie Ihrer Haut **Vitamin C.**

Der sichtbare Unterschied.

Elizabeth Arden

2.3. Vocabulary extension

In the following ads familiar phrases have been punned or twisted.

Task 10 – idioms

Use your dictionary to identify the original phrases and the double meanings. Decide whether it would be possible to translate any of them into German, and suggest solutions.

1 Handy Witch Hazel acts 'on the spot' (antiseptic)
2 Stain Devils – Now each stain has met its match (stain remover)
3 Perfect wholesome pastry is no longer just pie in the sky (pastry mix)
4 More to smile about when you say 'cheese' (supermarket ad for cheese section)
5 Don't put a foot wrong (Clark's shoes)
6 Talk a lot of tripe to your dog and he'll love it (Butcher's tripe mix for dogs)
7 Are you in clover? (Clover butter)
8 Our cock-a-leekie soup is well worth crowing about (soup)
9 You'll never take a shot in the dark at Boots (cameras)
10 Fine wine at plonky prices. Have Sainsbury's got a corkscrew loose? (wine discounts at Sainsbury's)
11 New Togs with the elasticated waist – you can test them without spending a penny (free sample of disposable nappies)
12 Croydex Weeder Kneeler – the open and shut case for easy gardening (a kneeler that can be folded up like a case when not in use)
13 Keep a drop of Guiness by in case friends do (stout beer)
14 Enjoy your Salad Days with Cyprus Food and Wine. Cyprus – a taste of the sun (Cyprus)
15 The Early Bird catches the deal (Earlybird care hire scheme)

Task 11 – word play

Find all the references to head and hair in the following ad from W.H. Smith's (bookstore/newsagent). With the help of a good dictionary, explain the double meanings.

Now kids can get a head start when going back to school. The chance to brush up on everything from how human hair grows to working out square roots, revision tips when exams crop up and stationery in hair-raising colours. Everything at neatly trimmed prices, too.

They'll also find all the latest music (so they can let their hair down after school).

As a translation text, it is enough to make your hair curl, so if you can manage a German version, you can certainly hold your head up.

Task 12 – synonyms

Complete the following advertisement by choosing one of the so-called 'synonyms' in brackets.

LANCASTER

___ (improve, maximize, increase) the tan ___ (lessen, reduce, minimize) the damage.

A ___ (new, fresh, novel), ___ (avant-garde, revolutionary, radical) after-sun booster which ___ (increases, improves, maximizes) your tan by up to 50% in just four days and rejuvenates your skin as you turn more ___ (tanned, golden, bronze). Tan Maximizer is ___ (soothing, calming, palliative), moisturising, conditioning and ___ (guards, protects, preserves) the skin from sun ageing whilst ___ (reducing, lessening, minimising) dryness and ___ (sunburn, redness, inflammation). A ___ (wonderful, remarkable, extraordinary) product that works with the skin's own ___ (natural, innate, inborn) tanning and repair system so that you can prolong your tan while ___ (improving, maximizing, increasing) the overall ___ (condition, state, plight) of your skin.

Check your solution with the original advertisement in the answer notes. If you have different answers, use a monolingual dictionary to find out whether the alternatives are only synonyms in certain situations. If more than one word seems possible, explain why the original one was chosen.

Task 13 – adjective replacement

Find as many synonyms as you can for the adjectives in the following four advertisements. Replace the original adjectives with some of those you have found and discuss whether the ads sound as good.

1 Glistening. Gleaming. Glorious. Gold. The Panthene Gold Cap Collection.
2 Dior Diorlight... A flawless look. Imperceptible, undetectable.
3 Ravishing on your lips, glamorous in your handbag, the new Lancome lip glosses will leave your lips shimmery, soft and gorgeous.
4 Provamel Soya Yofu is the most delicious alternative to yoghurt, full of succulent morsels of fruit and with a pleasing taste and texture.

Task 14 – compounds

Find translations for the following German compounds taken from advertisements.

1 magenmilder Kaffee
2 hauteigene Feuchtigkeit
3 ein Kleid mit Weitenregulierung
4 tropfengenau dosierbare Tropfen
5 anlagebedingter Haarausfall
6 die erste zartschmelzende Schokolade der Welt
7 volles Verwöhnaroma
8 der neue vollmundig-sanfter Geschmack

3.1 Quick texts

Practise translating advertisements with the following examples, spending no more than fifteen to twenty minutes on each.

VI.3
Independent
translation

1

Movida
color

Entdecken Sie das neue **Movida:** Die verbesserte **Intensiv-Tönung-Pflege-Creme** schenkt Ihrem Haar noch leuchtendere **Farben** und noch mehr **Geschmeidigkeit.** Natürlich ohne Ammoniak – super **sanft.** Jetzt neu mit **fruchtigem Duft.** Ganz einfach – mit dem **COLORCLIC-System.** Nur 15 Minuten Einwirkzeitfür bis zu 6 Wochen intensive Tönung. In 14 leuchtenden **Trend-Nuancen.**

TOLL DAS NEUE MOVIDA GRANATROT - VOLLER LEUCHTKRAFT, GANZ SANFT.

MIT DER GARANTIE VON LABORATOIRES GARNIER PARIS

2

D as Geheimnis vieler schöner Frauen
ist ihre glatte duftende Haut.
Wenn sie baden, baden sie in Fenjal.
Das Creme-Oelbad mit dem einzigartigen Fenjal-Oel,
das im Wasser einen betont weiblichen Duft entfaltet
und zugleich die Haut so glättet, daß das Wasser an ihr abperlt.
Selbst der Duft ist Pflege.
Fenjal Creme-Oelbad erhalten Sie in zwei Duftnoten
Die klassische ist die intensivere

Als hätten Sie nie trockene Haut gehabt
Fenjal Creme-Oelbad

166

3.2 45-minute texts

Take no more than 60 minutes to translate the following two advertisements from a series for PEUGEOT 106.

The ads are obviously targeted at young women and, because of the gender system of German, work particularly well. Although products can sometimes be personified in English (eg "New Jif Microliquid. He's the best, he outshines the rest") you cannot assume this is possible in all cases.

1

"Ich habe ihn über eine Anzeige kennen gelernt."

Er suchte eine hübsche Begleitung. Sie ein Lebensabschnittgefährt. Sie erkannte ihn sofort an der Chiffrenummer 106. Und er lachte sie gleich an. Aufgeschlossen, dynamisch, weltgewandt – der wollte kein Heimchen am Herd. Und auch sein Äußeres! Da war weit mehr drin als nur Kino, Kneipe und Kultur. Nach diesem ersten Treffen beim PEUGEOT Händler war ihr klar: Das Glück liegt auf der Straße. Und schon nach der ersten Fahrt mit ihm bedeutete das für sie vor allem eins: PEUGEOT. Mit Sicherheit mehr Vergnügen.

168

2

"Mein 106 und ich: Der Schöne und das Biest."

Kein Märchen: Schon als sie ihn das erste mal bei Ihrem PEUGEOT Händler sah, war sie wie verzaubert. Die schönen Farben, die schöne Ausstattung – es war zu schön, um wahr zu sein. Bei der Probefahrt war ihr dann sofort klar; Den muß ich haben. Denn er war weit mehr als nu schön stark, schön sicher – und schön erfolgreich. Seit diesem Tag hat er einen festen Platz in ihrem Herzen.
Aber das muß ja niemand wissen.
Vor allem nicht Kai, Uwe, Thomas.
PEUGEOT MIt Sicherheit mehr Vergnügen.

Car advertisements often have longer body copy.

Translate each of the following two advertisements for Mercedes-Benz within 45 minutes.

3

▶ Am 15. August 1934 drang der erste Mensch etwa 800m in die Tiefsee vor. Der amerikanische Zoologe William Beebe entdeckte ein Geisterreich, das voller wundersamer Wesen war. Eines davon war der kleine Anglerfisch, der in dieser dunklen Welt von ganz allein leuchtete, ohne einen Knopf betätigen zu müssen. Ein Phänomen, das man heute auch in der neuen S-Klasse findet: Sobald es ihr auf der Straße zu dunkel wird, schaltet sie automatisch ihre Scheinwerfer ein. Dies ist nur eine von vielen Ideen, um es Ihnen im Straßenverkehr noch ein bißchen komfortabler und sicherer zu machen. Am besten besuchen Sie uns selbst und entdecken all die anderen hilfreichen Neuheiten, die wir hier nicht aufzählen können. Mercedes-Benz. Die Zukunft des Automobils ·

Sinn und Sinnlichkeit. Die neue S-Klasse

Laura freut sich auf die Affen, Johanna freut sich auf die Elefanten, Jakob und Stefan freuen sich auf die Strauße. Und Papa freut sich auf die Rückfahrt.

Die V-Klasse. Jetzt neu mit 6-Zylinder-Motor.

Mercedes Benz

Kinder wollen immer alles ganz genau wissen. Zum Beispiel, warum Giraffen so lange Hälse haben oder wie schnell ein Leopard laufen kann. Gut, wenn man ein Auto hat, das einen schnell von der Theorie in die Praxis fährt. Wie die V-Klasse von Mercedes-Benz. Die bringt alle unermüdlichen Fragesteller dahin, wo einem die Antworten von selbst über den Weg laufen – beispielsweise in den Zoo. Aber damit Sie nicht nur am Ausflugsort viel Spaß haben, sondern auch schon auf der Fahrt dorthin, gibt es die V-Klasse jetzt mit einem kräftigen 2,8 Liter 6-Zylinder Motor. Und, keine Frage, jeder sitzt auf seinem eigenen Einzelsitz – im Fond mit integriertem Sicherheitsgurt. Wieso, weshalb, warum?
Mehr Informationen bekommen Sie unter Tel. 0180/22336 oder Fax 0180/22337.

4

The following advertising texts are about the length of examination texts in German universities.

Translate each into English within two and a half hours.

1

HOLLYWOODS NEUER JUNGBRUNNEN IST ÜBER 2000 JAHRE ALT.

In China ist Kombucha schon seit der Tsin-Dynastie (221 v. Chr.) bekannt. Dort hat ihn seine einzigartige Wirkung nahezu in den Rang eines magischen Wundergetränks erhoben.

Inzwischen erobert Kombucha auch die Neue Welt. In Hollywood gilt das mythenumwobene Naturgetränk als Schönheitselixir und Jungbrunnen, so berichten renommierte Magazine. Zahlreiche Film- und Popgrößen schwören auf Kombucha und trinken ihn regelmäßig.

Die ganzheitliche Wirkung von Kombucha kann nicht vollauf erklärt werden. Aber viele positive Teilwirkungen sind allein schon durch seine Inhaltsstoffe verständlich.

Kombucha entsteht durch die kontrollierte Fermentation von ausgewählten Kräutertees, Saccharose und mittels einer speziellen Kultur aus Hefe und Milchsäurebakterien.

Wissenschaftliche Erkenntnisse bestätigen den Beitrag, den Kombucha zu Gesundheit, Schönheit und Wohlbefinden leisten kann.

● Kombucha hilft durch seinen Enzymgehalt bei der Aufspaltung von Nahrungsstoffen und kann so die Darmfunktion verbessern.

● Durch seinen Gehalt an wertvollen Lactobazillen (Milchsäurebakterien) kann Kombucha die Erhaltung der Darmflora fördern und die körpereigenen Abwehrkräfte unterstützen.

● Kombucha kann durch seine Hefen zu einer reinen Haut beitragen.

Aber eben nicht nur das – Kombucha schmeckt auch noch unvergleichlich erfrischend. So wird es zum prickelnden Vergnügen, sich täglich etwas Gutes zu tun.

Kombucha sollte man regelmäßig trinken oder einfach dann, wenn es das Wohlbefinden verlangt. Und man fühlt sich rundum wohl und spürt seine Lebenskraft.

Körper und Seele sind in Harmonie.

KOMBUCHA REINIGT
UND ERFRISCHT
DEINEN KÖRPER. DEINE SEELE

Feuchtigkeit

braucht die Haut zum Leben Tag für Tag!

„Einfach ein tolles Gefühl: Den ganzen langen Tag bleibt die Haut topfit und rundum gepflegt".

„Täglich Hydro-Parts und viel VitaminE: frei öl-Feuchtigkeits-Creme bringt meine Haut in Form und stärkt ihre Immunkraft".

„Apotheke? Na klar: Beim Kauf von Wirkstoff-Kosmetik fühle ich mich dort besonders gut beraten".

Hydro-Parts für glatte, vitale Haut

Das A und O bei einer wirksamen Tagespflege ist die Zufuhr von Feuchtigkeit. Denn durch Umweltbelastungen wird der Haut sehr viel Feuchtigkeit entzogen. Das Ergebnis: Eine trockene Haut mit deutlicher Neigung zur Faltenbildung! Deshalb enthält ‚frei öl Feuchtigkeits Creme' spezielle Feuchthalter (Hydro-parts).

Diese Feuchthaltesubstanzen geben der Gesichtshaut ihre natürliche Feuchtigkeit zurück. Die Arbeitsweise der „Hydroparts" ist einfach, aber genial: Sie werden mit ‚frei öl-Feuchtigkeits-Creme' in die oberen Hautschichten eingeschleust. Dadurch rücken die Hautzellen enger zusammen. Sie sorgen aber auch dafür, daß die hauteigene Feuchtigkeit in den oberen Zellregionen festgehalten wird. So wird selbst sehr trockene Haut zarter und glatter!

Hautschutz-Vitamin E

Keine wirksame Tagespflege ohne Vitamin E. Als Schönheits-Wirkstoff kommt es immer dann zum Einsatz, wenn die natürliche Abwehrkraft der Haut geschwächt ist: ‚frei öl-Feuchtigkeits-Creme' verhindert mit hochdosiertem Vitamin E die Bildung der gefährlichen „freien Radikale" und stärkt dadurch nachhaltig die hauteigenen Abwehrkräfte. Damit ist die Haut gegen negative Umwelteinflüsse den ganzen Tag über prima geschützt.

NUR IN APOTHEKEN

„Schlimm ist nicht die Prüfung, schlimm ist die **Angst** davor."

Eine anstehende Prüfung, Probleme im Job, eine unvermeidbare Konfrontation – ganz gleich, was auch der Grund sein mag, es gibt viele Situationen im Leben, die einem einfach Angst einjagen. Man fängt an, sich Sorgen zu machen wird unsicher und deprimiert. In dieser Stimmung stellt sich häufig das Gefühl ein, am Ende einer Sackgasse zu stehen. Und dann?

Irgendwas mache ich vielleicht falsch, denken Sie, und suchen nach der Ursache, auf die Sie allerdings von allein nicht so leicht kommen werden. Denn oft entstehen solche Alltagsängste durch einen Mangel an Botenstoffen. Wenn sie im Körper nicht ausreichend vorhanden sind, kann der Stoffwechsel im Gehirn und damit die Psyche aus dem Gleichgewicht kommen. Und die Angst stellt sich ein.

Durch Esbericum® wird der Effekt der Botenstoffe erhöht. Dieses pflanzliche Präparat aus Johanniskraut sorgt dafür, daß der gestörte biochemische Prozeß im Gehirn wieder ins Gleichgewicht kommen kann. Esbericum® wirkt nach ca. 14 Tagen. Ihr Verhalten wird ausgeglichener, Probleme und Beklemmungen gehen zurück, und Sie haben wieder mehr Freude am Leben.

Vertrauen Sie auf Esbericum®. Denn das darin enthaltene Johanniskraut wirkt bei Verstimmungszuständen und ist besonders gut verträglich. Esbericum® gibt es rezeptfrei in Ihrer Apotheke.

Esbericum®
Ihr natürliches Mittel bei Verstimmungszuständen

Appendix

Answer Key   176

Glossary   192

Further Reading   196

I Recount – biographical

Task 1 – identifying grammatical THEME

Text 1   Margriet de Moor, sie, Kunstgeschichts- und Architekturstudium, mit ihren beiden Erzählungsbänden *Rückenansicht* (1988) und *Doppelporträt* (1989), es folgte, 1993

Text 2   Robert Schneider geb. 1961 in Bregenz, außerdem, sein Monolog *Dreck*

Text 3   Tilman Spengler geboren 1947 in Oberhausen, studierte, 1980 und 1981, lebt

In German various elements come in THEME position: the author, their work, CIRCUMSTANCES of time and manner, PROCESSES, PARTICIPANTS that are not the grammatical subject of the clause, and lexically dense phrases.

Text 1   Carol Shields, she, author of six novels, Carol Shields, she

Text 2   Keith Oatley, he, he, he, *The case of Emily V.*, it

Text 3   Jeanette Winterson, she

Text 4   Eva Hoffman, she, she, she

In English THEME position is occupied by the author, by name or pronoun, and their books.

Task 2 – identifying stylistic problems in German text
E

Task 3 – identifying stylistic problems in English text
C

Task 4 – identifying situational context

- The three texts come from academic publications, not works of narrative fiction.
- They were, like the biographical texts presented at the beginning of the chapter, printed on the back of their books, but their function is not to recount a career for general interests sake so much as to establish the credentials of the books authors. The purpose is to tell the reader what gives this writer authority to be writing the book in question. The focus is thus on who the writer is professionally in the present, and so the use of tenses differs to the other type of biographies presented previously.
- *Er wurde* should be translated with a present tense form, either simple present or present perfect. For example, "he is known", "he

has been made known", "he has become well known" or "his reputations has been established by such publications as ...".

- The tense chosen must include the link to the present. The previous biographies begin in the simple past, these biographies are dominated by the present simple and present perfect.

Task 5 – completing gap tranlation text

(1) raised (is concise and rhythmic)
(2) omit reference to parents or use "daughter of"
(3) is one of
(4) popular, widely read or well known
(5) NOT anything with "youth book" in it!
(6) have won
(7) have been translated
(8) has written
(9) currently lives

Task 6 – evaluating student translations

All have several problems, but overall **C** is probably the best version. Word order of the first clause should put final focus on when or where, not on the parents. In the examples at beginning of the chapter students should notice that WHERE the person was born tends to come straight after their name. "Leave behind" – the preposition is not necessary or elegant. "Abandon" is hardly appropriate. "Native land" is better than homeland (think of reserves) but perhaps it is better to leave it out altogether. "ing"-structure is more elegant. Final focus of text – in the German text it is on *monatenlang* so put that element last in English for end focus. "Even in Germany" makes it sound surprising that this should be the case in Germany, which is not a meaning intended in the original.

II News item – in brief

Task 1 – identfifying grammatical differences

Word order – in English the grammatical SUBJECT comes first, in German a CIRCUMSTANCE of place. Lexis is more 'neutral' in German, English plays word games and has high 'affect'. The use of the gerund in English needs to be remembered by students, and the use of present perfect in German.

Text 1

Task 4 – identifying situational context

The first text is from a newspaper, but includes commentary and lexical choices that express opinion and mock the minister spoken about (eg "dance a jig of rage, minions, elbowed out, snout, peppery rival, get his way, planted on, none other than"). The use of the interrogative, rhetorical question, is also evidence of sarcasm that would not occur in the sort of news item previously presented. The text makes no attempt or pretence to be an objective piece of news writing. It sounds like hearsay – "Robin Cook is said to have danced a jig of rage", so it is by no means sure that he actually did. The writer is being humorous.

Text 2

The second text is an excerpt from a narrative fiction text (Ken Follett, *Dangerous Fortune*, New York 1994.). The opening sentence with a CIRCUMSTANTIAL element in THEME position is not typical of a news report. Like a news report it starts with the result, but it contains details that would be unlikely in a text of this kind. The second sentence is also too long for a news story. The passive voice is also used too frequently. A "hot Saturday in May" puts it too far in the past and is too indefinite for a news report.

Task 5 – headlines

"headlinese"

1. Word play is involved in "count cost" and "innumeracy". The idiom "to count the cost" means to start having problems as a result of earlier mistakes. The mistake in this case is that the students have not been taught basic mathematical skills, ie have not been taught to count.
2. POWs is an abbreviation meaning "prisoners of war"; "to sue" is future (near future) time.
3. Double alliteration is evident here. Gas is still sometimes used in Britain to render patients unconscious during teeth extractions.
4. The headline can be deciphered by working backwards, ie: There is hope for the bride who hid as a stowaway. A "stowaway" is someone who hides on a ship or plane to travel secretly/illegally or to avoid paying.
5. Word play on the phrase "in top gear". Top gear is the gear used to drive at a high speed, but the phrase also means to do something with the greatest possible energy and effort.
6. Again you must work backwards, ie there is secrecy in connection with the investigation into examinations. "Probe" is a very common word in headlines.

7 Alliteration. The reference is to Paul Simon who put on a show that was a total flop. There is word play involved in *Sound of silence*, one of the most popular songs of Simon and Garfunkel. There was silence for the show in the sense of no applause.

8 "Lords a-fuming" recalls the "lords a-leaping" in *The Twelve days of Christmas*. To fume means to be angry or to smoke. The sense is that the members of the House of Lords are enraged about proposals to ban smoking in the House.

9 Rhyme. The Ouse is a river in Britain.

10 An example of long pre-modification which can again be deciphered from back to front. There is an MP who is a millionaire and has a son who drove a car with nine people in it and for this was banned from driving.

Amusing suggestions from students to translate the German headlines into English include:

1 Love sick lad loves no longer / Deadly love
2 Have a cuppa / A cup of abuse / Mug massacre / mug muggins
3 Tornado tears through Minnesota
4 Kiddie crime increases / Crime catches kids / kids catching up on crime / Child crime climbing
5 Lousy lorries fail the test / Truck test – half fail
6 Killer trout / Knockout trout / Fisher killed by catch
7 Family saved by the bottle
8 28 m moonlighters
9 pyro psycho in pyjamas / pyro pyjama psycho / pyro pj looney lets loose / pyromaniac in pyjamas
10 Tentative tête à tête / US and Iran tread tentatively

Task 6 – completing gap translation text

(1) have attacked
(2) NOT a few
(3) nothing
(4) boy
(5) according to B police reports
(6) broke into
(7) assaulted
(8) victims
(9) simple past, whichever verb is chosen
(10) was thrown

Task 9 – modal verbs

1 Is said to have, is believed to have
2 Boys and girls are to have the option of segregated classes in some subjects, should be allowed to
3 The referendum will hopefully bring peace

sollen/ wollen

4 This novel proved to be, turned out to be
5 There ought to be law banning smoking in restaurants
6 The seventh commandment says thou shalt not steal
7 Are you serious, you're not serious are you?
8 Her baby's due in May
9 I should have given it more water
10 Her one and only novel was to secure her place in the history of English literature
11 Edinburgh is said to be
12 His talk is intended to contribute to
13 We were supposed to fly out at 8, we were meant to, we should have flown...

1 In a new book, the author claims to have discovered Shakespeare's true identity.
2 I was just about to leave when the phone rang.
3 She says she didn't mean it like that.
4 He claims to have seen a UFO.
5 Let's make things up again.
6 She thinks she can always behave as she likes.
7 That doesn't mean much.
8 As fate would have it, she met her ex-husband at the party.
9 She was mugged on the train but no one was prepared to help her.
10 I just can't believe it.

Task 10 – verbal groups and participles

Text 2

Hamburg and Berlin following in third and fourth place,
Magdeburg ... Schwerin being way ahead of larger towns in the west

Text 7

Lay Catholic organisations in Germany are united in the ZdK, their events including the ...

III Report – generalised

Hans-Dieter Gelfert, *Einführung in das Studium, studium kompakt,*
Anglistik · Amerikanistik, Berlin, 1998.
Großer Atlas des Tierlebens, August 1995.
Greenpeace – Broschüre

III Report – generalised

Text 1

Text 2
Text 3

Task 1 – identifying lexical features

written English	–	spoken English
indigestible	–	inedible
adequate, sufficient	–	enough
infrequent	–	rare
efficient	–	working well

Task 2 – identifying grammatical features

written English	–	spoken English
the Euros home range	–	where the Euro lives, the area it lives in
plants with sufficient water content	–	plants that have enough water in them
prolific bacteria and protozoan fauna	–	lots of bacterial and one celled animals

CIRCUMSTANCES

1 in Stil und Denkweise eines englischsprachigen Autors, Gemessen am Arbeitsaufwand, im Allgemeinen, in der Regel, in Frage — Text 1

2 in vielen Teilen der Welt, an geschützten tropischen Küsten, zwischen Meer und Land, im Gewirr der stelzenatrigen Wurzeln der Mangrovenbäume und -sträucher, an den Strand, am unteren Rand der Gezeitenzone, weiter höher landeinwärts, ein- oder zweimal, im Jahr, durch besonders hohe Flutwellen, unter Wasser, in Südostasien, im allgemeinen, in unterschiedlichem Ausmaß, an das Seewasser, in den oberen Bereichen der Flußmündungen, in den oberen Schlammschichten, aus den eigentlichen Wurzeln, aus dem Schlamm, an die Mangroven, an mangrovenfreien Küsten, in diesem schlammigen Wald, andernorts, von Land-, von Meerestieren, an ein Leben halb im Wasser und halb auf dem Lande — Text 2

3 vor 60 Millionen Jahren, zurück ins Wasser, auf dem Land, zu den größten Lebewesen, im Vergleich, mit 30 Metern Länge und dem Gewicht von 25 Elefanten, im Sommer, in ihren Nahrungsgründen in arktischen und antarktischen Zonen, aus Krill, zur Paarungszeit, in wärmere Gewässer, in dieser Zeit, ohne Nahrung, im Jahr, zu den Rätseln, neben der sozialen Sprache, in den Paarungsgründen, ständig, in einer Umwelt, sehr rasch, vom Körper, über eine lange Periode, sicher, wahrscheinlich, nach Art, zwischen 30 und — Text 3

50 Jahre, durch dichten Nebel, zurück in den sicheren Hafen, vor dem Tod, gegenseitig, in größter Not

Text 1

1 in education, on small units, in different contexts, on the individual's mental capacity to acquire language, with little reference, to context of use, in a functional model, in the linguistic system.

Text 2

2 right across the arid zone, to a multi-storey, high-density housing development for birds, along the Cooper, for instance, to this habitat, on the Cooper, evenly, in pairs, along the Creek, with the woodland habitat.

Text 3

3 in appearance, by having shorter and redder hair, in caves and rock piles, on grasses and shrubs, in the evenings, in common with other kangaroos, in a sac-like development of the alimentary tract, in the natural diet of the Euro, from urea, with water, on a diet full of fibre and low on nitrogen, on spinifex, in the Euro's home range, with sufficient water content, with infrequent access to free water, during dry periods, on its efficient metabolism and ability to digest poor food to survive.

Task 3 – identifying problems in English text
C

Task 4 – identifying situational context

Text 2

The second text is an explanation of historical events. It uses past tense and focuses on the causal relations between events, expressed in such cohesive ties and lexical choices as: although, also, brought an end, made, forged, stimulated, inspired, as, otherwise.

Text 3/4

The third and fourth texts are not just giving information but arguing, interpreting, commenting and include much modality and personal reference to do so.

Text 1 was written by a primary school student learning the report genre. It is printed in David Butt et al., *Using Functional Grammar*, National Centre for English Language Teaching and Research, Macquarie University (Sydney), 1995 p. 21.

Text 2, written by a high school student for a history class, is printed in Martin, Matthiessen and Painter, reprinted in *Working with Functional Grammar*, London, 1997, p. 155.

Text 3 is by Egon Schwarz, *Der Reiz der Wörter*, Frankfurt a. M., 1978.

Text 4 was used as an examination text at Potsdam University, 1990.

Task 5 – completing gap translation text
(1) suffering
(2) malignant diseases

(3) get, or are affected by or become ill with
(4) for which a healthy donor is needed
(5) is compatible with
(6) are most likely to be found
(7) among
(8) can only
(9) donor outside the family
(10) of two unrelated people having the same tissue features
(11) when a very large number of people are willing to donate bone marrow
(12) can still not

IV Narrative – fictional
Task 1 – identifying grammatical features

2 ... Krankenwagen, alle rotbärtigen Bürger, Die Funkstreifen, der Befehl, sie, Zwei von ihnen, Wagen, zwei andere, den Geburtstag des Wirtes, drei, einem Kameraden, die übrigen, Einkäufe, sie, sie, Sie, Straßen, sie, Sie, sie, einen Rotbart, sie, ihn, der Verkehr, Das Geheul der Sirenen, die Bevölkerung, Gerüchte, die Hetzjagd, einem Massenmörder

3 ... der Mond, man, er, Augenblicke der Abwesenheit, ich, ich, ich, ich, diesem unbekannten schemenhaften Wesen, ihm, es, Das Kind, wir, uns, Wir, unsere Freunde, wir, eine größere Wohnung, uns, ich, alles, ich, man, ich, ich, Hanna, mich, ich, der Kinderwagen, Räder, ich, Ich, du, ich, ich, sie, Hauben, Jäckchen, Windeln, sie, ich, ich

1 ... the bush, what it was that would make Hush seen, They, Anzac biscuits, mornay, Minties, steak, salad, pumpkin scones, Hush , Grandma Poss, us, what we can find, they, a vegemite sandwich, Hush, A tail, both possums, A brand new visible tail, they, a piece of pavlova, Hush's legs, her body, You, Grandma Poss, they, they, a lamington, Hush, her eyes, Grandma Poss, her breath, she, she, Hush, Grandma Poss, Hush, they, Hush, she, Grandma Poss, a vegemite sandwich, a piece of pavlova, a half a lamington, Hush, she

2 ... some unfinished business, Hanford, the booze, the shotgun, The war, It, a fact, I, you, know, He, a soldier, They, kids, They, nothing, you, you, them, Buckridge, Hanford, no stopping this, This, something, He, fires, a football, their children's hair, darkness, the moon, his own son

3 ... his predecessor, twenty miles outside the little seaport, the commercial outlet of the district, this, Joseph's eager temperament, he, his footing, a little experience, he, Simmondsen, a bad fellow, glimpses of his manly nature, This, a decent welcome, he, a good distance, the weather, everybody, a horse, him, The Rev. Joseph, the roughness of the back country

Task 2 – identifying problems in English text
B

Task 3 – identifying situational context

Text 1

Text 1 is a short history of England by Christopher Hibbert, *The Story of England*, London, 1992.

Text 2

Text 2 is an Australian Aboriginal Dreaming story *The Beginning of Life*, explaining the origins of life, told by Oodgeroo in her book *Stradbroke Dreamtime*, Sydney, 1993.

Text 3

Text 3 is a personal life story by Eva Leanne Johnson, published in Roberta Sykes, ed., *Murrawina*, New York, 1993.

Task 4 – completing gap translation text

(1) wanted to show the cows how tough they were
(2) one of them
(3) cried
(4) than you
(5) could run the pants of you, if I wanted to
(6) the other one
(7) cried
(8) could toss you in the air with my horns, if I wanted to
(9) stood
(10) were amazed
(11) went on crying out
(12) cried
(13) could stomp you into porridge if I wanted to
(14) the other one
(15) cried
(16) could pummel you til your skin burned, if I wanted to
(17) mooed and wondered
(18) cried out til they were hoarse
(19) could only squeak and squeal
(20) got bored with all the silly yelling
(21) turned their backs on the bulls
(22) let them go on shouting on their own

Task 7 – prepositional phrases in German text 3

– (Two people) turned to stone
– Her bowed head before my eyes and her silence in my ears
– The moon as it begins to wax
– A larger apartment

- I came (chanced) upon thoughts as one comes upon landmines
- Explosive force
- Without thinking of the danger / without a thought for the danger / no thought of the danger
- Not paying attention

Task 8 – verbal groups in German text 3
- without saying goodnight
- I escpaped to my room / I took refuge in my room
- was she lying down and trying to sleep or awake and waiting?
- we furnished the apartment more comfortably and permanently
- I should have recoiled
- because I couldn't decide
- whatever you say / as you like
- I **am** listening
- she accused me of letting my mind wander / she accused me of not paying attention
- but I wasn't, far from it / but I was, only too well

V Procedure – constructional
Task 3 – identifying stylistic problems in English text

All the texts make no use of ellipsis, one of the major ways of achieving conciseness in instructional texts.
Since the ad appeared in a teenage magazine, the use of "your hair" is possible. The use of the definite article with hair is completely wrong. The use of "it" and "them" is often confused and confusing. The texts all contain wrong lexical choices, eg in text **C** strand/ hairband/ to roll up/ snail/ pin". "String" is also a wrong lexical choice in this context. Expressions chosen are often too long-winded, eg "Put the flowers with the help of little hairgrips in your hair", "by the use of little hairgrips".
Nominalisation, eg "for decoration" in this kind of text is unusual.

Task 4 – identifying situational context
- Instructions for games are written in chronological order but do not make use of the imperative mood. Passives are often found, or in German the pronoun *man*. Ellipsis is not usual. Clauses are finite and more complex than in constructional procedure. If-clauses are common. Modality is usual, eg "must", "may", "can".

- The diet rules are taken from a cookery book issued by *Weightwatchers*. The recipes in this book are all written in the infinitive with imperative function and show the features of constructional procedure discussed at the beginning of the chapter. With the 'rules', the TENOR becomes more personal. The reader feels that s/he is being addressed individually. In a book intended to help people lose weight, it is important to establish a relationship of trust.

Task 5 – completing gap translation text

(1) How to organise
(2) talk
(3) presentation
(4) introduction
(5) topic
(6) arouse interest in
(7) the readings
(8) audience's (or listeners')
(9) prior knowledge
(10) body
(11) keep making the structure clear
(12) audience's (or listeners')
(13) summarise
(14) sub-points
(15) link
(16) topics
(17) speak
(18) clearly
(19) vague
(20) terms
(21) use
(22) devices
(23) lively
(24) use
(25) conclusion
(26) summarise
(27) information
(28) present
(29) conclusions
(30) last line

Task 8 – recipe vocabulary

(1) stir
(2) cut
(3) cube
(4) fold
(5) take
(6) arrange
(7) shred
(8) serve
(9) spoon
(10) garnish

Task 9 – translating *man*

1 We could go to the cinema this evening.
2 People will talk / There'll be talk.
3 Have we the right to destroy our environment in this way?
4 It is assumed that children from dysfunctional families have more problems.
5 Don't count your chickens before they are hatched.
6 You (one) can rely on his word. / He's as good as his word/ He's a man of his word.
7 Have they caught the criminal yet?
8 You can easily get there by bus from here.
9 Today it's known (they know) that a baby in the womb can already hear.
10 How can anyone be so tactless (insensitive)!
11 It has to be taken into consideration that well-known critics disagree on this point.
12 Everyone in the firm knows that he always reacts like that.
13 It is rumoured that she is having an affair with the boss.
14 One has to admit that he knows how to make the best of every situation.
15 There's work needs doing / There's a lot to be done / I've a lot to do.

How to stand when talking to someone

When you are talking to someone, you should follow certain rules that signal to the other person that you are really interested in him or her ie that you are listening. This begins with the way you stand. Stand upright and composed, your body turned towards the person you are talking to. You should look at him/her while speaking and refrain from looking around at other people or things during the conversation.

Task 10 – translating *wer*

1 Anyone in New York for the first time (Any/every first time visitor to new York) is amazed at the number of homeless people.

2 First come, first served.

3 Whoever wants / anyone wanting to get on in their job has to be competent in several foreign languages.

4 Whoever wants to/ Everyone/Anyone who wants to can take part in the competition

5 Those students wanting to take their examination in the summer must put their names down now.

6 Ask a lot of questions, get a lot of answers.

7 Whoever did it must be punished.

8 Remember the boy who cried "Wolf"!

9 No way do I believe you.

10 If you have done this exercise, you now know that you have to be very careful when translating sentences beginning with the German word wer.

VI Advertising – product

VI Advertising – product
Task 2 – identifying grammatical and poetic features

word play

"From Hair to Eternity" recalls the book/film title "From Here to Eternity"/ "to make waves" is to be understood in the sense of loose curls in the hair but is also a play on the phrase "to make waves" which can mean to cause problems or here to create a sensation.

ad 3

ad 4

"Spot-on"– is an informal phrase meaning "exactly right". Here "on the spot/on the stain" is also meant. "No marks for spotting" contains double word play. "Mark" and "spot" both mean "stain", but the verb "spot" also means to notice or recognise. The phrase "No marks for" means something is so obvious that you cannot be praised for doing/guessing it.

Text 6

"to put your Athlete's Foot down" – echoes the idiom "to put one's foot down "meaning to be firm, but Athlete's Foot is also a medical condition in which the skin cracks between the toes.

Text 8

"When everything else comes off" – literally refers to other lipsticks not staying on the lips, but the suggestion is that clothes are taken off. The accompanying picture was of a naked couple. This is an example of the erotic suggestiveness found in many of today's ads.

pun

"Ohm and Away" – Ohm is literally a unit of electrical resistance but is intended to be read as "Home".

Home and Away is a very, very popular Australian soap series shown twice a day on British television.

"Ohmward Bound" = *Homeward Bound*, which is a well-known song. The ads only work because of the pronunciation of "Ohm" and "Home".

"I think therefore IBM" – is a play on the English version of "Cogito ergo sum" – "I Think therefore I am" – and only works as an ad for IBM computers because of the sound of the letters.

H2O – the chemical formula for water could not work as an ad for "Eau Perrier" in German because the letter "O" would not sound like the French word for water, "eau".

Task 4 –brand names

The products would not sell well in English-speaking countries because BONKER would recall the British adjective "bonkers", which means "crazy".

KRAPP is reminiscent of the slang adjective "crap" meaning "of bad quality", but is particularly funny here as "to crap" as a verb means to do just what one needs a lot of toilet paper for.

PSCHITT sounds like "shit" which needs no explanation.

SKUM looks like "scum", which is the dirty substance that forms on a liquid.

SKINABLE brings to mind the verb "skin" (*enthäuten*) rather than suggesting the smooth skin of a baby.

SOD is an informal and rude word meaning stupid or annoying person.

Task 5 – identifying stylistic problems in German text

A suggestion keeping five parallel constructions in German might be something like

Liebe ist........den Regen nicht merken

Liebe ist........zu Hause kuscheln

Liebe ist........gar nichts bereuen

Liebe ist........seine Hobbies teilen

Liebe ist........L'Aimant

This is not put forward as an ideal solution but might provide a starting point for an improved version.

Task 7 – multiple choice translation

1 "Original" seems to be a good word to use in advertisements. It is also better to make the cheese recipe the THEME rather than France.

2 Both 2(a) and 2(b) collocate well, but mean something slightly different. 2(b) means that something surprisingly good was made known by God, 2(a) means that the monks got the idea of making cheese from God.

3 (a)

4 (c) The use of the progressive form conveys the idea of repeated

action and is to be preferred to the simple form. The use of the passive is clumsy and takes the emphasis away from the monks' actions.

5 "Cheeses" is a plural meaning "kinds of cheese" and is correct here. "Betray" has negative connotations.

6 (c) is neater than the constructions with "like" which sound rather clumsy.

7 English speakers would probably add "its". Connoisseur is used not only for people who know a lot about music and art but also about food. As a French word, it seems particularly suitable here.

8 Compound adjectives are often used in advertisements and seem to fit well here, *Larousse Gastronomique* speaks of the "pungent flavour sought after by connoisseurs" when describing Roquefort, so this adjective seems to be the correct one to use. "Spicy" and "aromatic" do not go well with cheese.

9 The German repeats *göttlich* from the heading but it seems better to use "heavenly" to contrast with "earth" here. It is strange to talk about cheese as an "invention" as this is usually used with machines, tools and instruments. "Concoction" means a mixture of things not usually combined.

10 No one would understand (a). Solution (c) is somewhat better but (b) echoes a phrase often used in English and often used together with "God".

Task 10 – idioms

1 on the spot = meaning immediately, but "spot" also to be understood as "pimple"

2 to meet one's match = meaning to have an opponent who is stronger or more skilful, ie that can here get rid of the stain. Since there is a whole series of Stain Devils, for ink, grass, rust, etc; each stain also has its "match" in the sense of suitable stain remover.

3 pie in the sky = meaning something good which is hardly likely to happen, ie a kind of dream. But pie is made from pastry so with this pastry the dream of perfect pie comes true.

4 to say cheese = is a popular phrase said by photographers so that people will smile.

5 not to put a foot wrong = means to do everything right and make no mistakes. This is what you do if you put your feet in Clark's shoes.

6 to talk tripe = means to talk rubbish, but tripe is also the stomach of a pig or cow used for food and is contained in this particular brand of dog food.

7 to be in clover = is an informal expression meaning to live very well and comfortably. The play involves the name of the product "Clover" butter.

8 to crow about something = means to boast about something. Since the product advertised is a soup made from chicken and vegetables called "cock-a-leekie", the word play involves "cock" and "crow", the loud sound made by a cock.

9 a shot in the dark = means an attempt to guess without the facts, but "shot" is also another word for photo or snap.

10 plonky prices = "plonk" is an informal word for cheap wine./ to have a screw loose = means to be slightly crazy; a corkscrew is the tool you use to pull the cork out of bottles.

11 spend a penny = is a colloquial British euphemism for "to urinate". The connection with nappies is obvious. Since the nappy samples are free of charge, you can get them <u>literally</u> without spending a penny.

12 an open and shut case = you talk about an open and shut case when something is completely obvious and needs no discussion. In this ad, the kneeler weeder is literally a case (container) than can be opened up for use and shut again for storage.

13 to drop by/in = means to pay an informal unarranged visit. A drop often refers to alcohol. Here it means several bottles of Guiness.

14 salad days = refers to the time of your life when you are young and not very experienced. Since the weather in Cyprus is sunny, you can enjoy light salad meals during the days you spend there on holiday.

15 The early bird catches the worm = is the proverb echoed.

Task 11 – word play
- to get a head start = an advantage that helps you be successful
- to brush up on = to practise/revise
- square roots = a mathematical problem; root also refers to the part of the hair that joins to the scalp
- revision tips = advice; also the ends of your hair
- to crop up = to happen unexpectedly, also to cut very short
- hair raising = frightening or exciting
- neatly-trimmed prices = reduced; trim is also the act of cutting off a little to make something look neater
- to let one's hair down = to enjoy yourself and relax

Task 12 – synonyms

Maximize the tan. Minimize the damage

A new revolutionary after sun booster which increases your tan by up to 50% in just four days and rejuvenates your skin as you turn more golden. TAN MAXIMIZER is soothing, moisturising, conditioning and protects the skin from sun ageing whilst reducing dryness and redness. A remarkable product that works with the skin's own natural tanning and repair system, so you can prolong your tan while improving the overall condition of your skin.

LANCASTER

Task 13 – adjective replacement

The point is that adjectives are chosen for reasons of alliteration, phonetic repetition, rhythm, etc and not for meaning alone.

compounds

Task 14 – compounds

1 *magenmild* = mild or gentle to the stomach
2 *hauteigene Feuchtigkeit* = the skin's natural moisture
3 *Weitenregulierung* = adjustable width
4 *tropfengenau dosierbar* = for drops without drips
5 *anlagebedingter Haarausfall* = genetically determined hair loss
6 d*ie erste zartschmelzende Schokolade* = world's first …
7 *volles Verwöhnaroma* = the aroma of total indulgence
8 *vollmundig-sanfter Geschmack* = new mild yet full flavoured taste

Glossary

ADJUNCT

An optional element in a clause. There are three kinds of Adjunct: Circumstantial (where, when, how, with whom, etc), Modal (possibility, probability, frequency, obligation) and Conjunctive (furthermore, however, nevertheless, on the other hand, meanwhile, thus, therefore, consequently, for example, firstly, etc).

ATTIDUDINAL LEXIS

Words which indicate the speaker's attitude to their subject. If there is none in a given text, the translator must be careful about word choice so the result does not have inappropriate connotations. (eg "bourgeois" is attitudinal, *bürgerlich* is not).

CIRCUMSTANCE

Clause element that represents where, when, why, how, etc the event occurred.

CLAUSE

The key unit of a language's lexicogrammar, structured around an action and involving PARTICIPANTS and perhaps also CIRCUMSTANCES. It realises several semantic functions simultaneously, and so can be analysed in several ways depending on what type of meaning the analysis is interested in. The types of functional structure a clause represents are:

PROCESS, PARTICIPANTS and CIRCUMSTANCES (Ideational meaning)
SUBJECT, FINITE, PREDICATOR, COMPLEMENT and ADJUNCT (Interpersonal meaning)
THEME and RHEME/Given and New information (Textual meaning)

CLAUSE COMPLEX

A group of two or more clauses linked or bound together (by a relation of coordination or subordination)

COHESION/COHESIVE DEVICES

The quality of connected language that makes text. Language which does not use cohesive devices fails to produce sensible text for the reader. Cohesive devices are:
Conjunction, reference, substitution and ellipsis, and lexical choices whereby words throughout a text are repeated or related to one another by synonymy, etc.

COMPLEXITY/DENSITY

It is typical of spoken language to have many simple clauses strung together in often complex ways, and typical of written language to have less and much denser clauses – whereby all the information is packed into one complex noun group, rather than strung out over a series of clauses. In very concise text, the aim is to get much information into short structures, so nominalisation is useful.

CONCISENESS

Textual compactness achieved through such devices as lecical density, nominalisation and ellipsis.

DETERMINER

The, a/an, this, these, that, those.

ELLIPSIS

Cohesive device whereby words are left out of a clause and the reader has to refer back to previous text to make sense of the clause.

FIELD
– see REGISTER

FINITE
Form of the verb, modal or auxiliary verb in a clause that shows tense and agrees with the SUBJECT in person and number. (I **am** a teacher/ I **am** eating/ I **eat** too much/ I **have** not eaten yet/ **did** you eat it?).

GENRE
A recognised cultural activity, structured into steps to achieve a specific purpose. (The degree to which language is involved in any instance of a genre is a variable of REGISTER. A story, for example, can be told without language by using pictures).

GRAMMAR
The grammar of a language is its mechanism by which meanings are realised by wordings - it is the interface between social context and the material of linguistic expression.

LEXIS
Word with 'content', not just grammatical function. Dictionary items (the **cat sat** on the **mat**).

LEXICAL DENSITY
A calculation of a text's informational compactness, by comparing the ratio of clauses to lexical items. Written language is typically much denser than spoken language, as the number of clauses is lower and the number of lexical items per clause higher.

MARKED
Any pattern or choice of word or word ordering that is unusual, not the typical or most common choice (eg THEME position in an English language clause is typically occupied by the SUBJECT. When a CIRCUMSTANTIAL ADJUNCT is THEME, that is less usual and draws attention).

Modality
Refers to expressions between positive and negative, in verbs or adjuncts (might, could, probably, possibly, etc.). Some genres use much modality, others use none. Most modal verbs (eg can, may, might, sollen) can express a range of meanings, so translation of them demands a good understanding of the possibilities of meaning and the options available for their realisation.

MODE
– see REGISTER

MOOD
The three possible clause moods in English are imperative (do it), declarative (you did it) and interrogative (did you do it?).

NOUN GROUP
Group of words functioning in the clause as either SUBJECT or OBJECT. The Head word is typically a noun or pronoun. (eg **the cat** sat **on the filthy old green mat**).

NOMINALISATION
Representation of what is in reality a process as a thing (eg the train's departure).

PARTICIPANT
Clause element typically realised by a noun group. Who or what is involved in the PROCESS of the clause. The 'affected' PARTICIPANT in a clause is the one to whom something is done.

PROCESS
The representation in a clause of an event or state.

PROCESS TYPES
Mental processes include verbs like: think, know, feel, hope
Material processes include: make, do, hit, write, drive, lose, save, receive, work, study, give;
Relational: be, have, be from, be at;
Verbal: say, express, opine, shout, whisper;
Behavioural: jump, leave, emigrate, return;
Existential: there is, exist.

REGISTER
A text's configuration of FIELD, TENOR and MODE variables. (eg the REGISTER of this book can be described as formal written text about language and translation by a university lecturer for colleagues and students of English Studies).

SUBJECT
Clause function that acts together with FINITE. Typically expressed as a noun group (the cat sat on the mat).

TENOR
– see REGISTER

THEME

The "point of departure" for the message. Simple THEMES are Topical, complex THEMES include Interpersonal and/or Textual elements as well. Marked THEMES are unusual patterns, such as beginning the message with some other element than the grammatical SUBJECT in English.

Further Reading

Functional Grammar

Bloor, Thomas/ Bloor, Muriel, *Functional analysis of English*, London, 1995.

Butt, David et al., *Using Functional Grammar*, Sydney, 1995.

Eggins, Suzanne, *Introduction to Systemic Functional Linguistics*, London, 1994.

Halliday, Michael A. K., *An Introduction to Functional Grammar*, London, 1985.

Halliday, Michael A. K., *Spoken and Written Language*, Deakin, Australia, 1985.

Halliday, Michael A. K. / Hasan, Ruqaiya, *Language, Context and Text*, Deakin, Australia, 1985.

Halliday, Michael / Hasan, Ruqaiya, *Cohesion in English*, London, 1976.

Hasan, Ruqaiya / Cloran, Carmel / Butt, David, eds., *Functional Descriptions: Theory in Practice*, Amsterdam, 1996.

Lock, Graham, *Functional English Grammar*, Cambridge, 1996.

Martin, James, *Factual Writing*, Deakin Australia, 1985.

Martin, James / Matthiessen, Christian / Painter, Clare, *Working with Functional Grammar*, London, 1997.

Martin, James, *English text*, Amsterdam, 1992.

Matthiessen, Christian, *Lexicogrammatical cartography, English systems*, Tokyo, 1995.

Swales, J. A., *Genre analysis*, Cambridge 1990.

Thompson, Geoff, *Introducing Functional Grammar*, London, 1996.

Advertising

Leech, Geoffrey, *English in Advertising*, London, 1966.

Römer, Ruth, *Die Sprache der Anzeigenwerbung*, Düsseldorf, 1968/73.

Cook, Guy, *The Discourse of Advertising*, London, 1992.

Myers, Greg, *Words in Ads*, London, 1994.

Nash, Walter / Carter, Ronald, *Seeing Through Language*, Oxford 1990.